Ric

Best of
ITALY

*Make the Most of Every Day
and Every Dollar*

John Muir Publications
Santa Fe, New Mexico

Other JMP travel guidebooks by Rick Steves
Asia Through the Back Door (with Bob Effertz)
Europe Through the Back Door
Europe 101: History, Art, and Culture for the Traveler
  (with Gene Openshaw)
Kidding Around Seattle
Mona Winks: Self-Guided Tours of Europe's Top Museums
  (with Gene Openshaw)
Rick Steves' Best of the Baltics and Russia
  (with Ian Watson)
Rick Steves' Best of Europe
Rick Steves' Best of France, Belgium, and the Netherlands
  (with Steve Smith)
Rick Steves' Best of Germany, Austria, and Switzerland
Rick Steves' Best of Great Britain
Rick Steves' Best of Scandinavia
Rick Steves' Best of Spain and Portugal
Rick Steves' Phrase Books for French, German, Italian,
  Spanish/Portuguese, and French/Italian/German

John Muir Publications, P.O. Box 613, Santa Fe, NM 87504
© 1995 by Rick Steves
Cover © 1995 by John Muir Publications
All rights reserved.

Printed in the United States of America
First printing January 1995

ISSN 1078-8026
ISBN 1-56261-198-4

Distributed to the book trade by
Publishers Group West
Emeryville, California

Editor Risa Laib
Editorial Support Elizabeth Wolf, Jean Teeters
Production Kathryn Lloyd-Strongin, Sarah Johansson
Design and Typesetting Linda Braun
Maps Dave Hoerlein
Research Assistance Steve Smith
Printer Quebecor/Kingsport
Cover Photo Leo de Wys Inc./Fridmar Damm

ITALY'S TEN BEST DESTINATIONS

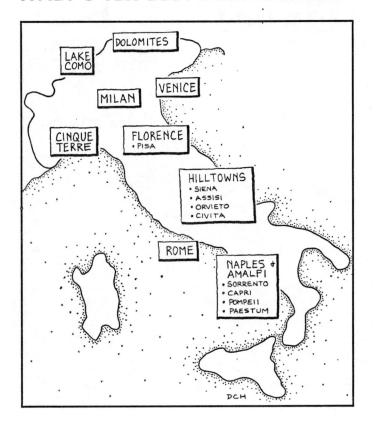

CONTENTS

HOW TO USE THIS BOOK

This book breaks Italy into its top ten big city, small town, and rural destinations. It then gives you all the information and opinions necessary to wring the maximum value out of your limited time and money in each of these destinations.

If you plan a month or less in Italy, and have a normal appetite for information, this lean and mean little book is all you need. If you're a travel info junkie (like me), this book sorts through all the superlatives and provides a handy rack upon which to hang your supplemental information.

Experiencing Italy's culture, people, and natural wonders economically and hassle-free has been my goal for 20 years of traveling, researching, and tour guiding. With this book, I pass on to you the lessons I've learned, updated (in mid-1994) for 1995.

Rick Steves' Best of Italy is a tour guide in your pocket. Places covered are balanced to include a comfortable mix of exciting big cities and cozy small towns, from brutal but *bello* Rome to *tranquillo* and traffic-free Riviera villages. It covers the predictable biggies and mixes in a healthy dose of Back Door intimacy. Along with the masterpieces of Michelangelo, you'll enjoy a "bruschetta" snack as a village boy pours oil and rubs fresh garlic on your toast. I've been selective, including only the most exciting sights. For example, of the many hill towns, I recommend the best five.

I don't recommend anything just to fill a hole. If you find no tips on eating in a town, I've yet to find a restaurant worth recommending above the others. For hassle-free efficiency, I favor hotels and restaurants handy to your sightseeing activities. Rather than list hotels scattered throughout a city, I describe my favorite two or three neighborhoods, and recommend the best accommodations values in each, from $8 bunks to fancy-in-my-book $120 doubles.

The best is, of course, only my opinion. But after two busy decades of travel writing, lecturing, tour guiding, and hearing well-meaning friends who don't travel say "get a life, Rick," I've developed a sixth sense of what tickles the traveler's fancy.

This Information Is Accurate and Up-to-Date

This book is updated every year. Most publishers of guide-books that cover a country from top to bottom can afford an update only every two or three years (and even then, it's often by letter). Since this book is selective, covering only the places I think make the top month or so in each country, I'm able to personally update it each summer. Even with an annual update, things change. But if you're traveling with the current edition of this book, I guarantee you're using the most up-to-date information available. If you're packing an old book, you'll learn the seriousness of your mistake . . . in Italy. (Your trip costs about $10 per waking hour. Your time is valuable. This guidebook saves lots of time.)

2 to 22 Days Out . . . Modularity In! Italy's Top Destinations

This book used to be called *2 to 22 Days in Italy*. It was orga-nized as a proposed 22-day route. It's now restructured into a more flexible modular system. Each recommended module, or "destination" (as they're referred to in this book), is cov-ered as a mini-vacation on its own, filled with exciting sights, homey, affordable places to stay, and hard opinions on how to best use your limited time. As before, my goal remains to help you get the most travel experience out of each day and each dollar. Each destination is broken into these sections:

Planning Your Time, a suggested schedule with thoughts on how to best use your time.

Orientation, including transportation within a destina-tion, tourist information, and a DCH map designed to make the text clear and your entry smooth.

Sights with ratings: ▲▲▲—Don't miss; ▲▲—Try hard to see; ▲—Worthwhile if you can make it; no rating— Worth knowing about.

Sleeping and **Eating**, with addresses and phone numbers of my favorite budget hotels and restaurants.

Transportation Connections to nearby destinations by train or car with ideas on road-side attractions along the way.

The **Appendix** is a traveler's tool kit, with information on climate, telephone numbers, youth hostels, and public transportation.

You can browse through this book, then choose your favorite destinations, link them up, and have a great trip. You'll travel like a temporary local, getting the absolute most out of every mile, minute, and dollar. You won't waste time on mediocre sights because, unlike other guidebooks, I cover only my favorites. Since a major financial pitfall is lousy-though-expensive hotels, I've worked hard to assemble the best accommodations values for each stop. And, as you travel the route I know and love best, I'm happy you'll be meeting some of my favorite Italian people.

Costs

Five components make up your trip cost: airfare, surface transportation, room and board, sightseeing, and shopping/entertainment/miscellany.

Airfare: It's confusing and you can't save by going direct. Get and use a good travel agent. A basic round-trip U.S.A.-to-Milan (or Rome) flight should cost $600 to $1,000, depending on where you fly from and when. Consider "open-jaws" (into one city and out of another) and remember, there's no free lunch in the airline industry.

Surface Transportation: For a 3-week whirlwind trip of all my recommended destinations, allow $300 per person for public transportation (train and buses), or $500 per person (based on two people sharing car and gas) for a 3-week car rental, tolls, gas, and insurance.

Room and Board: While Italy is one of Europe's most expensive countries, you can still eat and sleep well there in 1995 for $60 a day plus transportation costs (that's $35 for a double with breakfast, $10 for lunch, and $15 for dinner). Students and tightwads do it on $40 a day ($15 to $20 per bed, $20 a day for meals and snacks). That's doable. But budget sleeping and eating requires the skills and information covered below.

Sightseeing: In big cities, figure $5 to $10 per major sight, $2 for minor ones, $25 for splurge experiences (e.g., tours or gondola rides). An overall average of $15 a day works for most. Don't skimp here. After all, this category directly powers most of the experiences all the other expenses are designed to make possible.

Shopping/Entertainment/Miscellany: This can vary from

nearly nothing to a small fortune. Figure $1 per coffee, $2 per beer and ice cream cone, $1 per postcard, and $10 to $20 for evening entertainment. Good budget travelers find that this category has little to do with assembling a trip full of lifelong and wonderful memories.

Prices and Discounts

I've priced things in lire (about L1,600 = $1). To figure lire quickly and easily, cover the last three digits and cut what's left by a third (e.g., a L24,000 dinner costs $16). Prices, hours, and telephone numbers are accurate as of mid-1994—but once you pin Italy down it wiggles. While discounts are not listed in this book, seniors (60 and over), students (with International Student Identity Cards), and youths (under 18) may snare a discount—although many discounts are limited to European residents.

Sample Itineraries
Priority of Italian Sightseeing Stops

3 days:	Florence, Venice
5 days, add:	Rome
7 days, add:	Cinque Terre, Siena
10 days, add:	Città di Bagnoregio and slow down
14 days, add:	Sorrento, Naples, Pompeii, Amalfi, Paestum
18 days, add:	Milan, Lago di Como, Varenna, Assisi
21 days, add:	Dolomites, Verona, Ravenna (this includes everything on the route map that follows)

Itinerary considerations: Considering how you're likely to go both broke and crazy driving in big Italian cities, and how handy and affordable the trains are, I'd do most of Italy by public transportation. If you want to drive, consider doing the big intense stuff (Rome, Naples area, Milan, Florence, and Venice) by train/bus and renting a car for the hill towns of Tuscany and Umbria and for the Dolomites. A car is a worthless headache on the Riviera and in the Lake Como area.

By train, consider seeing everything but Venice on the way south and sleeping through everything you've already

Whirlwind Three-Week Tour of Italy

seen by catching the night train from Rome (or Naples) to Venice. (This saves you a day, gives you a late night in Rome, and an early arrival in Venice.)

While you can fly easily into either Milan or Rome, I'd start in Milan (less crazy) and consider either starting or finishing the trip easy in Varenna on Lake Como (a quick hour by train from Milan).

General strategies (such as homebasing in Siena to do Florence, and drivers parking in Orvieto and training into Rome) are covered in the text.

Scheduling

Your day-by-day itinerary strategy is a fun challenge. Sundays have the same pros and cons as they do for travelers in the

Italy's Best 22-Day Trip

Days	Plan	Sleep in
1	Arrive and see Milan	Milan
2	See Milan	Milan
3	Milan to the Riviera	Vernazza
4	Beach day in Cinque Terre	Vernazza
5	Riviera to Florence via Pisa	Florence
6	See Florence	Florence
7	To Siena via San Gimignano	Siena
8	Free day in Siena	Siena
9	Free day for hill towns or Assisi	Assisi or ?
10	To Città di Bagnoregio	Bagnoregio
11	To Rome, see Rome	Rome
12	See Rome	Rome
13	See Rome	Rome
14	Survive Naples	Sorrento
15	Pompeii, Amalfi Coast	Sorrento
16	Amalfi Coast, Paestum	night train
17	Venice	Venice
18	Venice	Venice
19	To Bolzano, into Dolomites	Castelrotto
20	Free day in mountains	Castelrotto
21	To Lake Como via Verona	Varenna
22	Relax on Lake Como	Varenna

U.S.A. Sightseeing attractions are generally open but with shorter hours, shops and banks closed, and minor transportation connections more frustrating. City traffic is light. Rowdy evenings are rare on Sundays. Saturdays are virtually weekdays with earlier closing hours. Hotels in tourist areas are often booked out at Easter, in August, and on Fridays and Saturdays.

Read through this book and note the days when most museums are closed. (Mondays are bad in Milan, Florence, and Rome.) Museums and sights, especially large ones, usually stop admitting people 30 to 60 minutes before closing time.

Plan ahead for banking, laundry, post office chores, and picnics. Mix intense and relaxed periods. Every trip needs at least a few slack days. Pace yourself. Assume you will return.

When to Go

Italy's best travel months are May, June, September, and
October. November through April usually has pleasant
weather with generally none of the sweat and stress of the
tourist season. Peak season (July and August) offers the
longest hours and the most exciting slate of activities—but
terrible crowds and, at times, suffocating heat. In resort
areas, hotels often require dinner in peak times. August, the
local holiday month, isn't as bad as many make it out to be,
but big cities tend to be quiet and beach and mountain
resorts are jammed. If you anticipate crowds, arrive early in
the day or call hotels in advance (call from one hotel to the
next; your fluent-in-Italian receptionist can help you).
Summer temperatures range from the 70s in Milan to the
high 80s and 90s in Rome. In the winter it often drops to the
30s and 40s in Milan and the 40s and 50s in Rome.

Italy has more than its share of holidays. Each town
has a local festival honoring its patron saint. February is
Carnevale time in Venice. Italy (including most major sights)
closes down on these national holidays: January 1, January 6
(Epiphany), Easter Sunday and Monday, April 25 (Liberation
Day), May 1 (Labor Day), May 20 (Ascension Day), August
15 (Assumption of Mary), November 1 (All Saints Day),
December 8 (Immaculate Conception of Mary), and
December 25 and 26.

Travel Smart

Many people travel through Italy thinking it's a chaotic mess.
Any attempt at organization is seen as futile and put off until
they get to Switzerland. This is dead wrong—and expensive.
Italy, a living organism that on the surface seems as orderly
as spilled spaghetti, functions quite well. Only those who
understand this and travel smart can enjoy Italy on a budget.
Upon arrival in a new town, lay the groundwork for a smooth
departure. Buy a phone card and use it for reservations,
reconfirmations, and to double-check hours. Reread this
book as you travel. Utilize local tourist information offices.
Enjoy the friendliness of the local people. Ask questions.
Seek and accept help. Wear your money belt, learn the local
currency, and develop a simple formula to quickly estimate
rough prices in dollars. Keep a sheet of paper in your pocket

for organizing your thoughts and practice the virtue of simplicity. Those who expect to travel smart, do.

Tourist Information

Before your trip, send a letter to an Italian National Tourist Office (TI) telling them of your general plans and asking for information.

Italian Government Tourist Offices: 630 Fifth Avenue, #1565, New York, NY 10111, tel. 212/245-4822; 12400 Wilshire Boulevard, #550, Los Angeles, CA 90025, tel. 310/820-0098; or 500 North Michigan Avenue, #1046, Chicago, IL 60611, tel. 312/644-0990. They'll send you the general packet, and if you ask for specifics (individual city maps, a publication called "General Information for Travelers to Italy," the calendars of festivals, good hikes around Lake Como, wine-tasting in Umbria, or whatever), you'll get an impressive amount of help. If you have a specific problem, they are a good source of assistance.

Local Tourist Offices: During your trip, your first stop in each town should be the tourist office (turismo, EPT). While Italian tourist offices are about half as helpful as those in other countries, their information is twice as important. Prepare. Have a list of questions and a proposed plan to double-check. If you're arriving late, telephone ahead. Be wary of the travel agencies or special information services that masquerade as tourist information offices but serve fancy hotels and tour companies. They are crooks and liars, selling things you don't need.

While the TI is eager to book you a room, use their room-finding service only as a last resort. Across Europe, room-finding services are charging commissions from hotels, taking fees from travelers, and blacklisting establishments that buck their materialistic rules. They are unable to give hard opinions on the relative value of one place over another. The accommodations stakes are too high to go potluck through the TI. And with the listings in this book, there's generally no need to.

Recommended Guidebooks

Especially if you'll be traveling beyond my recommended destinations, you may want some supplemental information.

When you consider the improvements they'll make in your $3,000 vacation, $25 or $35 for extra maps and books is money well spent. Especially for several people traveling by car, the weight and expense are negligible.

The Lonely Planet Guide to Italy is thorough, well-researched, and packed with good maps and hotel recommendations for low-to-moderate-budget travelers. The hip *Rough Guide to Italy* (British researchers, more insightful), and the highly opinionated *Let's Go: Italy* (by Harvard students, better hotel listings) are great for students, vagabonds, and those planning to go beyond my recommended destinations. If you're a low-budget train traveler interested in the youth and night scene (which I have basically ignored), get *Let's Go: Italy. Let's Go: Europe's* Italy pages are pretty sketchy.

Cultural and sightseeing guides: The tall green Michelin guides to Italy and Rome have nothing on room and board, but do have great maps for drivers and lots on sights, customs, and culture (sold in English in Italy). Among several good books specializing on Venice, Florence, and Rome, overachievers love the slick and user-friendly Insight guides, which are packed with art and historical background. The Cadogan guides to various parts of Italy offer an insightful look at the rich and confusing local culture. Those heading for Florence or Rome should read Irving Stone's *The Agony and the Ecstasy* for a great—if romanticized—rundown on Michelangelo, the Medici, and the turbulent times of the Renaissance.

Rick Steves' books: *Europe Through the Back Door, 13th Edition* (John Muir Publications, 1995) gives you budget travel skills and information on minimizing jet lag, packing light, driving or train travel, finding budget beds without reservations, changing money, theft, terrorism, hurdling the language barrier, health, travel photography, what to do with your bidet, Ugly Americanism, laundry, itinerary strategies, and more. The book also includes chapters on nearly 40 of my favorite "Back Doors."

Rick Steves' Country Guides are a series of eight guidebooks (formerly the 2 to 22 Days Itinerary Planners) covering Great Britain; France; Spain and Portugal; Germany, Austria, and Switzerland; Scandinavia; the Baltics and Russia; and Europe, as this one covers Italy.

Europe 101: Art for Travelers (co-written with Gene Openshaw, John Muir Publications, 1993), which gives you the story of Europe's people, history, and art, is heavy on Italy's ancient, Renaissance, and modern history. A little "101" background knowledge carbonates your Caesar shuffle.

Mona Winks: Self-Guided Tours of Europe's Top Museums (co-written with Gene Openshaw, John Muir Publications, 1993) gives you 1- to 3-hour self-guided tours through Europe's 20 most exhausting and important museums. Nearly half the book is devoted to Italy, with tours covering Venice's St. Mark's, the Doge's Palace, and Accademia Gallery; Florence's Uffizi Gallery, Bargello, Michelangelo's *David*, and a Renaissance walk through the town center; and Rome's Colosseum, Forum, Pantheon, the Vatican Museum, and St. Peter's Basilica. If you want to enjoy the great sights and museums of Italy, *Mona* will be a valued friend.

Italy is one country where a phrase book is as fun as it is necessary. My *Rick Steves' Italian Phrase Book* (John Muir Publications) is the only book of its kind, designed to help you meet the people and stretch your budget. It's written by a monoglot who, for 20 years, has fumbled happily through Italy, struggling with all the other phrase books. This is a fun and practical communication aid to help you make accurate hotel reservations over the telephone, ask for a free taste of cantaloupe-flavored gelato, and have the man in the deli make you a sandwich.

Maps

Don't skimp on maps. Excellent Michelin maps are available (cheaper than in the U.S.A.) throughout Italy at bookstores, newsstands, and gas stations. Train travelers can do fine with a simple rail map (such as the one that comes with your train pass) and free city maps picked up at TIs as you travel. However, drivers should invest in good 1/200,000 maps to really get the most out of their miles. Study the key to get the most sightseeing value out of your map.

The maps in this book, drawn by Dave Hoerlein, are concise and simple. Dave, who is well-traveled in Italy, has designed the maps to help you locate recommended places and the tourist offices, where you'll find more in-depth maps (usually free) of necessary cities or regions.

Transportation in Italy

By Car or Train?

Each mode of transportation has pros and cons. Public transportation is one of the few bargains in Italy. Trains and buses are inexpensive and good. City-to-city travel is faster, easier, and cheaper by train than by car. Trains give you the convenience and economy of doing long stretches overnight. By train I arrive relaxed and well-rested—not so by car.

Parking, gas, and tolls are expensive in Italy. But drivers enjoy more control, especially in the countryside. Cars carry your luggage for you, generally from door to door—especially important for heavy packers (such as chronic shoppers and families traveling with children). And groups know that the more people you pack into a car or minibus, the cheaper it gets per person.

Train Travel in Italy

You can travel cheaply in Italy simply by buying tickets as you go and avoiding the more expensive express trains. A second-class Rome-to-Venice ticket costs about $45 (with express supplement). But Italy's train ticket system confounds even the locals, and for convenience alone, I'd go with the Italian State Railway's BTLC "Go Anywhere" pass (see box, page 13). Unlike the BTLC pass, Italy's Kilometric pass is a headache because it doesn't cover fast train supplements. For travel exclusively in Italy, a Eurailpass is a bad value.

You'll encounter four types of trains in Italy: the *accelerato* or *locale* is the miserable milk-run train. The *diretto* is faster. The *espresso* zips along very fast, connecting only major cities. *Rapido* and Intercity trains are the sleek, air-conditioned top-of-the-line trains that charge a supplement (covered by the Eurail and BTLC train passes). First-class tickets cost 50 percent more than second-class tickets. While second-class cars go exactly as fast as their first-class neighbors, Italy is one country where I would consider the splurge of first class. The easiest way to upgrade a second-class ticket once on board an impossibly crowded train is to nurse a drink in the snack car. Newsstands sell up-to-date regional and all-Italy timetables (L4,000).

Italian trains are famous for their thieves. Never leave a bag unattended. There have been cases of bandits gassing an entire car before looting the snoozing gang. I've noticed recently that police ride the trains and things seem more controlled. Still, for an overnight ride, I'd feel safe only in a *cuccetta* (a $15 bunk bed in a special sleeping car with an attendant who keeps track of who comes and goes while you sleep).

Avoid big-city train station lines whenever you can. For about a L4,000 fee you can buy tickets and reserve a *cuccetta* at a travel agency. Plan your rail journey with the fun and clever new computer train schedule terminals. Watch the locals use one and then give it a try yourself. Because of the threat of bombs, you won't find storage lockers in train stations. But each station has a *deposito* (or *bagagli*) where you can safely leave your bag for L2,000 a day (payable when you pick up the bag).

Car Rental

Research car rental before you go. It's cheaper to arrange for car rentals through your travel agent while still in the U.S. Rent by the week with unlimited mileage. If you'll be renting for more than three weeks, leasing, which is a scheme to save on insurance and taxes, is cheaper. Explore your drop-off options.

Your car rental price includes minimal insurance with a very high deductible. A CDW (Collision Damage Waiver) insurance supplement covers you for this deductible. Since deductibles are horrendous, usually the entire value of the car, I usually splurge for the CDW. Ask your travel agent about money-saving alternatives to this car rental agency rip-off. The way I understand it, the car rental agency makes up for its highly competitive, unprofitably low, weekly rental rates with the approximate $12 a day you'll spend for CDW.

A rail 'n' drive train pass can be put to thoughtful use. Certain areas (like the Dolomites and the hill towns of Tuscany and Umbria) are great by car, while most of the rest of Italy is best by train.

Driving in Italy

Driving in Italy is frightening—a video game for keeps and you only get one quarter. All you need is your valid U.S.

Cost of Public Transportation

ITALIAN KILOMETRIC TICKETS

Also known as the Biglietto Chilometrico, this features coupons for up to 20 trips for up to 3,000 kilometers that can be split by up to 5 people for about $264 first class and $156 second class (1994 prices). Like the Go Anywhere pass, this is sold in the USA through the Italian State Railways (1-800-248-8687 for a busy signal) or cheaper and easy in Italy at CIT travel agencies and major train stations.

Italy: Point-to-point 2nd class rail fares in $US.

ITALIAN "GO ANYWHERE" RAILPASSES (BTLC)

	1st cl	2nd cl
8 days	$236	$162
15 days	294	200
21 days	340	230
30 days	406	274
Any 4 days out of 9	180	126
Any 8 days out of 21	260	174
Any 12 days out of 30	324	220

Passes cover all supplements and surcharges except for the very uppity TR450 trains. This is retailed in the USA through travel agents, direct from the Italian State Railways in NYC (1-800-248-8687), or cheaper and easy in Italy at CIT travel agencies and major train stations. Flexi passes are sold only in the USA. The 1994 prices above include an extra $10 per pass tacked on by the ISR folks in New York.

driver's license and a car. (According to everybody but the Italian police, international drivers' licenses are not necessary.)

Italy's freeway system is as good as our interstate system. But you'll pay about a dollar for every ten minutes of use. While I favor the autoroutes for the time and gas saved, and because I find them safer and less nerve-racking than the smaller roads, savvy local drivers know which toll-free highways are actually faster and more direct than the autoroute (e.g., Florence to Pisa). You'll pay more to park in Italy than in a comparable American town. Garages are safe, save time, and help you avoid the stress of parking tickets. Take the parking voucher with you to pay the cashier before you leave.

Cars are routinely vandalized and stolen. Try to make your car look locally owned: hide the "tourist-owned" rental company decals and put a local newspaper in your back window.

Sleeping in Italy

It's expensive. Cheap big-city hotels can be sleazy, depressing, dangerous, and rented by the hour. Tourist information services cannot give opinions on quality. A major feature of this book is its extensive listing of good value hotels with doubles ranging from $30 to $120 a night. I like places that are clean, small, central, quiet at night, traditional, inexpensive, friendly, with firm beds, and not in other guidebooks. (In Italy, I'm happy to score six out of these nine.) Budget travelers have a wide range of money-saving alternatives to choose from—convents, youth hostels, campgrounds, and private homes. Whenever applicable, I've listed these.

The Accommodations Description Code

To save space while giving more specific information for people with special concerns, I've described my recommended hotels with a standard code. When there is a range of prices in one category, the price will fluctuate with the season, size of room, or length of stay.

S—Single room or price for one person using a double.

D—Double or twin room. Double beds are usually big enough for non-romantic couples.

T—Three-person room (often a double bed with a single bed moved in).

Q—Four-adult room (an extra child's bed is usually cheaper).

B—Private shower (most likely) or bath in the room. Most B rooms have a WC (toilet). All rooms have a sink. B rooms are often bigger and renovated while the cheaper rooms without B often will be on the top floor or yet to be refurbished. Any room without B has access to a B on the corridor (free unless otherwise noted). Rooms with baths often cost more than rooms with showers.

WC—I include this only to differentiate between rooms that have only a B and those with BWC. With no WC mentioned, B rooms generally have a WC.

CC—Accepts credit cards: **V**=Visa, **M**=Mastercard, **A**=American Express. Many also accept Diners (which I ignored). If CC is not mentioned, assume they accept only cash.

SE—The likelihood that an English-speaking staff person is available is graded A through F.

Hotels

Double rooms listed in this book will range from about $30 (very simple, toilet and shower down the hall) to $120 (maximum plumbing and more), with most clustering around $60. It's higher in big cities and heavily touristed cities and less off the beaten path. Three or four people can economize by requesting larger rooms. Solo travelers find that the cost of a *camera singola* is often only 25 percent less than a *camera doppia*. Most listed hotels have rooms for anywhere from one to five people. If there's room for an extra cot, they'll cram it in for you.

Italy has a five-star rating system, but while the stars can give you a general idea of price range, the government no longer regulates hotel prices. Prices are pretty standard, and you normally get close to what you pay for. Shopping around earns you a better location and more character but rarely a cheaper price. You'll save $10-$20 if you ask for a room without a shower and just use the public shower down the hall (although in many cases the rooms with the extra plumbing are larger and more pleasant). Generally, rooms with a bath or shower also have a toilet and a bidet (which Italians use for a quick "sponge bath"). Double beds (called *matrimoniale* even though hotels aren't interested in your marital status) are cheaper than twins (*due letti singoli*). The cord that dangles over the tub or shower is not a clothesline. You pull it when you've fallen and can't get up. A few places have kept the old titles, *locanda* or *pension*. These indicate they offer budget beds. The Italian word for "hotel" is *albergo*.

Ancient Romans ate no breakfast at all, and the breakfast scene has improved only marginally. Except for the smallest places, a very simple continental breakfast is normally available. If you like juice and protein for breakfast, supply it yourself. I enjoy a box of juice in my hotel room and often supplement the skimpy breakfasts with a piece of fruit and a separately wrapped small piece of cheese. (A zip-lock baggie is handy for petite eaters to grab an extra breakfast roll and

slice of cheese, when provided, for a fast and free light lunch.)
The hotel breakfast, while convenient, is usually a bad value—
$6-$8 for a roll, jelly, and usually unlimited *cafe con latte*.
Legally, it's supposed to be optional. You can always request
cheese or salami (L5,000 extra). I enjoy taking breakfast at
the corner café. It's okay to supplement what you order with
a few picnic goodies.

Rooms are safe. Still, zip cameras and money out of
sight. More pillows and blankets are usually in the closet or
available on request. Remember, in Italy towels and linen
aren't always replaced every day—drip dry and conserve.
Towels are as thin as tempers in Italy.

To reserve a hotel room from the U.S.A, write or fax
(simple English is usually fine) to the address listed and iden-
tify clearly the dates you intend to be there. (A two-night
stay in August would be "one room, two people, two nights,
16/8/95 to 18/8/95"—European hotel jargon uses your day
of departure and European date system.) You may receive a
letter response requesting one night's deposit. Send a $50
signed traveler's check or a bank draft in the local currency.
More and more frequently, travelers can reserve a room with
a simple phone call or fax, leaving a credit card number as a
deposit. You can pay with your card or by cash when you
arrive, and if you don't show up, you'll be billed for one
night anyway. Ideally, the hotel receptionist will hold a room
for you without a deposit if you promise to arrive by mid-
afternoon and call to reconfirm two days before arrival.

Except during the busiest summer times, long-distance
hotel reservations are not usually necessary. But when you
know where you'll be tomorrow night, life on the road is
easier if you telephone ahead to reserve a bed. My most
highly recommended hotels get lots of my likable and reliable
readers, and will usually hold a room with a phone call until
17:00 with no deposit. They are usually accustomed to us
English-speaking monoglots. Use the telephone! I've listed
numbers with area codes. See the appendix for long-distance
dialing instructions.

When you reserve or confirm through a tourist office,
they often get a fee from you and a percentage from the hotel.
Go direct when you can.

Upon arrival, the receptionist will normally ask for your

passport. Hotels are legally required to register each guest with the local police. Relax. Americans are notorious for making this chore more difficult than it needs to be.

While bed and breakfasts (*affitta camere*) and youth hostels (*ostello della gioventu*) are not as common in Italy as elsewhere in Europe, I've listed quite a few in this book. While big city hostels are normally overrun with the *Let's Go* crowd, small town hostels can be a wonderfully enjoyable way to save money and make friends.

Eating Italian

The Italians are masters of the art of fine living. That means eating . . . long and well. Long, multi-course lunches and dinners and endless hours sitting in outdoor cafés are the norm. Americans eat on their way to an evening event and complain if the check is slow in coming. For Italians, the meal is an end in itself, and only rude waiters rush you. When you want the bill, scratch your raised palm and ask, "*Il conto?*"

Even those of us who liked dorm food will find that the local cafés, cuisine, and wines become a highlight of our Italian adventure. Trust me, this is sightseeing for your palate, and even if the rest of you is sleeping in cheap hotels, your buds will want an occasional first-class splurge. You can eat well without going broke. But be careful; you're just as likely to blow a small fortune on a disappointing meal as you are to dine wonderfully for $20.

Restaurants

When restaurant hunting, choose places filled with locals, not the place with the big neon signs boasting, "We speak English and accept credit cards." Look for menus posted outside. For unexciting but basic values, look for a "menu turistico," a three- or four-course set-price menu. Galloping gourmets order à la carte with the help of a menu translator. (The *Marling Italian Menu Master* is excellent. *Rick Steves Italian Phrase Book* has enough phrases for intermediate eaters.)

A full meal consists of an appetizer (antipasto, L5,000 and up), a first course (*primi piatto*, pasta or soup, L6,000-L12,000), and a second course (*secondo piatto*, expensive meat and fish dishes, L12,000-L20,000). Vegetables (*contorno*, *verdure*) may come with the *secondo* or be available for extra lire (L5,000) as a side dish. Restaurants normally pad the bill with a cover charge (*pane e coperto*, about L2,000) and a service charge (*servizio*, 15%). These days, service is usually automatically added to the bill. Tipping beyond that is unnecessary.

As you can see, the lire will add up in a hurry. Light and budget eaters can get by with a *primi piatto*. Hungry paupers can even go with two: a minestrone and a pasta. Self-service places and a few lower-class eateries feed you without the add-ons. Family-run places operate without hired help and can offer cheaper meals. An *osteria* is normally a simple local-style restaurant.

Many modern Italian fast food places slam-dunk pasta, rather than burgers, cheap and fast. *Rosticceria* are like delis with great cooked food to go. Pizza places (often called *Pizza Rustica*) sell fresh pizza by the weight. Two hundred grams with a beer or soft drink makes a good, cheap lunch. American-style fast food is reasonable and often a good bet for a salad bar.

The Italian bar is not just a place to drink. It is a local hangout serving coffee, mini-pizzas, sandwiches, cartons of milk from the cooler, and plates of fried cheese and vegetables under the glass counter, ready to reheat, as well as alcoholic drinks. This is my budget choice, the Italian equivalent of English pub grub. It's cheap, friendly, very local, and edible. Don't be limited by what you can see. If you feel like a salad with a slice of cantaloupe and a hunk of cheese, they'll whip that up for you in a snap.

Bar procedure can be frustrating: 1) decide what you want; 2) check the price list on the wall; 3) pay the cashier; and 4) give the receipt to the bartender (whose clean fingers handle no dirty lire), and tell him what you want. *Panini* and *tramezzini* are sandwiches. *Da portar via* is "for the road." You'll notice a two-tiered price system. A cup of coffee at the bar is cheaper than at a table. If on a budget, don't sit without checking out the financial consequences.

Picnic

In Italy, picnicking saves lots of lire and is a great way to sample local specialties. In the process of assembling your meal, you get to deal with the Italians in the local market scene.

On days you choose to picnic, gather supplies early. You'll probably visit several small stores or market stalls to assemble a complete meal, and many close around noon. While it's fun to visit the small specialty shops, a local *alimentari* is your one-stop corner grocery store. *Supermercatos* give you decent quality with less color, less cost, and more efficiency.

Juice lovers can get a liter of O.J. for the price of a Coke or coffee. Look for "100% *succa* (juice)" on the label or suffer through a sickly-sweet orange drink. Buy juice in less-expensive liter boxes, and store what you don't drink in your reusable water bottle for nipping between sights. Hang onto the twist-top half-liter mineral water bottles (sold everywhere for about L1,000).

Remember, picnics can be an adventure in high cuisine. Be daring. Try the smelly cheeses, midget pickles, ugly olives, and any UFOs the locals are excited about. Local shopkeepers are happy to sell small quantities of produce, and will even slice and stuff a sandwich for you. In a busy market, a merchant may not want to weigh and sell small, three-carrot-type quantities. In this case estimate generously what you think it should cost, and hold out the lire in one hand and the produce in the other. Wear a smile that says, "If you take the money, I'll go." He'll grab the money. A typical picnic for two might be fresh rolls, two tomatoes, three carrots, 100 grams of cheese, 100 grams of meat (100 grams = about a quarter pound, called *etto* in Italy), two apples, a liter box of juice, and a yogurt. Total cost—$10.

Red Tape and Business Hours
You currently need a passport but no visa and no shots to travel in Italy. In Italy—and in this book—you'll be using the 24-hour clock. After 12:00 noon, keep going—13:00, 14:00, and so on. For anything over 12, subtract 12 and add p.m. (e.g., 14:00 is 2 p.m.).

This book lists in-season hours for sightseeing attractions. Off-season, roughly October through April, generally expect shorter hours, more lunchtime breaks, and fewer activities.

Italians arrange dates by day/month/year, so Christmas

would be 25-12-95. What we Americans call the second floor
of a building is the first floor in Europe. Commas and periods
are often switched, so there are 5.280 feet in a mile, and your
temperature is 98,6. In museums art is dated with A.C. (for
Avanti Cristo, or B.C.) and D.C. (for Dopo Cristo, or A.D.).

Mail service is miserable in Italy. Postcards get last
priority. It's best to tell your loved ones you're going
behind the dark side of the moon for a while or keep in
touch with a few phone calls. If you must have mail stops,
consider a few pre-reserved hotels along your route or use
American Express Mail Services. Most American Express
offices in Italy will hold mail for one month. (They mail
out a free listing of addresses.) This service is free to
anyone using an AmExCo card or traveler's checks (and
available for a small fee to others). Allow 14 days for
U.S.-to-Italy mail delivery, but don't count on it. Federal
Express makes two-day deliveries, for a price.

Culture Shock—Accepting Italy as a Package Deal

While we think shower curtains are logical, many Italians
just cover the toilet paper and let the rest of the room
shower with you. When writing numbers, Italians give their
"1s" an upswing and cross their "7s." If you don't adapt,
your "7" will be mistaken for a sloppy "1" and you'll miss
your train— and probably find a reason to be mad at the
local system. Fit in!

We travel all the way to Italy to enjoy differences—to
become temporary locals. You'll experience frustrations.
Certain truths that we find "God-given" or "self-evident,"
like cold beer, ice, a bottomless cup of coffee, long, hot
showers, body odor smelling bad, and bigger being better,
are suddenly not so true. One of the benefits of travel is the
eye-opening realization that there are logical, civil, and even
better alternatives. Travel tends to pry open one's hometown
blinders. If the beds are too short, the real problem is that
you are too long. Don't look for things American on the
other side of the Atlantic and you're sure to enjoy a good
dose of Italian hospitality.

Send Me a Postcard, Drop Me a Line

While I do what I can to keep this book accurate and up-to-date, things are always changing. If you enjoy a successful trip with the help of this book and would like to share your discoveries, please send any tips, recommendations, criticisms, or corrections to me at Europe Through the Back Door, Box 2009, Edmonds, WA 98020. To update the book before your trip or share tips, tap into our free computer bulletin board travel information service (206/771-1902:1200 or 2400/8/N/1). All correspondents receive a two-year subscription to our "Back Door Travel" quarterly newsletter (it's free anyway). Tips actually used get you a first-class railpass in heaven.

Judging from the positive feedback and happy postcards I receive from travelers using this book, it's safe to assume you're on your way to a great Italian vacation—independent, inexpensive, and done with the finesse of an experienced traveler. Thanks, and *buon viaggio!*

BACK DOOR TRAVEL PHILOSOPHY
As Taught in *Rick Steves' Europe Through the Back Door*

Travel is intensified living—maximum thrills per minute and one of the last great sources of legal adventure. Travel is freedom. It's recess, and we need it.

Experiencing the real Europe requires catching it by surprise, going casual . . . "Through the Back Door."

Affording travel is a matter of priorities. (Make do with the old car.) You can travel—simple, safe, and comfortable—anywhere in Europe for $50 a day plus transportation costs. In many ways, spending more money only builds a thicker wall between you and what you came to see. Europe is a cultural carnival, and time after time, you'll find that its best acts are free and the best seats are the cheap ones.

A tight budget forces you to travel close to the ground, meeting and communicating with the people, not relying on service with a purchased smile. Never sacrifice sleep, nutrition, safety, or cleanliness in the name of budget. Simply enjoy the local-style alternatives to expensive hotels and restaurants.

Extroverts have more fun. If your trip is low on magic moments, kick yourself and make things happen. If you don't enjoy a place, maybe you don't know enough about it. Seek the truth. Recognize tourist traps. Give a culture the benefit of your open mind. See things as different but not better or worse. Any culture has much to share.

Of course, travel, like the world, is a series of hills and valleys. Be fanatically positive and militantly optimistic. If something's not to your liking, change your liking. Travel is addicting. It can make you a happier American, as well as a citizen of the world. Our Earth is home to nearly six billion equally important people. It's humbling to travel and find that people don't envy Americans. They like us, but with all due respect, they wouldn't trade passports.

Globe-trotting destroys ethnocentricity. It helps you understand and appreciate different cultures. Travel changes people. It broadens perspectives and teaches new ways to measure quality of life. Many travelers toss aside their hometown blinders. Their prized souvenirs are the strands of different cultures they decide to knit into their own character. The world is a cultural yarn shop. And Back Door Travelers are weaving the ultimate tapestry. Come on, join in!

ITALY

- 116,000 square miles (the size of Arizona)
- 60 million people (477 people per square mile)
- 800 miles tall, 100 miles wide
- 1,600 lire = about US$1; 1,000 lire = about 65 cents
- Country telephone code: 39; international access code: 00

Bella Italia! It has Europe's richest, craziest culture. If I had to choose just one, Italy's my favorite. If you take it on its own terms and accept the package deal, Italy is a cultural keelhauling that actually feels good.

Some people, often with considerable effort, manage to hate it. Italy bubbles with emotion, corruption, stray hairs, inflation, traffic jams, body odor, strikes, rallies, holidays, crowded squalor, and irate ranters shaking their fists at each other one minute and walking arm in arm the next. Have a talk with yourself before you cross the border. Promise yourself to relax and soak in it; it's a glorious mud puddle.

With so much history and art in Venice, Florence, and Rome, you'll need to do some reading ahead to maximize your experience. There are two Italys: the north is relatively industrial, aggressive, and "time-is-money" in its outlook. The Po River basin and the area between Milan, Genoa, and Torino have the richest farmland and the heavy-duty industry. The south is more crowded, poor, relaxed, farm-oriented, and traditional. Families here are very strong and usually live in the same house for many generations. Loyalties are to the family, city, region, soccer team, and country—in that order. The Appenine Mountains give Italy a rugged north-south spine, while the Alps divide Italy from France, Switzerland, and Austria in the north.

Economically, Italy has had its problems, but somehow things work out. Today Italy is the Western world's seventh-largest industrial power. Its people earn more per capita than the British. Italy is the world's leading wine producer. It is sixth in cheese and wool output. Tourism (as you'll find out) is also big business in Italy. Cronyism, which complicates my work, is an integral part of the economy.

Italy, home of the Vatican, is Catholic, but the dominant religion is life—motor scooters, football, fashion, girl-watching, boy-watching, good coffee, good wine, and *la dolce far niente* ("the sweetness of doing nothing"). The Italian character shows itself on the streets with the skilled maniac drivers and the classy dressers who star in the ritual evening stroll, or *passeggiata*.

The language is fun. Be melodramatic and move your hand with your tongue. Hear the melody, get into the flow. Fake it, let the farce be with you. Italians are outgoing characters. They want to communicate, and they try harder than any other Europeans. Play with them.

Italy, a land of extremes, is also the most thief-ridden country you'll visit. Tourists suffer virtually no violent crime—but plenty of petty purse-snatchings, pickpocketings, and shortchangings. Only the sloppy get stung. Wear your money belt! Unfortunately, you'll need to assume many Gypsy women and children on the street are after your wallet or purse.

Traditionally, Italy uses the siesta plan: people work from 8:00 or 9:00 to 13:00 and from 15:30 to 19:00, six days a week. Many businesses have adopted the government's new recommended 8:00–14:00 workday. In tourist areas, shops are open longer.

Sightseeing hours are always changing in Italy, and (especially with the expected new austerity programs promised by the new right-wing government) many of the hours in this book will be wrong by the time you travel. Use the local tourist offices to double-check your sightseeing plans.

For extra sightseeing information, take advantage of the cheap, colorful, and dry but informative city guidebooks sold on the streets all over. Also, use the information telephones you'll find in most historic buildings. Just set the dial on English, pop in your coins, and listen. The narration is often accompanied by a brief slide show. Many dark interiors can be brilliantly lit for a coin. Whenever possible, let there be light.

Some important Italian churches require modest dress: no shorts or bare shoulders on men or women. With a little imagination (except at the Vatican), those caught by surprise can improvise something—a jacket for your knees and maps for your shoulders. I wear a super lightweight pair of long pants for my hot and muggy big-city Italian sightseeing.

While no longer a cheap country, Italy is still a hit with shoppers. Glassware (Venice), gold, silver, leather, and prints (Florence), and high fashion (Rome) are good souvenirs, but do some price research at home so you know what a good value is.

Many tourists are mind-boggled by the huge prices: 16,000 lire for dinner! 42,000 for the room! 126,000 for the taxi ride! That's still real money—it's just spoken of in much smaller units than a dollar. Since there are roughly L1,600 in a dollar, figure Italian prices by covering the last three zeros with your finger and taking about two-thirds of the remaining figure. That L16,000 dinner costs $10 in U.S. money; the L42,000 room, $28; and the taxi ride . . . uh-oh!

Beware of the "slow count." After you buy something, you may get your change back in batches. The salesperson (or bank teller) hopes you are confused by all the zeros and will gather up your money and say *grazie* before he or she finishes the count. Always do your own rough figuring before-hand and understand the transaction. Only the sloppy are ripped off. Try to enforce the local prices. It's only natural for them to inflate prices or assume you don't know what's a fair rate. Be savvy, firm, and friendly.

La dolce far niente is a big part of Italy. Zero in on the fine points. Don't dwell on the problems. Accept Italy as Italy. Savor your cappuccino, dangle your feet over a canal (if it smells, breathe through your mouth), and imagine what it was like centuries ago. Ramble through the rubble of Rome and mentally resurrect those ancient stones. Look into the famous sculpted eyes of Michelangelo's *David*, and understand Renaissance man's assertion of himself. Sit silently on a hilltop rooftop. Get chummy with the winds of the past. Write a poem over a glass of local wine in a sun-splashed, wave-dashed Riviera village. If you fall off your moral horse, call it a cultural experience. Italy is for romantics.

ROME (ROMA)

Rome is magnificent and brutal at the same time. Your ears will ring, your nose will turn your hankie black, the careless will be run down or pickpocketed, you'll be frustrated by chaos that only an Italian can understand. You may even come to believe Mussolini was necessary. But Rome is required. If your hotel provides a comfortable refuge; if you pace yourself, accept and even partake in the siesta plan; if you're well-organized for sight-seeing; and if you protect yourself and your valuables with extra caution and discretion, you'll do fine. You'll see the sights and leave satisfied.

Rome at its peak meant civilization itself. Everything was either civilized (part of the Roman Empire, Latin- or Greek-speaking) or barbarian. Today, Rome is Italy's political capital, the capital of Catholicism, and a splendid . . . "junkpile" is not quite the right word . . . of western civilization. As you wander, you'll find its buildings, people, cats, laundry, and traffic endlessly entertaining. And then, of course, there are its magnificent sights.

Tour St. Peter's, the greatest church on earth, and scale Michelangelo's 100-yard-tall dome, the world's largest. Learn something about eternity by touring the huge Vatican Museum. You'll find paradise—bright as the day it was painted—in the Sistine Chapel. Do the "Caesar shuffle" walk from the historic Colosseum through the ancient Forum, and over the Capitoline Hill. Enjoy the sweet life. Take an early evening "Dolce Vita Stroll" down the Via del Corso with Rome's beautiful people.

Planning Your Time

For most, Rome is best done fast. It's great, but exhausting. Time is normally short and Italy is more charming elsewhere.

To "do" Rome in a day, consider it as a side trip from Orvieto or Florence and maybe before the night train to Venice. Crazy as that sounds, if all you have is a day, it's a great one.

If you only have a day, be brutally selective: Vatican (2 hours in museum and Sistine and an hour in St. Peter's), march over river to Pantheon, then over the Capitoline Hill, through the Forum and to the Colosseum. Dinner on Campo di Fiori and evening stroll (Piazza Navona to Spanish Steps).

   With two days (the optimal first visit): To maximize open hours do odd sights that close at 13:00 first and finish the day with the "Caesar Shuffle" through the Forum and Colosseum. On the second day do the Vatican (St. Peters, climb the dome, tour the museum). After a siesta, join the locals strolling (Piazza del Popolo to Spanish Steps) or Trastevere to Campo di Fiori to Spanish Steps.

   With a third day consider adding a side trip to Ostia and another museum.

Rome Area

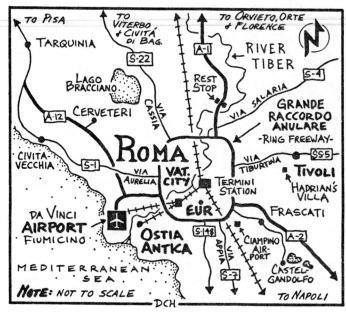

Orientation (tel. code: 06)

The modern sprawl of Rome is of no interest to us. Our Rome is the old core—within the triangle formed by the train station, Colosseum, and Vatican. Get a handle on Rome by considering it in these chunks: **The ancient city** had a million people. Tear it down to size by walking through just the core. The best of the classical sights stand in a line from the Colosseum to the Pantheon. In the time of **Medieval Rome**, the population dipped as low as 50,000, and a good part of them were thieves. The medieval city, a colorful tangle of lanes, lies between the Pantheon and the river. **Window-shoppers' Rome** twinkles with nightlife and ritzy shopping near medieval Rome, on or near Rome's main drag, the Via del Corso. **The Vatican City** is a compact world of its own with two great sights: a huge basilica and the museum. And **Trastevere**, the seedy/colorful wrong-side-of-the-river neighborhood-village, is Rome at its crustiest. **Baroque Rome** is an overleaf that embellishes great squares through-out the town with fountains and church facades.

Tourist Information

Rome offers less tourist information per capita than any city in the First World. Most available publications are two years old, and nobody seems to know or care what is actually going on. The Ente Provinciale Per il Turismo (EPT) has three offices (8:15-19:15): at the airport, in the train station (near track #1, very crowded, the only one open on Sunday), and the central office (5 Via Parigi, just a 5-minute walk out the front of the station, near Piazza della Republica's huge fountain, less crowded and more helpful, air-conditioned with comfortable sofas and a desk to plan on—or sit at to over-come your frustration, tel. 06/48899255 or 48899253). Get the free EPT city map (better than the free McDonald's ver-sion, ask for one with bus lines) and a monthly periodical guide if there is one. (If all you need is a map, forget the TI. Most hotels carry the EPT map.) Fancy hotels carry a free and helpful English monthly, *Un Ospite a Roma* (A Guest in Rome). All hotels list an inflated rate to cover the hefty commission any room-finding service charges. You'll save money by booking direct.

     Enjoy Rome (8:30-13:00, 15:30-18:00, closed Saturday afternoon and on Sunday, 3 blocks northeast of the station at Via Varese 39, tel. 4451843, English-speaking) is a free and friendly new information service providing maps, museum hours, and a room-finding service.

     Apart from the normal big bus tours, the ATAC city buses do a 3-hour orientation tour daily. And American

Rome

students in Rome lead "Secret Walks" (May-October).
Three or four different walks are given daily (L5,000 membership card required plus L12,000 per tour or L9,000 for students, children under 15 go free, tel. 39728728).

Trains and Buses

The Termini train station is a mine field of tourist services: a late-hours bank, a day hotel, luggage lockers, 24-hour thievery, the city bus station, and a subway stop. Handy multilingual charts make locations very clear. La Piazza is a bright and cheery self-service restaurant (open 11:00-22:30).

Getting Around Rome

Sightsee on foot, by city bus, or taxi. I've grouped your sightseeing into walkable neighborhoods. Public transportation is efficient, cheap, and part of your Roman experience.

Buses: Bus routes are clearly listed at the stops. Bus #64 is particularly useful, connecting the station, Victor Emmanuel Monument (near the Forum), and the Vatican. Ride it for a city overview and to watch pickpockets in action. Buy tickets at newsstands, tobacco shops, or at major bus stops but not on board (L1,200, good for 90 minutes, punch them yourself as you board). Buy a bunch so you can hop a bus without searching for an open tobacco shop. (Riding without a ticket, while relatively safe, is still stressful. Inspectors fine even innocent-looking tourists L50,000 if found on a bus or subway without a ticket.) If you hop a bus without a ticket, locals who use tickets rather than a monthly pass can sell you a ticket from their wallet bundle. All-day bus/Metro passes cost L4,000. Learn which buses serve your neighborhood.

Buses, especially the touristic #64, and the subway, are havens for thieves and pickpockets. Assume any commotion is a thief-created distraction. Watch your pack, wear no wallet, and keep your money belt out of sight. When it's crowded, a giggle or a jostle can be expensive. For six trips in a row, I've met a tourist who was pickpocketed. You are a target.

Subway: The Roman subway system (Metropolitana) is simple, with two clean, cheap, fast lines. While much of Rome is not served by its skimpy subway, these stops may be helpful to you: Termini (central train station, several recommended hotels, National Museum), Republica (main tourist office,

Metropolitana: Rome's Subway

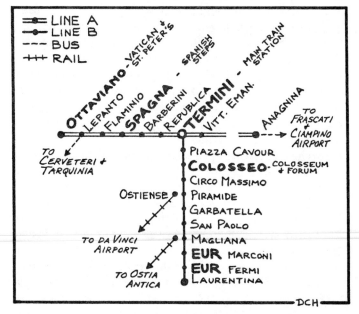

several recommended hotels), Barberini (Cappuccin Crypt, Trevi Fountain), Spagna (Spanish Steps, Villa Borghese, classiest shopping area), Flaminio (Piazza del Popolo, start of the Via del Corso Dolce Vita stroll), Ottaviano (the Vatican, recommended hotels), Colosseo (the Colosseum, Roman Forum, recommended hotels), and EUR (Mussolini's futuristic suburb). Buy your L1,000 subway tickets at subway ticket counters. (Attendants will try to short-change you.)

Taxis: Taxis' big drop-charge (L6,400) covers you for 3 kilometers. (L5,000 surcharge after 22:00.) From the train station to the Colosseo costs about L8,000, to the Vatican about L12,000. Three or four traveling together with more money than time should taxi almost everywhere. Rather than wave and wave, ask in local shops for the nearest taxi stand (*"Dov'e una fermata dei tassi?"*). The meter is fair.

Helpful Hints

General Museum Hours: 9:00-14:00, closed on Monday (except the Vatican) and at 13:00 on Sunday. Outdoor sights like the Colosseum, Forum, and Ostia Antica are open

9:00-19:00 (15:00 in winter), and are often closed one day a week. The Capitoline Hill museums, Rome's only nocturnal museums, are open Tuesday 17:00-20:00, and Saturday 20:00-23:00. There are absolutely no absolutes in Italy. These hours will vary. Confirm sightseeing plans each morning with a quick L200 telephone call asking, "Are you open today?" (*"Aperto oggi?"*) and "What time do you close?" (*"A che ora chuiso?"*). I've included telephone numbers for this purpose. The last pages of the daily "Messaggero" newspaper list current events, exhibits, and hours.

Churches: Churches open early, close for lunch, and reopen for a few hours around 16:00. Modest dress means no bare shoulders, mini-skirts, or shorts (men or women). Kamikaze tourists maximize their sightseeing hours by visiting churches before 9:00, seeing the major sights that don't close for siesta (St. Peter's and the Forum), when all good Romans are taking it cool and easy, and doing the nocturnal museums after dark.

Shop Hours: Usually 9:00-13:00 and 16:00-20:00. In the holiday month of August, many shops and restaurants close up for vacation—*Chiuso per ferie* (and closed for restoration) signs decorate locked doors all over town.

Theft Alert: With sweet-talking con artists, pickpockets on buses and at the station, and thieving gangs at the ancient sights, Rome is a gauntlet of rip-offs. Other than getting run down, there's no great physical risk. But green tourists will be ripped off. Thieves strike when you're distracted. Don't trust kind strangers and keep nothing important in your pockets. Assume you're being stalked.

Buyer Beware: I carefully understand the final price before I order *anything* and I deliberately count my change. Expect the "slow count." Wait for the last bits of your change to straggle over to you. There are legitimate extras (café prices skyrocket when you sit down, taxis get L5,000 extra after 22:00, and so on) to which paranoid tourists wrongly take offense. But the waiter who charges you L70,000 for the pizza and beer assumes you're too polite to involve the police. If you have any problem with a restaurant, hotel, or taxi, get a cop to arbitrate. Rome is trying to civilize itself.

Siesta: The siesta is a key to survival in summertime Rome. Lie down and contemplate the extraordinary power of gravity in the eternal city. I drink lots of cold, refreshing water from

Rome's many drinking fountains (the Forum has three). If you get sick, call the International Medical Center (tel. 4882371).

Sights—Rome
(These sights are in walking order.)

▲**St. Peter-in-Chains Church (San Pietro in Vincoli)**—
The original chains and Michelangelo's able-to-stand-and-toss-those-tablets *Moses* are on exhibit in an otherwise unexceptional church. Just a short walk uphill from the Colosseum (free, 6:30-12:30, 15:30-19:00, modest dress required).

Downtown Ancient Rome

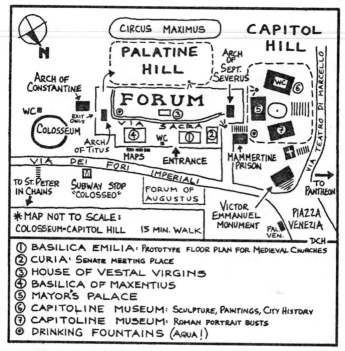

1. BASILICA EMILIA: Prototype floor plan for Medieval Churches
2. CURIA: Senate meeting place
3. HOUSE OF VESTAL VIRGINS
4. BASILICA OF MAXENTIUS
5. MAYOR'S PALACE
6. CAPITOLINE MUSEUM: Sculpture, Paintings, City History
7. CAPITOLINE MUSEUM: Roman portrait busts
8. DRINKING FOUNTAINS (Aqua!)

▲▲▲**Colosseum**—This is the great example of Roman engineering, 2,000 years old. The Romans, using concrete, brick, and their trademark round arches, were able to construct much larger buildings than the Greeks. But in deference to the higher Greek culture, notice how they finished their no-nonsense mega-structure by pasting all three orders (Doric, Ionic, and Corinthian) of Greek columns as decorations on the outside. The Flavian Amphitheater's popular name "Colosseum" comes from the colossal statue of Nero that used to stand in front of it.

Romans were into "big." By putting two theaters together, they created a circular amphitheater. They could fill and empty its 50,000 numbered seats as quickly and efficiently as we do our super-stadiums. They had teams of sailors who could hoist canvas awnings over the stadium to give the fans shade. This was where the ancient Romans, whose taste was nearly as violent as modern America's, enjoyed their Dirty Harry and Terminator. Gladiators, criminals, and wild animals fought to the death in every conceivable scenario. They could even flood the place to wage mock naval battles (free, L6,000 to go upstairs, daily 9:00-19:00, Sunday and Wednesday 9:00-13:00, less off-season, tel. 7004261.)

▲▲▲**Roman Forum (Foro Romano)**—Ancient Rome's birthplace and civic center, the Forum was the common ground between Rome's famous seven hills. To help resurrect this confusing pile of rubble, study the before-and-after pictures in the cheap city guidebooks sold on the streets. (Check out the small red *Rome, Past and Present* books with plastic overleafs to un-ruin the ruins. They're priced at L25,000—pay no more than L10,000.)

Start at the Basilica Aemilia, on your right as you walk down the entry ramp. This ancient palace's floor plan shows how medieval churches adopted the "basilica" design. Then walk the Via Sacra, the main street of ancient Rome, running from the Arch of Septimus Severus on the right, past Basilica Aemilia, up to the Arch of Titus and the Colosseum on the left. The plain, intact brick building near the Arch of Septimus Severus was the Curia where the Roman senate sat. (Peek inside.) Only the giant barrel vault remains of the huge Basilica Maxentius, looming crumbly and weed-eaten to the left of Via Sacra as you walk to the Arch of Titus (direction: Colosseum).

As you stand in the shadow of the Bas Max, reconstruct the place in your mind. The huge barrel vaults were just side niches. Extend the broken nub of an arch out over the vacant lot and finish your imaginary Roman basilica with rich marble and fountains. People it with plenty of toga-clad Romans. Yeow.

The Arch of Titus is carved with propaganda celebrating the defeat, in A.D. 70, of the Jews which began the Diaspora that ended only with the creation of Israel in 1947 (find the menorah).

From the Titus drinking fountain, walk up the Palatine Hill to the remains of the Imperial palaces. We get our word "palace" from this hill, where the emperors chose to live. The pleasant garden overlooks the Forum; on the far side, look down on the dusty old Circus Maximus. (L10,000, Forum open 9:00-19:00, Sunday 9:00-13:00, off-season 9:00-15:00, last tickets sold an hour before closing, tel. 6990110). Just past the entry, there's a WC and a handy headless statue for you to pose behind.

▲**Thief Gangs**—If you know what to look out for, the omni-present groups of children picking the pockets and handbags of naive tourists are no threat but an interesting, albeit sad, spectacle. Gangs of city-stained children, too young to pros-ecute but old enough to rip you off, troll through the tourist crowds around the Forum, Colosseum, and train and Metro stations. Watch them target tourists distracted with a video camera or overloaded with bags. They look like beggars and use newspapers or cardboard signs to distract their victims. Every year they get bolder, but they'll still scram like stray cats if you're on to them. A fast-fingered mother with a baby is often nearby.

▲**Mammertine Prison**—The 2,500-year-old converted cistern that once imprisoned Saints Peter and Paul is worth a look. On the walls are lists of prisoners (Christian and non-Christian) and how they were executed: Strangolati, Decapitato, Morto di Fame . . . (donation requested, 9:00-12:00, 14:30-18:00). At the top of the stairs leading to the Campidoglio, you'll find a refreshing water foun-tain. Block the spout with your fingers; it spurts up for drinking.

▲▲**Capitoline Hill (Campidoglio)**—This hill was the reli-gious and political center of ancient Rome. It's still the home of the city's government. Michelangelo's lovely Renaissance square is bounded by two fine museums and the mayoral palace.

The Capitoline Museum (Musei Capitolini) in the Palazzo Nuovo (the building closest to the river) is the world's oldest museum (500 years old) and more important than its sister (opposite). Outside the entrance, notice the marriage announcements (and, very likely, wedding party photo ops). Inside the courtyard, have some photo fun with chunks of a giant statue of Emperor Constantine. (A rare public toilet hides near the museum ticket-taker.) The museum is worthwhile, with lavish rooms housing several great statues including the original (500 B.C.) Etruscan Capitoline wolf and the enchanting Commodus as Hercules. Across the square is a museum full of ancient statues—great if you like portrait busts of forgotten emperors or want to see the restored equestrian statue of Marcus Aurelius that used to sit on the pedestal in the square. (L10,000, Both open Tuesday-Saturday 9:00-13:30, Tuesday 17:00-20:00, Saturday 20:00-23:00, Sunday 9:00-13:00, closed Monday, tel. 67102475.) There's a fine view of the Forum from the terrace just past the mayor's palace on the right.

To approach the great square the way Michelangelo wanted you to, walk halfway down the grand stairway toward Piazza Venezia, spin around, and walk back up. At the bottom of the stairs, look up the long stairway to your right for a good example of the earliest style of Christian church and be thankful it's not worth climbing up to see.

Way down the street on your left, you'll see a modern building actually built around surviving ancient pillars and arches. Farther ahead (toward Piazza Venezia), look into the ditch (on the right), and see how everywhere modern Rome is built on the countless bricks and forgotten mosaics of ancient Rome.

Piazza Venezia—This square is the focal point of modern Rome. The Via del Corso, starting here, is the city's axis, surrounded by the classiest shopping district. From the Palazzo di Venezia's balcony above the square (to your left with back to Victor Emmanuel Monument), Mussolini whipped up the nationalistic fervor of Italy. Fascist masses filled the square screaming, "Four more years!" or something like that. (Fifteen years later, they hung him from a meat hook in Milan.)

Victor Emmanuel Monument—This oversize monument

to an Italian king loved only by his relatives and the ignorant
is known to most Romans as "the wedding cake," "the type-
writer," or "the dentures." It wouldn't be so bad if it weren't
sitting on a priceless acre of Ancient Rome. Soldiers guard
Italy's Tomb of the Unknown Soldier as the eternal flame
flickers.

▲▲▲**Pantheon**—For the greatest look at the splendor of
Rome, antiquity's best-preserved interior is a must (free,
normally open 9:00-18:00, Sunday and Monday 9:00-13:00,
less in winter, tel. 369831). Walk past its one-piece granite
columns and through the original bronze door. Sit inside
under the glorious skylight and study it. The dome, 140 feet
high and wide, was Europe's biggest until Brunelleschi's
dome was built in Florence 1,200 years later. You'll understand why this wonderfully harmonious architecture was so
inspirational to the artists of the Renaissance, particularly
Raphael; along with Italy's first two kings, he chose to be
buried here. As you walk around the outside of the Pantheon,
notice the "rise of Rome"—about 15 feet since it was built.

▲**Curiosities near the Pantheon**—The only Gothic church
you'll see in Rome is Santa Maria sopra Minerva. On a little
square behind the Pantheon to the left, past the Bernini ele-
phant and the Egyptian obelisk statue, it was built *sopra*, or
over, a pre-Christian temple of Minerva. Rome was at its low
ebb, almost a ghost town through much of the Gothic period,
and the little building done from this time was later redone
Baroque. This church is a refreshing exception. St. Catherine's
body lies under the altar (her head is in Siena) and a little-
known Michelangelo statue, *Christ Bearing the Cross*, stands
to the left. Fra Angelico's tomb is in the left, or north,
transept.

   Nearby (head out the church's rear door behind the
Michelangelo statue and turn left) you'll find the **Chiesa di
St. Ignazio** church, a riot of Baroque illusions. Study the
ceiling in the back of the nave. Then stand on the yellow
disk on the floor between the two stars. Look at the central
(black) dome. Keeping your eyes on the dome, walk under
and past it. Church building project runs out of money?
Hire a painter to paint a fake (and flat) dome. Turn around
and look at the fresco over the entry. Walk left, then right
. . . then look at the altar. What would you say if I told you

it was a flat painting? (free, churches open until 19:00, take a 12:30-16:00 siesta, and welcome modestly dressed visitors.)

A few blocks away, back across Corso Victor Emmanuel, is the very rich and Baroque **Gesu Church**, headquarters of the Jesuits in Rome. The Jesuits powered the Church's Counter-Reformation. With Protestants teaching that all roads to heaven didn't pass through Rome, the baroque churches of the late 1500s were painted with spiritual road maps that said they did.

▲▲**The Dolce Vita Stroll down Via del Corso**—The city's chic and hip "cruise" from the Piazza del Popolo (Metro: Flaminio) down a wonderfully traffic-free section of the Via del Corso and up Via Condotti to the Spanish Steps each evening around 18:00. Shoppers, take a left on Via Condotti for the Spanish Steps and Gucci (shops open after siesta, 16:30-19:30). Historians, start with a visit to the Baroque Church of Santa Maria del Popolo (with Raphael's Chigi Chapel and two Caravaggio paintings), continue down the Via del Corso to the Victor Emmanuel Monument, climb Michelangelo's stairway to his glorious Campidoglio Square, and visit Rome's Capitoline Museum, open Tuesday and Saturday evenings. Catch the lovely view of the Forum (from past the mayor's palace on right) as the horizon reddens and cats prowl the unclaimed rubble of ancient Rome.

▲**Villa Borghese**—Rome's unkept "Central Park" is great for people-watching (plenty of modern-day Romeos and Juliets). Take a row on the lake, or visit its fine museums. The **Borghese Gallery** has some world-class Baroque art, including the exciting Bernini statue of Apollo chasing Daphne, and paintings by Caravaggio and Rubens (L4,000, 9:00-14:00, Sunday 9:00-13:00, closed Monday, tel. 8548577; for a few years the paintings will be in Trastevere at via de San Michele 22, 10:00-13:00, 16:00-20:00, closed Monday and Sunday afternoon). The nearby Museo di Villa Giulia is a fine Etruscan museum (L8,000, 9:00-19:00, Sunday 9:00-13:00, closed Monday, also often closed, tel. 3201951).

▲**National Museum of Rome (Museo Nazionale Romano delle Terme)**—Directly in front of the station, it houses much of the greatest ancient Roman sculpture

(L3,000, 9:00-14:00, Sunday until 13:00, closed Monday, tel. 4880530). This collection is being moved to the nearby Palazzo Massimo, so call before visiting.

▲▲▲**Floodlit Rome Hike: Trastevere to the Spanish Steps**—Rome can be grueling. But a fine way to enjoy this historian's fertility rite is an evening walk lacing together Rome's flood-lit night spots. Fine urban spaces, real-life theater vignettes, sitting close enough to the Bernini fountain to hear no traffic, water flickering its mirror on the marble, jostling with local teenagers to see all the gelati flavors, enjoying lovers straddling more than the bench, jay-walking past flak-vested *polizia*, marveling at the ramshackle elegance that softens this brutal city for those who were born here and can imagine living nowhere else—these are the flavors of Rome best tasted after dark.

Taxi or ride the bus (#23 from the Vatican area) to Trastevere, the colorful neighborhood across (*tras*) the Tiber (*tevere*). Start your hike at Santa Maria in Trastevere. Trastevere offers the best look at medieval-village Rome. The action all marches to the chime of the church bells. Go there and wander. Wonder. Be a poet. This is Rome's Left Bank.

Santa Maria in Trastevere from the third century (free, 8:00-12:00, 16:00-19:00) is one of Rome's oldest churches. Notice the ancient basilica floor plan and early Christian symbols in the walls near the entry.

From the square, Via del Moro leads to the river and Ponte Sisto, a pedestrian bridge with a good view of St. Peter's dome. Cross the bridge and continue straight ahead for one block. Take the first left, which leads through the scary and narrow darkness to Piazza Farnese with the imposing Palazzo Farnese. The palace's beautiful interior, designed in part by Michelangelo, is closed to the public. One block from there is **Campo di Fiori** (Field of Flowers), which is an affordable outdoor dining room after dark (Trattoria Virgilio is one of several decent restaurants).

If the statue on the square did a hop, step, and a jump forward and turned right, he'd cross the busy Corso Vittorio Emanuele and find Piazza Navona. Rome's most interesting night scene features street music, artists, fire-eaters, local Casanovas, ice cream, outdoor cafés (splurge-worthy if you've got time to sit and enjoy the human river of Italy), and three fountains by Bernini, the father of Baroque art. This oblong square is molded around the long-gone stadium of Domitian, an ancient chariot race track that was often flooded so the masses could enjoy major water games.

Leave Piazza Navona directly across from the Tre Scalini café, go past rose peddlers and palm readers, jog left around the guarded building, and follow the yellow sign to the Pantheon straight down Via del Salvatore (cheap pizza place on left just before the Pantheon). From the obelisk (facing the Pantheon), head left to Casa del Caffe, then left down Via degli Orfani. At the square, pass the church on the left down Via Aquiro. At the obelisk (if it's gelati time, take a detour left behind Albergo Nazionale), turn right, walk between the Italian parliament and the huge Il Tempo newspaper building to the busy Via del Corso. You'll pass the huge second-century column honoring Marcus Aurelius, cross the street, and go into the lofty gallery. Take the right branch of this Y-shaped gallery and exit continuing straight down Via de Crociferi to the roar of the water, light, and people of the Trevi fountain.

The **Trevi fountain** is an example of how Rome took full advantage of the abundance of water brought into the city by its great aqueducts. This watery Baroque avalanche was built in 1762. Romantics toss two coins over their shoulder thinking it will give them a wish and assure their return to Rome. That may sound stupid, but every year I go through this touristic ritual . . . and it seems to work very well.

Take some time to people-watch (whisper a few breathy *bellos* or *bellas*) before leaving. Facing the fountain, go past it on the right down Via delle Stamperia to Via del Triton. Cross the busy street and continue to the Spanish Steps (ask, '*Dové Piazza di Spagna?*') a few short blocks and thousands of dollars of shopping opportunities away.

The **Piazza di Spagna**, with the very popular Spanish Steps, got its name 300 years ago when this was the site of the Spanish Embassy. It's been the hangout of many romantics over the years (Keats, Wagner, Openshaw, Goethe, and others). The Boat Fountain at the foot of the steps was done by Bernini's father, Bernini.

Facing the steps, walk to your right about a block to tour one of the world's biggest and most lavish McDonald's.

Vatican City, St. Peter's, and the Museum

Ⓞ yds 100 200 300
Ⓞ m 100 200 300

CONVENT
VIA ANDREA DORIA
OTTAVIANO SUBWAY STOP
PIAZZA EROI
MARKET
PENSIONE ALIMANDI
VIA LEONE
VIA CANDIA
VIA SCIPIONI
VIA SEB. VEN.
LOTS OF BUSES
VIA ANG. EMO
VIA COLA
VIA CRES.
VATICANO WALL
WALL
PIAZZA RISORGI-MENTO
VATICAN MUSEUM
PAPAL APT.
ITAL. POST
TO TIBER RIVER, PANTHEON FORUM, ETC.
SISTINE CHAPEL
BUS 64
GARDENS
RADIO VAT.
P.O.
OBELISK VIA CONCILIAZIONE
ST. PETER'S
WALL
PIAZZA S. PIETRO
TUNNEL
❶ ENTRANCE to VAT. MUSEUMS
❷ TOURIST INFO, POST, W.C. & BUS STOP FOR VAT. MUSEUM
—DCH—

About a block on the other side of the steps is the subway, or *Metropolitana*, which (until 23:30) will zip you home.

▲▲**Ostia Antica**—Rome's ancient seaport (80,000 people in the time of Christ, later a ghost town, now excavated), less than an hour from downtown, is the next best thing to Pompeii. Start at the 2,000-year-old theater, buy a map, explore the town, and finish with its fine little museum. To get there, take the subway's B Line to the Magliana stop, catch the Lido train to Ostia Antica (twice an hour), walk over the overpass, go straight to the end of that road, and follow the signs to (or ask for) "scavi" Ostia Antica. Open daily from 9:00 to one hour before sunset. The L8,000 entry fee includes the museum (which closes at 14:00). Just beyond is the filthy beach (Lido), an interesting anthill of Roman sun-worshipers.

▲▲**Vatican City**—This tiny independent country of just over 100 acres is contained entirely within Rome. Politically powerful, the Vatican is the religious capital of 800 million Roman Catholics. If you're not one already, become a Catholic for your visit. Start by dropping by the helpful tourist office just to the left of St. Peter's Basilica (Monday-Saturday, 8:30-19:00, tel. 69884466.) Check out the glossy L5,000 guidebooklet (crowded piazza on cover), which doubles as a classy souvenir. Telephone them if you're interested in the pope's schedule (Sundays at noon for a quick blessing of the crowds in Piazza San Pietro from the window of his study above the square, or Wednesday mornings when a reservation is necessary), or in their sporadic but very good tours of the Vatican grounds or the church interior. If you don't care to see the pope, remember that the times he appears are most crowded. Handy buses shuttle visitors between the church and the museum (L2,000, twice an hour, 8:45 until about 13:00). This is far better than the exhausting walk around the Vatican wall, and it gives you a pleasant peek at the garden-filled Vatican grounds.

▲▲▲**St. Peter's Basilica**—There is no doubt: this is the richest and most impressive church on earth. To call it vast is like calling God smart. Marks on the floor show where the next largest churches would fit if they were put inside. The ornamental cherubs would dwarf a large man. Birds roost

St. Peter's Basilica

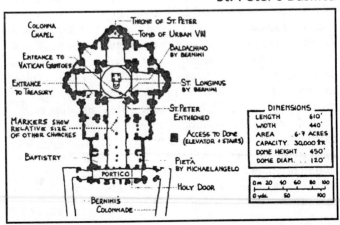

inside, and thousands of people wander about, heads craned heavenward, hardly noticing each other. Don't miss Michelangelo's *Pietà* (behind bullet-proof glass) to the right of the entrance. Bernini's altar work and huge bronze canopy (*baldacchino*) are brilliant.

While for most the treasury (in the sacristy) is not worth the admission, the crypt is free and worth a wander. Directly under the dome, stairs will lead you down to the level of the earlier church and the tombs of many of the popes, including the very first one . . . Peter.

The dome, Michelangelo's last work, is (you guessed it) the biggest anywhere. Taller than a football field is long, it's well worth the sweaty climb (330 steps after the elevator, allow an hour to go up and down) for a great view of Rome, the Vatican grounds, and the inside of the Basilica—particularly heavenly while there is singing. (Last entry is about an hour before closing. Catch the elevator just outside the church to the right as you face it.) The church strictly enforces its dress code. Dress modestly—a dress or long pants, shoulders covered. You are usually required to check any bags at a cloak room near the entry. St. Peter's is open daily 7:00-19:00, 18:00 in winter; ticket booths to the treasury and dome close an hour early. All are welcome to join in the mass (most days at the front altar, 17:00).

The church is particularly moving at 7:00 while tourism is still sleeping. Volunteers who want you to understand and appreciate St. Peter's give free 90-minute "Pilgrim Service" tours in English often at 10:15 and 15:00. Check at the desk just after the dress code check as you're entering for the day's schedule. Seeing the *Pietà* is neat, understanding it is divine.

▲▲▲**The Vatican Museum**—Too often, the immense Vatican Museum is treated as an obstacle course, with four nagging miles of displays, separating the tourist from the Sistine Chapel. Even without the Sistine, this is one of Europe's top three or four houses of art. It can be exhausting, so plan your visit carefully, focusing on a few themes, and allow several hours. The museum uses a nearly-impossible-not-to-follow, one-way system.

Required minimum stops, in this order: Etruscan Gallery (impressive for 500 B.C. and well-explained in English), Egyptian mummies and statues; *Apollo Belvedere* and *Laocoön* in Octagonal Courtyard, *Belvedere Torso* (all three showing the Classical mastery of the body and very influential to Renaissance artists); past the rooms of animals, the giant porphyry hot tub, between the porphyry sarcophagi of Constantine's mother and daughter, then down the hall of broken penises and past the corridor of maps to huge rooms plastered with church propaganda (Constantine's divine vision and his victory at Milvian Bridge which led him to become Christian, and the 19th-century Vatican declaration of the immaculate conception of the Virgin Mary), past a small chapel frescoed by Fra Angelico and into the Raphael rooms.

The masterpiece here is the School of Athens, remarkable for its blatant pre-Christian Classical orientation wallpapering the apartments of Pope Julius II. Raphael honors the great pre-Christian thinkers—Aristotle, Plato, and company—who are portrayed as the leading artists of Raphael's day: the bearded figure of Plato is Leonardo da Vinci, and Michelangelo broods in the foreground—supposedly added late, after Raphael snuck a peek at the Sistine Chapel and decided that his arch-competitor was so good he had to put their personal differences aside and include him in this tribute to the artists of his generation. Today's St. Peter's was under construction as Raphael was working. In this fresco he gives us a sneak preview of the unfinished church. (The School of Athens is likely to be scaffolded up through 1995.)

Next (unless you detour through the refreshing modern Catholic art section) is the newly restored Sistine Chapel. Michelangelo's pictorial culmination of the Renaissance shows the story of Creation with a powerful God weaving in and out of each scene through that busy week. This is an optimistic and positive expression of the high Renaissance. Later, after the Reformation wars had begun and after the Catholic army of Spain had sacked the Vatican, the reeling church began to fight back. As part of its Counter-Reformation, Michelangelo was commissioned to paint the Last Judgment (behind the altar). Newly restored, the message is as brilliant and clear as the day Michelangelo finished it: Christ is returning, some will go to hell and some to heaven, and some will be saved by the power of the rosary.

The Vatican's small but fine collection of paintings, the Pinacoteca (with Raphael's *Transfiguration* and Caravaggio's *Deposition*) is near the entry/exit. Early Christian art is the final possible side trip before exiting via the souvenir shop.

The museum clearly marks out four color-coded visits of different lengths. Rentable headphones (L6,000) give a recorded tour of the Raphael rooms and Michelangelo's Sistine masterpiece. (Easter, July, August, September, and first half of October hours: 8:45-16:30, Saturday 8:45-14:00, closed Sunday, except last Sunday of month when museum is free; the rest of the year it's open 8:45-13:45. Last entry an hour before closing. Many minor rooms close 13:45-14:45 or from 13:30 on. The Sistine Chapel is closed 30 minutes before the rest of the museum. A small door at the rear of the Sistine Chapel is used by speedy tour groups to escape via St. Peter's. If you squirt out here you're done with the museum. The Pinacoteca is the only important part left. Consider doing it at the start. Otherwise, it's a 10-minute heel-to-toe slalom through the tourists from the Sistine to the entry/exit, L13,000, tel. 69883333. The museum is closed on 5/1, 6/29, 8/15, 11/1, 12/8, and on church holidays.)

The museum's excellent book and card shop offers a priceless (L10,000) black-and-white photo book of the *Pietà*— great for gifts. The Vatican post has an office in the museum and one on Piazza San Pietro (comfortable writing rooms, Monday-Friday 8:30-19:00, Saturday 8:30-18:00); the Vatican post is the only reliable mail service in Italy, and the stamps are a collectible bonus (Vatican stamps are good throughout Rome, Italian stamps are not good at the Vatican). The Vatican bank has sinful rates.

▲**Cappuccin Crypt**—If you want bones, this is it: below Santa Maria della Immaculata Concezione on Via Veneto, just off Piazza Barberini, are thousands of skeletons, all artistically arranged for the delight—or disgust—of the always wide-eyed visitor. The monastic message on the wall near the entry explains that this is more than just a macabre exercise. Pick up a few of Rome's most interesting postcards (9:00-12:00, 15:00-18:30). A bank with long hours and good exchange rates is next door and the American Embassy is just up the street.

▲**E.U.R.**—Mussolini's planned suburb of the future (60

years ago) is a 10-minute subway ride from the Colosseum to Metro: Magliana. From the Magliana subway stop, walk through the park uphill to the Palace of the Civilization of Labor (Pal. d. Civilta d. Concordia), the essence of Fascist architecture with its giant, no-questions-asked, patriotic statues and its this-is-the-truth simplicity. On the far side is the Museo della Civilta Romana (history museum, Piazza G. Agnelli; Metro: EUR Fermi; L5,000, 9:00-13:30, Tuesday and Thursday 15:00-18:00, closed Monday, tel. 5926041), including a large-scale model of ancient Rome.

Overrated Sights—The Spanish Steps (with Italy's first, and one of the world's largest, McDonald's—McGrandeur at its greatest—just down the street) and the commercialized Catacombs, which contain no bones, are way out of the city, and are not worth the time or trouble. The venerable old Villa d'Este garden of fountains near Hadrian's Villa outside of town at Tivoli is now run-down, overpriced, and a disappointment.

Entertainment in Rome

Nighttime fun in Rome is found in the piazzas, along the river, and at its outdoor concerts and street fairs. Pick up a local periodical entertainment guide for a rundown on special events.

Sleeping in Rome
(L1,600 ≈ about $1, tel. code: 06)

The absolute cheapest doubles in Rome are L50,000, without shower or breakfast. You'll pay L22,000 in a sleazy dorm or hostel. A nicer hotel (L100,000 doubles), providing an oasis/ refuge, makes it easier to enjoy this intense and grinding city. If you're going door to door, prices are soft—so bargain. Official prices that hotels list assume an agency or room- finding service kick-back which, if you're coming direct, they avoid. Many hotels have high season (mid-March through October) and low season prices. Easter and September are the crowded times. July and August are too hot for crowds. Most of my recommended hotels are small with huge, murky entrances that make you feel like a Q-tip someone dropped. The amount of English spoken drops with the price. Most places speak some and will hold a room with a phone call.

I've listed mostly places with minimal traffic noise. Many prices here are promised only to people who use no credit card, use no room-finding service, and show this book. Prices are generally guaranteed through 1995 (except for a few holiday times).

Sleep code: **S**=Single, **D**=Double/Twin, **T**=Triple, **Q**=Quad, **B**=Bath/Shower, **WC**=Toilet, **CC**=Credit Card (Visa, Mastercard, Amex), **SE**=Speaks English (graded **A**-**F**). Breakfast is normally included only in the expensive places (as noted).

Sleeping near the Train Station

The cheapest hotels in town are near the station. Avoid places on the seedy south (Colosseum) side of the station. The first two bunches of listings are closest in a safe and decent area (which gets a little weird and spooky late at night), two blocks northeast of the station. The next are a 5-minute walk in front of the station near the Via Nazionale.

Via Magenta 39: These odd ducks are about as cheap as the youth hostel and much handier (no breakfast). **Albergo Sileo** is a shiny chandeliered ten-room place with an elegant touch that has a contract to house train conductors who work the night shift, so they offer rooms from 17:00 to 9:00 only. If you can handle this, it's a great value (D-L40,000, cheap breakfasts, elevator, Via Magenta 39, fourth floor, tel. 4450246, Allesandro and Maria Savioli, SE-D). **Pensione Stefanella** is a dark, homey, quiet place with trampoline beds in four very simple rooms run by an elderly lady named Stefanella (S-L35,000, D-L45,000, SE-F, tel. 4451646). **The Faulty Towers** is a backpacker-type place run by the folks from Enjoy Rome. It's young, hip, and English-speaking, with a rooftop terrace and lots of information (shared triples or quads for L22,000-L25,000 per bed, D-L60,000, DB-L80,000, tel. 4450374).

Via Milazzo 20: Hotel Magic is a tiny, simple place run by a friendly mother-daughter team (Carmella and Rosanna). It's clean and high enough off the road to have no traffic problems (S-L50,000, D-L60,000, DB-L70,000, T-L90,000, TB-L105,000, with this book, no breakfast, Via Milazzo 20, third floor, 00185 Roma, tel. 4959880, little English spoken). In the same building these places are about the same price, good values for cheap rooms but mustier: **Hotel Fenicia** (owner Anna promises my readers a discount, tel. 490342), **Hotel Galli** (tel. 4456859), **Soggiorno Spagna** (tel. 4941191). A self-serve Lavanderia is at 8 via Milazzo (daily, 8:00-22:00 6 kilos washed and dried for L12,000).

Hotel Nardizzi Americana (D-L100,000, DB-L120,000, T-L140,000, TB-L160,000, including breakfast, rates promised through 1995, also 4- and 5-bed rooms, Via Firenze 38, 00184 Roma, elevator, tel. 4880368, fax 4880035, Nik, Fabrizio, and Rugero speak English) is a fine splurge in the station area. Traffic noise in the front rooms is a problem in the summer when you'll want the window open, but it's a tranquil haven, safe, handy, central, and a short walk from the central station and Piazza Barberini on the corner of Via Firenze and Via XX Septembre. (Parking is actually workable here. Double-park below the hotel until a space without yellow lines becomes available and grab it. The defense ministry is across the street, and you've got heavily armed guards all night.

The nearby **Residence Adler** (D-L100,000, DB-L125,000, T-L120,000, TB-L150,000, including breakfast, CC:VM, elevator, Via Modena 5, 00184 Roma, tel. 484466, fax 4880940), with 16 big, quiet, and elegant rooms in a great locale, is another worthwhile splurge.

Hotel Pensione Italia (SB-L75,000, DB-L120,000 with this book and cash only, including breakfast, elevator, Via Venezia 18, just off Via Nazionale, tel. 4828355, fax 4745550), in a busy, interesting, handy locale, placed safely next to the Ministry of the Interior, is pleasant, clean, and thoughtfully run by English-speaking Andrea.

Hotel Aberdeen (DB-L180,000, less off-season, CC:VMA, Via Firenze 48, 00184 Roma, tel. 4819340, fax 4821092, SE-A) with mini-bars, phones, TVs, and showers in its modern rooms, a first-class breakfast buffet, and no traffic noise, is my classiest hotel listing and a good value for Rome.

Sleeping near the Colosseum

A couple of stops on the subway from the train station, these places are out-of-the-station sleaze and buried in a very Roman world of exhaust-stained medieval ambience.

Hotel Flavio (S-L60,000, D-L85,000, DB-L105,000, CC:VM, no breakfast, hiding almost torch-lit under vines on a tiny street a block toward the Colosseum from Via Cavour at Via Frangipane 34, 00184 Roma, tel. 6797203, fax 6796246, not much English) is a real hotel with a classy TV-lounge/lobby, an elevator, and elegant furnishings throughout in a quiet setting. Its weakness is lousy tub-showers down the hall for the five cheap doubles.

Albergo Perugia (S-L38,000, D-L60,000, DB-L90,000, no breakfast, near the corner of Via Cavour and Via Fori Imperiali at Via del Colosseo 7, tel. 6797200, fax 6784635, only Maria speaks English) is yellow, peely, and filled with furniture not fit for a garage sale, but family-run, friendly, peaceful, and beautifully located. Poor couples might offer to share the large-bedded single (for L50,000).

Suore di Sant Anna (S-L35,000, D-L70,000, including breakfast, monkish lunch or dinner for L18,000 more, off the corner of Via dei Serpenti and Via Baccina at Piazza Madonna dei Monti 3, 00184 Roma, tel. 485778, fax 4873903) was built for Ukrainian pilgrims. The sisters are sweet, but the male staff doesn't seem to want your business. It's clumsy and difficult, but once you're in, you've got a comfortable home in a classic locale.

The **YWCA Casa Per Studentesse** (L26,000 per person in 3- and 4-bed rooms, D-L64,000, breakfast included, Via C. Balbo 4, 00184 Roma, 5 blocks toward the Colosseum from the station, tel. 4880460, fax 4871028) accepts women, couples, and couples with children. It's a grey and institutional place, filled with maids in white, more colorful Third World travelers, and 75 single beds.

In old Rome but nowhere near these others, the **Albergo del Sole** (D-L90,000, DB-L120,000, no breakfast, Via del Biscione 76, 00186 Roma, tel. 68806873, fax 6893787) is just off the colorful Campo dei Fiori, right in the Roman thick of things. It's clean and impersonal; has 65 rooms, a roof garden, and lots of Germans; and is spoiled by its success.

Sleeping Two Blocks from the Vatican Museum
Pension Alimandi (D-L97,000, DB-L113,000, TB-L143,000, 5% discount off these prices with this book and cash, CC:VM, elevator to most rooms, optional hearty L10,000 breakfast, great roof garden; just down the stairs in front of the Vatican Museum, Via Tunisi 8, 00192 Roma,

tel. 39726300, fax 39723943, credit card by telephone or fax accepted to secure reservation, SE-A) is a good value, run by friendly and entrepreneurial Paolo and Enrico. From the train station follow Metro line A to last stop, Ottaviano, exit subway station to "V. le G. Cesare," walk straight up that street four or five blocks (it becomes Via Candia), and turn left at Via Tunisi.

Hotel Spring House (D-L110,000, DB-L130,000, including breakfast, CC:VMA, Via Mocenigo 7, a block from Alimandi, tel. 39720948, fax 39721047) offers clean, quiet rooms with balconies, TVs, refrigerators, and a fine sixth-floor breakfast terrace.

Sleeping in Convents near the Vatican
Suore Oblate dell Assunzione (via Andrea Doria 42, 3 blocks in front of the Vatican Museum entrance, tel. 3729540) and a convent across the street from the museum (Viale Vaticano 92, tel. 39723797, fax 39723792) are clean, peaceful, and inexpensive, but no English is spoken and it's hard to get in.

Sleeping in Youth Hostels and Dorms
Rome has only one real youth hostel—big, institutional, not central or worth the trouble. For cheap dorm beds, consider **Pensione Ottaviano** (25 beds in 2- to 6-bed rooms, L23,000 per bed with sheets, depending on the season and their mood, call from the station), free showers, no lockers but a storage room, a fun, laid-back clubhouse feel, close to the Ottaviano Metro stop (near the Vatican) at Via Ottaviano 6, tel. 39737253 (reservations held until noon). The same slum visionaries run the dumpier **Pensione Sandy** (south of station, up a million depressing stairs, Via Cavour 136, tel. 4884585, L20,000 beds).

Eating in Rome
The cheapest meals in town are picnics (from *alimentari* shops or open-air markets), self-serve **Rostisseries**, and stand-up or take-out meals from a **Pizza Rustica** (pizza slices sold by the weight, 100 grams is a hot cheap snack, 200 grams or 2 *etti* make a light meal). Most *alimentari* will slice and stuff your sandwich (*panini*) for you if you buy the stuff there.

Eating in Trastevere or on the Campo di Fiori

My best dinner tip is to go for Rome's Vespa street ambience and find your own place in Trastevere (bus #23 from the Vatican area) or on Campo di Fiori. Guidebooks list Trastevere's famous places, but I'd wander the fascinating maze of streets around the Piazza Santa Maria in Trastevere and find a mom-and-pop place with barely a menu. For the basic meal with lots of tourists, eat amazingly cheaply at **Mario's** (three courses with wine and service for L15,000, near the Sisto bridge at via del Moro 53, tel. 5803809, closed Sunday). For the ultimate romantic square setting, eat at whichever place looks best on Campo di Fiori (**Virgilio's** setting makes up for its service, tel. 68802746, closed Wednesday).

Eating near the Pantheon

Il Delfino is a handy self-service cafeteria on the Largo Argentina square (7:00-21:00, closed Monday, not cheap but fast). The alimentari on the Pantheon square will make you a sandwich for a temple porch picnic.

Eating on Via Firenze, near Hotel Nardizzi and Hotel Alder

Lon Fon, at #44, serves reasonably priced Chinese food with elegant atmosphere, **Snack Bar Gastronomia** (#34, really cheap hot meals dished up from under glass counter, open until 24:00, closed Sunday), and an *alimentari* (grocery store, at #54). McDonald's on Piazza della Republica has free piazza seating and a great salad bar that no American fast-food joint would recognize.

Eating near the Vatican Museum and Pension Alimandi

Viale Giulio Cesare is lined with cheap, fun eateries (such as **Cipriani Self-Service Rosticceria** near the Ottaviano subway stop at Via Vespasiano, with pleasant outdoor seating). Don't miss the wonderful **Via Andrea Doria** open-air market in front of the Vatican Museum, two blocks between Via Tunisi and Via Andrea Doria (closed by 13:30, Monday-Saturday).

Train Connections

Rome to: Amsterdam (2/day, 20 hrs), **Bern** (5/day, 10 hrs), **Brindisi** (2/day, 9 hrs), **Florence** (12/day, 2 hrs), **Frankfurt** (4/day, 14 hrs), **Genova** (7/day, 6 hrs, overnight possible), **Milan** (12/day, 5 hrs, overnight possible), **Munich** (5/day, 12 hrs), **Naples** (12/day, 2-3 hrs), **Nice** (2/day, 10 hrs), **Paris** (5/day, 16 hrs), **Pisa** (8/day, 3-4 hrs), **Venice** (6/day, 5-8 hrs, overnight possible), **Vienna** (3/day, 13-15 hrs). **Città:** Take the Rome-Orvieto train (every 2 hrs, 75 min), catch the bus from Orvieto to Bagnoregio, walk to Città.

Rome and Its Airport

Rome's new rail-air link connects Rome's Leonardo airport with the Termini Station in 30 minutes for L12,000 (non-stop, hourly departures from about 7:00 until 21:00, lobby at track 22). This is far better than the Metro link via Tiburtina. Your hotel can arrange a taxi to the airport at any hour for about L70,000.

Driving in Rome

Greater Rome is circled by the *Grande Raccordo Anulare*. This ring road has spokes that lead you into the center (much like the strings under the skin of a baseball). Entering from the north, take the Via Salaria and work your way doggedly into the Roman thick-of-things (following the black-and-white Rome bull's-eye *centro* signs). Avoid rush hour. Drive defensively: Roman cars stay in their lanes like rocks in an avalanche. Parking in Rome is dangerous. Park near a police station or get advice at your hotel. My favorite hotel is next to the Italian defense ministry—guarded by machine-gunners. You'll pay about L30,000 a day in a garage. In many cases, it's well worth it.

Consider this. Your car is a worthless headache in Rome. Avoid a pile of stress and save money by parking it at the huge, new, easy, and relatively safe lot behind the Orvieto station (drive around about a half-mile south), and catch the train to Rome. The town of Orte, closer to Rome, has easy parking and more frequent trains into Rome (40- to 80-minute rides at least hourly).

VENICE (VENEZIA)

Soak all day in this puddle of elegant decay. Venice is Europe's best-preserved big city, a car-free urban wonderland of 100 islands, laced together by 400 bridges and 2,000 alleys.

Born in a lagoon 1,500 years ago as a refuge from barbarians, Venice is overloaded with tourists and slowly sinking (unrelated facts). In the Middle Ages, after the Venetians created a great trading empire, they smuggled in the bones of St. Mark (San Marco), and Venice gained religious importance as well.

Today, Venice is home to about 75,000 people in its old city, down from a peak population of around 200,000. While there are about 500,000 in greater Venice (counting the mainland, not counting tourists), the old town has a small-town feel. To see small-town Venice through the touristic flak, explore the back streets and try a Stand-Up-Progressive-Venetian-Pub-Crawl-Dinner.

Planning Your Time

Venice is worth at least a day on even the speediest tour. Train travelers can be most efficient by taking the night train in and/or out. Sleep in the old center to experience Venice at its best: early and late. For a one-day visit: cruise the Grand Canal, do the major San Marco sights (square, palace, church), see the Church of the Frari for art, and wander the back streets on a pub crawl. Venice's greatest sight is the city itself. Make time to simply wander. While doable in a day, Venice is worth two. It's a medieval cookie jar, and nobody's looking.

Orientation (tel. code: 041)

The island city of Venice is shaped like a fish. Its major thoroughfares are canals. The Grand Canal snakes through the middle of the fish, starting at the mouth where all the people and food enter, passing under the Rialto Bridge, and ending at St. Mark's Square (San Marco). Park your 20th-century perspective at the mouth, and let Venice swallow you whole.

Venice is a car-less kaleidoscope of people, bridges, and odorless canals. The city has no real streets, and addresses are hopelessly confusing. There are six districts, each with about 6,000 address numbers. Luckily, it's easy to find your way, since many street corners have a sign pointing you to the nearest major landmark (such as San Marco, Accademia, and Rialto). To find your way, navigate by landmarks, not streets. Obedient visitors stick to the main thoroughfares as directed by these signs and miss the charm of back-street Venice.

Parking in Venice
At Venice, the freeway ends like Medusa's head. Follow the green lights directing you to a parking lot with space. The standard place is Tronchetto (across the causeway and on the right) with a huge new multi-storied garage (L36,000 per day, half off with a discount coupon from your hotel; Hotel Guerrato has them). From there you'll find travel agencies masquerading as TIs and *vaporetto* docks for the boat connection (#82) to the town center.

Tourist Information
The best tourist information office (TI) is on St. Mark's Square (tel. 5226356, open maybe 8:30-19:00, closed Sunday). Pick up a city map, public transit map, the latest museum hours, and confirm your sightseeing plans. Drop into any fancy hotel (as if you're sleeping there) and pick up the free periodical entertainment guide, *Un Ospite de Venezia* (a handy listing of events and the latest museum hours). The cheap Venice map on sale at postcard racks has much more detail than the TI map. Also consider the little sold-with-the-postcards guidebook with a city map and explanations of the major sights.

Trains and Buses
A long causeway connects Venice to the mainland. Venice's Santa Lucia train station plops you right into the old town on the Grand Canal, an easy *vaporetto* ride or fascinating 40-minute walk from San Marco. Mestre is the sprawling mainland industrial base of Venice. While there are fewer crowds and cheaper hotels and parking lots here, Mestre has no charm. Don't stop here. The Santa Lucia station is a thriving center of information, but I'd go directly to the center.

Venice

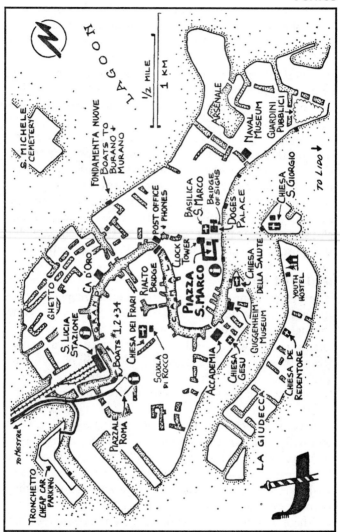

Getting Around Venice

The public transit system is a fleet of bus-boats called *vaporetti*. They work like city buses except that they never get a flat, the stops are docks, and if you get off between stops you may drown. While route numbers seem to change every year, for now only three lines matter: #1 is the slow boat, taking 45 minutes to make every stop along the entire length of the Grand Canal (tickets L2,500), #82 is the fast boat down the Grand Canal, stopping only at the car park, train station, Rialto, and San Marco, making the trip in 20 minutes (tickets L3,500), and #52 gives you an interesting circular tour of the island city (L3,500). Buy tickets before boarding or for an extra fee from a conductor on board. There are one-day and three-day passes, but I've never sailed enough to merit purchasing one.

Only three bridges cross the Grand Canal, but seven *traghetti* (little L500 ferry gondolas, marked on better maps) shuttle locals and in-the-know tourists across the canal, where necessary. Take advantage of these time savers.

Good city maps show boat stops, routes, and *traghetti* crossings. The TI, boat information office at Piazzale Roma, and some hotels can give you the free ACTV Venice public transportation map (which has a good city map on the back).

Helpful Hints

The Venice fly-trap lures us in and takes our money, any way it can. Expect to be shortchanged by any ticket-taker. Wait through the delayed-payment-of-change trick. Count your change carefully. Accept the fact that Venice was a tourist town 400 years ago. It was, is, and always will be crowded. Eighty percent of Venice is actually an untouristy place; 80% percent of the tourists never notice. Hit the back streets.

Get Lost: Venice is the ideal town to explore on foot. Walk and walk to the far reaches of the town. Don't worry about getting lost. Get as lost as possible. Keep reminding yourself, "I'm on an island and I can't get off." When it comes time to find your way, just follow the directional arrows on building corners, or simply ask a local, "*Dové* (DOH-vay) *San Marco?*" ("Where is St. Mark's?") People in the tourist business (that's most Venetians) speak some English.

Money: Bank rates vary. I like the Banco di Sicilia a block towards San Marco from Campo San Bartolomio. AmExCo has bad rates. Non-bank exchange bureaus will cost you $10 more than a bank for a $200 exchange. There's a 24-hour cash machine near the Rialto *vaporetto* stop that exchanges U.S. dollars and other currencies into lire at a fair rate.

The "Rolling Venice" Youth Discount Pass: This gives anyone under 30 discounts on sights, transportation, information on cheap eating and sleeping, and a handy guide-booklet to the city—but for L5,000, it's barely worthwhile (behind the AmExCo at Corte Contarina 1529, Monday-Saturday 9:30-13:00).

Water: Venetians pride themselves on having pure, safe, and tasty tap water, which is piped in from the foothills of the Alps (which you can actually see from Venice on a crisp winter day).

Pigeon Poop: If bombed by a pigeon, resist the initial response to wipe it off immediately—it'll just smear into your hair. Wait until it dries and flake it off cleanly.

Laundry: A handy *lavanderia* (laundromat) near St. Mark's and most of my hotel listings is the full-service Laundry Gabriella (Monday-Friday 8:00-19:00, Rio Terra Colonne, one bridge off the Merceria near San Zulian church, tel. 5221758). There, you can get nine pounds of laundry washed and dried for L15,000. Near the Rialto: Lavanderia SS. Apostoli (8:30-12:00, 15:00-19:00, closed Saturday, tel. 26650, on Campo SS. Apostoli). At either place you can drop it by in the morning, pick it up that afternoon.

Sights—Venice

▲▲▲**Grand Canal Tour**—Grab a front seat on boat #82 (fast, 20 minutes) or #1 (slow, 45 minutes) to cruise the entire Canale Grande from the car park (*Tronchetto*) or train station (*Ferrovia*) to San Marco. While Venice is a barrage on the senses that hardly needs a narration, these notes give the cruise a little meaning and help orient you to this great city. Some city maps (on sale at postcard racks) have a handy Grand Canal map on the back side.

Venice, built in a lagoon, sits on pilings—pine trees driven 15 feet into the mud. Over 100 canals, about 25 miles in length, drain the city, dumping like streams into the Grand Canal.

Venice is a city of palaces. The most lavish were built fronting this canal. This cruise is the only way to really appreciate the front doors of this unique and historic chorus line of mansions from the days when Venice was the world's richest city. Strict laws prohibit any changes in these buildings,

Downtown Venice

O M ____400
O YDS ____400

#'S REFER TO VAPERETTO LINES

SCUOLA S. ROCCO
CHIESA DEI FRARI
MARKET
RIALTO
PTT
CAMPO S. GIO. + PAOLO - COLLEONI-MON.
FOND. NUOVE
HOSP.
CAMPO S. BART.
CANALE
CAMPO S. LUCA
SALIZ. S. LIO
CAMPO S. MARIA FORMOSA
S. ZAC.
PAL. GRASSI
CAMPO S. ANGELO
MERCERIE
CALLE S. FINE
BASILICA S. MARCO
CAMPO MOROSINI
LA FENICE
SAN MARCO
T.I.
RIVA SCHIA.
AMEX
CALLE LARGA
WC
GRANDE
DOGE'S PAL.
LIDO
ACCADEMIA
TO RIALTO STAZIONE + P. ROMA
ZATTERE
PEGGY GUGGENHEIM MUSEUM
CHIESA DELLA SALUTE
CHIESA S. GIORGIO
HOSTEL
DCH

❶ ALBERGO GUERRATO   ❸ HOTEL S. GALLO
❷ LOCANDA STURION   T TRAGHETTI

so while landowners gnash their teeth, we can enjoy Europe's best-preserved medieval city—slowly rotting. Many of the grand buildings are now vacant. Others harbor chandeliered elegance above mossy basements.

Start at Tronchetto (the bus and car park) or the train station. FS stands for "Ferrovie dello Stato," the Italian state railway system. The bridge at the station is one of only three that cross the Canale Grande.

Vaporetto stop #4 (San Marcuola-Ghetto) is near the world's original ghetto. When this area was set aside as the local Jewish quarter in 1516, it was a kind of urban island which developed into one of the most closely knit business and cultural quarters of any Jewish community in Italy.

As you cruise, notice the traffic signs. Venice's main thoroughfare is busy with traffic. You'll see all kinds of boats: taxis, police boats, garbage, even brown-and-white UPS boats.

Venice's 500 sleek, black, graceful gondolas are a symbol of the city. They cost about $35,000 apiece and are built with a slight curve so that one oar propels them in a straight line.

At the Ca d'Oro stop, notice the palace of the same name. For years it's been under a wooden case of scaffolding for reconstruction. Named the "House of Gold," and considered the most elegant Venetian Gothic palace on the canal, today it's an art gallery with a few important paintings. Unfortunately its interior shows nothing of its palatial origins.

Just before the Rialto Bridge, on the right, the outdoor produce market bustles with people in the morning, but is quiet with only a few grazing pigeons the rest of the day. Can you see the *traghetto* gondola ferrying shoppers back and forth? The huge post office, usually with a postal boat moored at its blue posts, is on the left.

A symbol of Venice, the Rialto Bridge, is lined with shops and tourists. Built in 1592, with a span of 42 meters, it was an impressive engineering feat in its day. Locals call the summit of this bridge the "icebox of Venice" for its cool breeze.

The Rialto, a separate town in the early days of Venice, has always been the commercial district, while San Marco was the religious and governmental center. Today a street called the Merceria connects the two, providing travelers with a gauntlet of shopping temptations.

Take a deep whiff of Venice. What's all this nonsense about stinky canals? All I smell is my shirt. By the way, how's your captain? Smooth dockings? To get to know him, stand up in the bow and block his view.

Notice how the rich marble facades are just a veneer covering no-nonsense brick buildings. And notice the characteristic chimneys.

After passing the British consulate, you'll see the wooden Accademia Bridge, leading to the Accademia Gallery, filled with the best Venetian paintings. The bridge was put up in 1932 as a temporary fix for the original iron one. Locals liked it and it became permanent.

Cruising under the bridge, you'll get a classic view of the Salute Church, built as a thanks to God when the devastating plague of 1630 passed. It's claimed that over a million trees were used for the foundation alone. Much of the surrounding countryside was deforested by Venice. Trees were needed both to fuel the furnaces of its booming glass industry and to prop up this city in the mud.

The low white building on the right (before the church) is the Peggy Guggenheim Gallery. She willed the city a fine collection of modern art.

The building on the right with the golden dome is the Dogana da Mar, a 16th-century customs house. Its two bronze Atlases hold a statue of Fortune riding the dome.

As you prepare to de-boat at stop #15—San Marco—look from left to right out over the lagoon. A wide harbor-front walk leads past the town's most elegant hotels to the green area in the distance. This is the public gardens, the only sizable park in town. Farther out is the Lido, tempting with its beaches and casinos. The dreamy church that seems to float is the architect Palladio's San Giorgio (interesting visit, fine Tintoretto paintings, great view from its bell tower, L2,000, 9:30-12:30, 14:00-18:00 daily). And farther to the right is a residential chunk of Venice called the Guidecca.

For more *vaporetto* fun, ride boat #52 around the city. Plenty of boats leave from San Marco for the beach (Lido), as well as speedboat tours of Burano (a quiet, picturesque fishing and lace town), Murano (the glassblowing island), and Torcello (has the oldest churches and mosaics, but is an otherwise dull and desolate island). Boat #12 takes you to these remote points slower and cheaper.

▲▲▲**St. Mark's Square (Piazza San Marco)**—Surrounded by splashy and historic buildings, Piazza San Marco is filled with music, lovers, pigeons, and tourists from around the world by day and is your private rendezvous with the Middle Ages late at night. Europe's greatest dance floor is the romantic place to be. This is the first place to flood, has Venice's best tourist information office (rear corner), and fine public rest rooms (Albergo Diorno, WC, shower, L3,000 baggage check, behind the TI).

With your back to the church, survey one of Europe's great urban spaces and the only square in Venice to merit the title "Piazza." Nearly two football fields long, it's surrounded by the offices of the republic. On the right are the "old offices," (16th century, Renaissance). On the left are the "new offices" (17th century, Baroque style). Napoleon enclosed the square

St. Mark's Square

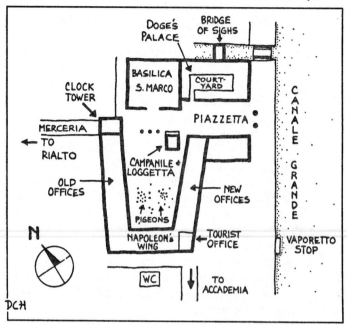

with the more simple and austere Neoclassical wing across the far end and called this "the most beautiful drawing room in Europe."

For a slow and pricey thrill, invest L8,000 in a beer or coffee in one of the elegant cafés with the dueling orchestras. If you're going to sit awhile and savor the scene, it's worth the splurge. Caution: ask if there's an extra music fee. For the most thrills L1,500 can get you in Venice, buy a bag of pigeon seed and become very popular in a flurry.

▲▲**Doge's Palace (Palazzo Ducale)**—The seat of the Venetian government and home of its ruling duke or "doge," this was the most powerful half acre in Europe for 400 years. It was built to show off the power and wealth of the republic and remind all visitors that Venice was number one. Built in Venetian Gothic style, the bottom has pointy arches and the top has an eastern or Islamic flavor. Its columns sat on pedestals, but in the thousand years since they were erected the palace has settled into the mud and they have vanished.

Entering the palace (before the ticket booth) notice a grand staircase (with nearly naked Moses and Paul Newman at the top). Even the most powerful visitors climbed this to meet the doge. This was the beginning of an architectural power trip. The doge, the elected king of this "dictatorial republic," lived on the first floor (now used for special exhibits). You'll tour the public rooms of the top floor. The place is wallpapered with masterpieces by Veronese and Tintoretto. Don't worry much about the great art. Enjoy the building.

In room 12, the Senate Room, the 200 senators met, debated, and passed laws. From the center of the ceiling, Tintoretto's Triumph of Venice shows the city in all her glory. Lady Venice, in heaven with the Greek Gods, stands high above the lesser nations who swirl respectfully at her feet with gifts.

The Armory shows the military might of the empire which was employed to keep the east-west trade lines open (and the local economy booming). Squint out the window at the far end for a fine view of Palladio's San Georgio church and the Lido in the distance.

After the huge old globes, you'll enter the giant Hall of the Grand Council (180 feet long, capacity 2,000) where the entire nobility met to elect the senate and doge. Ringing the room are portraits of 76 doges (in chronological order). One, who opposed the will of the Grand Council, is blacked out. Behind the doge's throne, you can't miss Tintoretto's monsterpiece, *Paradise*. At 1,700 square feet, this is the world's largest oil painting. Christ and Mary are surrounded by 500 saints.

Walking over the Bridge of Sighs, you'll enter the prisons. The doges could sentence, torture, and jail their opponents secretly and in the privacy of their own homes. As you walk back over the bridge, wave to the gang of tourists gawking at you. (L10,000, 9:00-19:00, last entry at 18:00, good WC near exit).

▲▲**St. Mark's Basilica**—For well over a thousand years, it has housed the saint's bones. The mosaic above the door at the far left of the church shows two guys carrying Mark's coffin into the church. Mark looks pretty grumpy after the long voyage from Egypt. The church has 4,000 square meters of Byzantine mosaics. The best and oldest are in the atrium (turn right as you enter and stop under the last dome). Face the piazza, gape up (it's okay, no pigeons), and study the story of Noah, the Ark, and the flood (two by two, the wicked drowning, Noah sending out the dove, happy rainbow, sacrifice of thanks). Now face the church and read clockwise the story of Adam and Eve that rings the bottom of the dome. Step inside the church (stairs on right lead to horses) and notice the rolling mosaic marble floor. Stop under the central dome and look up for the ascension. (Modest dress, no shorts or bare shoulders, free, 9:00-17:00, Sunday 14:00-17:00, tel. 5225205, see the schedule board in the atrium listing free English guided tours of the church, beautifully lit at the 18:45 mass on Saturday and 14:00-17:00 Sunday.)

Upstairs you can see an up-close mosaic exhibition, a fine view of the church interior, a view of the square from the horse balcony, and the newly restored original bronze horses (L3,000, 9:45-17:00). These horses, made during the days of Alexander the Great (4th century B.C.), were taken to Rome by Nero, to Constantinople by Constantine, to Venice by crusaders, to Paris by Napoleon, back "home" to Venice when Napoleon fell, and finally indoors out of the acidic air.

The treasures of the church (requiring two more L3,000 admissions) give you the best chance outside of Istanbul or Ravenna to see the glories of Byzantium. Venetian crusaders looted the Christian city of Constantinople and brought home piles of lavish loot (until the advent of TV evangelism, perhaps the lowest point in Christian history). Much of this plunder is stored in the treasury of San Marco (*tesaro*). As you view these treasures, remember most were made in A.D. 500, while western Europe was still rooting in the mud. Behind the high altar lies the body of St. Mark ("Marxus") and the Pala d'Oro, a golden altarpiece made (A.D. 1000-1300) with 80 Byzantine enamels. Each shows a religious scene set in gold and precious stones. Both of these sights are interesting and historic, but neither are as much fun as two bags of pigeon seed.

▲**Campanile di San Marco**—Ride the elevator 300 feet to the top of the bell tower for the best view in Venice. Photos on the wall inside show how this bell tower crumbled into a pile of bricks in 1902, one thousand years after it was built. For an ear-shattering experience, be on top when the bells ring (L4,000, 9:30-19:00). The golden angel at its top always faces into the wind.

Clock Tower—From Piazza San Marco you can see the bronze men (Moors) swing their huge clappers at the top of each hour. Notice the world's first "digital" clock on the tower facing the square (flips dramatically every 5 minutes).

▲▲**Galleria dell' Accademia**—Venice's top art museum is packed with the painted highlights of the Venetian Renaissance (Bellini, Giorgione, Veronese, Tiepolo, and Canaletto). It's just over the wooden Accademia Bridge (L10,000, 9:00-14:00, Sunday 9:00-13:00; expect delays, as they allow only 180 visitors at a time, tel. 5222247).

▲**Museo Civico Correr**—The interesting city history museum offers dusty bits of Venice's glory days and fine views of Piazza San Marco. Entry is on the square opposite the church (L5,000, 10:00-17:00, closed Tuesday).

▲▲▲**Chiesa dei Frari**—This great Gothic Franciscan church, an artistic highlight of Venice featuring three great masters, offers more art per lira than any other Venetian sight. Freeload on English-language tours to get the most out of the Titian Assumption above the high altar. Then move one chapel to the right to see Donatello's wood carving of St. John the Baptist almost live. And for the climax, continue right into the sacristy to sit before Bellini's *Madonna and the Saints*. Perhaps the greatest Venetian painter, Bellini's genius is obvious in the pristine clarity, believable depth, and reassuring calm of this three-paneled altarpiece. Notice the rich colors of Mary's clothing and how good it is to see a painting in its intended setting. For many, these three pieces of art make a visit to the Accademia Gallery unnecessary. Before leaving, check out the Neoclassical pyramid-shaped tomb of Canova and (opposite) the grandiose tomb of Titian, the Venetian. Compare the carved marble Assumption behind his tombstone portrait with the painted original above the high altar (L1,000, 9:00-12:00, 14:30-18:00, Sunday 15:00-18:00).

▲**Scuola di San Rocco**—Next to the Frari church, another lavish building bursts with art, including some 50 Tintorettos. The best paintings are upstairs, especially the *Crucifixion* in the smaller room. View the neck-breakingly splendid ceiling paintings with one of the mirrors (specchio) available at the entrance. (L8,000, 9:00-17:30, last entrance 17:00.)

▲**Peggy Guggenheim Collection**—A popular collection of far-out art, including works by Picasso, Chagall, and Dali, that so many try so hard to understand. (L10,000, 11:00-18:00, closed Tuesday.)

Ca' Rezzonico—This 18th-century Grand Canal palazzo is now open as the Museo del '700 Veneziano, offering the best look in Venice about the life of the rich and famous here 200 years ago. (L5,000, 10:00-16:00, closed Friday, tel. 5224543, at a *vaporetto* stop by the same name).

▲**Gondola Rides**—A traditional must for many but a rip-off for most; gondoliers charge about L70,000 for a 40-minute ride. You can divide the cost—and the romance—by up to six people (some take seven if you beg and they're hungry). For cheap gondola thrills, stick to the L500 1-minute ferry ride on a Grand Canal *traghetti*, or hang out on a bridge along the gondola route and wave at the romantics.

▲**Glassblowing**—It's unnecessary to go all the way to Murano Island to see glassblowing demonstrations. For the best show, wait near one of several glassworks near St. Mark's Square and follow any tour group into the furnace room for a fun and free 10-minute show. You'll usually see a vase and a *"leetle orse"* made from molten glass. The commercial that always follows in the showroom is actually entertaining. Prices around St. Mark's have a sizable tour-guide commission built in. Serious glass-shoppers buy at small shops on Murano Island.

Santa Elena—For a pleasant peek into a completely untouristy residential side of Venice, catch the boat from San Marco to the neighborhood of Santa Elena (at the fish's tail). This 100-year-old suburb lives as if there was no tourism. You'll find a kid-friendly park, a few lazy restaurants, and great sunsets over San Marco.

▲▲**Evening: The Stand-up Progressive Venetian Pub Crawl Dinner**—Venice's residential back streets hide plenty of characteristic bars with countless trays of interesting toothpick munchie food (*cicheti*). Partaking in the *"giro di ombre"* (pub crawl) tradition is a great way to mingle and have fun with the Venetians. Real *cicheti* pubs are getting rare in these fast-food days, but locals can point you in the right direction or you can follow the plan below.

Italian *cicheti* (hors d'oeuvres) wait under glass in bars; try fried mozzarella cheese, blue cheese, calamari, artichoke hearts, and anything ugly on a toothpick. Ask for a *piatto misto* (mixed plate). Drink the house wines. A small beer (*birrino*) or house wine costs about L1,000, meat and fish munchies are expensive, veggies are around L4,000 for a meal-sized plate. A good last drink is the local sweet red wine called Fragolino. To be safe, you might give each place L20,000 (or whatever) for your group and explain you want to eat and drink until it's *finito*. Bars don't stay open very late, and the *cicheti* selection is best early, so start your evening by 18:30.

First course: Start on Campo San Bartolomeo near the Rialto Bridge. If the statue walked backwards 20 yards, turned left, went under a passageway, over one bridge to Campo San Lio, took a left past Hotel Canada and over another bridge, he'd hit Alberto's Osteria, called simply Osteria on Calle Malvasia. This fine local-style bar has plenty of snacks and *cicheti*, available cheap from the bar. Say "hi" to Alberto, order with your best Italian (and by pointing), then sit or stand for same price (17:30-21:00, closed Sunday, tel. 5229038).

Second course: Leaving Alberto's, turn left on Calle Malvasia and go basically straight with a jog to the left through a couple of squares to Campo Santa Maria di Formosa. (Ask *"Dové Santa Maria di Formosa?"*) You could split a pizza with wine on the square (Piero's Bar all' Orologio, opposite the canal, has the worst pizza with the best setting.) *Capricioso* means the house specialty. You can get "pizza to go" on the square from Cip Ciap Pizza Rustica (over the bridge behind the SMF gelateria on Calle del Mondo Novo, open until 21:00, closed Tuesday).

Third course: Fresh fruit and vegetables from the stand on the square next to the water fountain (open until about 20:00).

Fourth course: *Cicheti* and wine. From Bar all' Orologio (on Campo S.M. di Formosa), with your back to the church (follow yellow sign to SS Giov e Paolo) head down the street to Osteria Mascaron (Gigi's bar, best selection by 19:30, closes at 23:00 and on Sunday).

Fifth course: More *cicheti* and wine. Go down the alley across from Gigi's bar (Calle Trevisana o Cicogua, yellow sign to SS G. e P.), over the great gondola voyeurism bridge (pause, sigh *"amoré"*), down Calle Bressana to Campo S. Giovanni e Paolo. Pass the church-looking hospital (notice the illusions

painted on its facade, maybe with a drink under the statue at
Sergio's Cafe Bar Cavallo). Go over the bridge to the left of
the hospital to Calle Larga Gallina, and take the first right to
Antiche Cantine Ardenghi de Lucia and Michael at #6369
under the red telephone (no sign for tax reasons, open until
21:00, closed Sunday, tel. 5237691). This *cicheteria* (munchie
bar supreme) also serves good sit-down meals.

Sixth course: Gelati. The unfriendly but delicious gelateria
on Campo di Formosa closes at about 20:00 and on Thursday. (The owner, Mario, promised me that even if you buy a
cone for the L1,000 take-away price, you can sit on his
chairs for 5 minutes.) Or head toward San Marco where the
gelaterias stay open later (the best is opposite the Doge's
Palace, by the two columns, on the bay). There's also a good
late-hours gelateria (L1,000 small cones) a block in front of
the Rialto Bridge.

You're not a tourist, you're a living part of a soft Venetian night . . . an alley cat with money. Streetlamp halos, live
music, floodlit history, and a ceiling of stars make St. Mark's
magic at midnight. Shine with the old lanterns on the gondola
piers where the sloppy Grand Canal splashes at the Doge's
Palace. Comfort the four frightened tetrarchs (ancient Byzantine emperors) under the moon near the Doge's Palace
entrance. Cuddle history.

There are also a lot of *cicheta* bars around the Rialto
market (between the bridge, Campo San Polo, Chiesa di San
Cassiano and recommended hotel Guerrato). You could
track down: Do Mori, Cantina Do Spade, Vini da Pinto, All'
Arco, Ostaria Antico Dolo, and Osteria Enoteca Vivaldi
(most closed on Sunday). You'll notice the same local crowd
popping up at each of these characteristic places for *chicheti*
and *bon vin*.

Sights—Venice's Lagoon

Several interesting islands hide out in the Venice Lagoon.
Burano, famous for its lace-making, is a sleepy island with
a sleepy community—village Venice without the glitz. Lace
fans enjoy Burano's Scuola di Merletti (L3,000, 9:00-18:00,
Sunday 10:00-16:00, closed Monday, tel. 730034). **Torcello,**
another lagoon island, is dead except for its church, which
claims to be the oldest in Venice (L3,000, 10:00-12:30,

Venice Lagoon

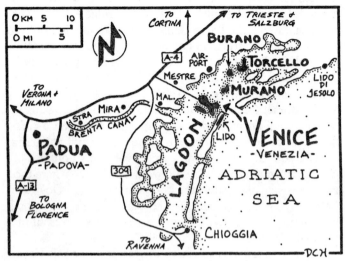

14:00-16:00, closed Monday, tel. 730084). It's impressive for
its mosaics but not worth a look on a short visit unless you
really have your heart set on Ravenna, but aren't able to make
it there. The island of **Murano**, famous for its glass factories,
has the Museo Vetrario, which displays the very best of 700
years of Venetian glassmaking (L5,000, 10:00-16:00, closed
Wednesday, tel. 739586). The islands are reached easily but
slowly by *vaporetto* (catch at Fondamente Nove). Four-hour
speedboat tours of these three lagoon destinations leave
twice a day from the dock near the Doge's Palace.

Sleeping in Venice
(L1,600 = about $1, tel. code: 041)
Finding a room in Venice is easy. Simply call one of my recommendations a few days in advance, reconfirm by telephone
the morning of your arrival day, and arrive by mid-afternoon.
While many stay in a nearby less-crowded place and side-trip
to Venice, I can't imagine not sleeping downtown. If you
arrive on an overnight train, your room may not be ready.
Drop your bag at the hotel and dive right into Venice.

Baths (*bagno*) are substantially more expensive than
showers (*doccia*). A toilet in the room knocks the price up.
Don't book through the tourist office (which pockets a

L15,000 per person "deposit"). The prices I've listed here are
for those who book direct (mention that you have this book
and insist on the listed price through 1995). Prices may be
cheaper (or soft), especially off-season. If on a budget, ask for
a cheaper room or a discount. I've let location and character
be my priorities.

Sleep code: **S**=Single, **D**=Double/Twin, **T**=Triple,
Q=Quad, **B**=Bath/Shower, **WC**=Toilet, **CC**=Credit Card
(Visa, Mastercard, Amex), **SE**=Speaks English (graded **A-F**),
breakfast is included unless otherwise noted.

Sleeping near the Rialto Bridge

Albergo Guerrato, near a handy and colorful produce mar-
ket, one minute from the Rialto action, is warmly run by
English-speaking Biba, her husband, Roberto (Bobby Drink-
water), and dog, Lord. Their 800-year-old building is Old
World simple, airy, and wonderfully characteristic
(D-L70,000, DB-L80,000, DBWC-L95,000, T-L92,000,
TB-L103,000, TBWC-L120,000, QB-L120,000, QBWC-
L160,000, including a big breakfast and city map, CC:VM,
walk over the Rialto away from San Marco, go straight about
3 blocks, turn right on Calle drio la Scimia and you'll see the
red sign, Calle drio la Scimia 240a, Rialto, tel. and fax
5227131 or 5285927).

Locanda Sturion (DB-L180,000, QB-L300,000 with
canal view, CC:VM, miles of stairs, S. Polo, Rialto, Calle
Sturion 679, 30125 Venezia, tel. 5236243, fax 5228378, SE-A),
with all the modern comforts, overlooks the Grand Canal.
Helen, Flavia, and Nicolette hold a room until 16:00 with
no deposit; 100 yards from the Rialto Bridge (opposite the
vaporetto dock).

Hotel Canada (two D with adjacent bath-L125,000,
DB-L160,000, CC:VM, Castello San Lio 5659, 30122
Venezia, tel. 5229912, fax 5235852, SE-B) has 25 rooms,
all with private showers, WC, and phones. In a "typical
noble Venetian home," it's ideally located on a quiet square,
between the Rialto and San Marco. (See directions to
Alberto's under Pub Crawl Evening, above.)

Sleeping near St. Mark's Square

Hotel Riva (two 4th-floor view D with adjacent showers-

L85,000, DB-L110,000, Ponte dell' Angelo, 5310, Venezia, tel. 5227034), with gleaming marble hallways and bright modern rooms, is romantically situated on a canal along the gondola serenade route. You could actually dunk your breakfast rolls in the canal (but don't). Sandro will hold a corner (*angolo*) room if you ask. It's behind San Marco where the canals Rio di San Zulian and Rio del Mondo Nouvo hit Rio Canonica o Palazzo.

Hotel San Gallo (S-L40,000, SB-L60,000, D-L90,000, DB-L140,000, T-L125,000, TB-L170,000, CC:VM, San Marco 1093/A, 30124 Venice, tel. 5227311 or 5289877, fax 5225702, SE-A, Luca and Franco promise these prices to those with this book) is about 100 yards off Piazza San Marco (with back to the church, take the second-to-last archway right off St. Mark's Square). Breakfast is on a chirpy, breezy roof garden.

Albergo Doni (D-L80,000, Riva Schiavoni, San Zaccaria N. #4656 Calle del Vin, tel. 5224267, SE-B) is a dark, woody, clean, and quiet place with 12 classy rooms run by a likable smart-aleck named Gina, who promises my readers one free down-the-hall shower each. It's two bridges behind the San Marco, or walk east along the San Marco waterfront (Riva Degli Schiavoni), over two bridges, take the first left (Calle del Vin), and follow the signs.

Albergo Corona is a squeaky-clean, Old World gem with nine rooms. (S-L38,000, D-L55,000, breakfast L8,000 extra, showers L3,000, find Campo SS Filippo e Giacomo behind San Marco, go down Calle Sacristia, go left on Calle Corona to #4464, tel. 5229174, lots of stairs, SE-F.)

Locanda Piave, with 12 fine rooms above a bright and classy lobby is a rare value (S-L55,000, D-L82,000, T-120,000, CC:VMA; from Campo Santa Maria Formosa go behind the church, over a bridge and down Parrocchia di San Zaccaria to the first corner, Ruga Giuffa 4838/40, 30122 Venezia, tel. 5285174, fax 5238512, SE-D).

Alloggi Masetto, incredibly well-located with four dirt-cheap rooms, is a homey place filled with birds, goldfish, and stacks of magazines, and run by Irvana Artico, a crusty landlady who surprises you with pretty good English (D-L40,000, DB-L45,000, TB-60,000, no breakfast, just off San Marco, from AmExCo head toward San Marco, first left, first left again through tunnel following yellow sign to Commmune di Venezia, jog left again and see her sign, Sotoportego Ramo Contarina, Frezzeria, San Marco 1520 A, tel. 5230505).

Locanda Casa Petrarca, wicker-cozy and bubbling jazz, hangs like an ivy-framed painting over a dead-end alley. Nelli is a friend as well as a host. (D-L80,000, DB-L100,000, Calle Schiavone #4386. With your back to St. Mark's, take last right off square. From Campo San Luco, go down Calle dei Fuseri, take left before red "restorante" sign, look right, tel. 5200430, SE-A.)

Locanda Gambero, with 30 rooms, is the biggest one-star hotel in the San Marco area. (S-L50,000, D-L80,000, DB-L100,000, T-L110,000, TB-L130,000, CC:VM, run by English-speaking Sandro and Sergio, a straight shot down Calle dei Fabbri from the Rialto *vaporetto* #1 dock, from Piazza San Marco walk down Calle dei Fabbri, over one bridge to #4685, tel. 5224384, fax 5200431, smoke-free rooms upon request). Gambero runs "La Bistro," a user-friendly French/ Italian eatery with a pleasant art-deco ambiance and good L7,000 pasta specials with no extra charges.

Sleeping in Other Parts of Venice

Hotel Marin is 3 minutes from the train station but completely out of the touristic bustle of the Lista di Spagna (S-L47,000, D-L74,000, DB-L100,000, T-L95,000, TB-L130,000, Q-L120,000, QB-L160,000, prices include breakfast and receive a 10% discount with this book, promised through 1995, CC:VMA, from the train station, cross the bridge and go behind the big green domed church. From the bridge go right, left, right, and right to San Croce 670b, tel. and fax 718022). Cozy, plain, and cheery, it will seem like a 19-bedroom home the moment you cross the threshold. It's family-run by helpful, English-speaking Bruno, Nadia, and son Samuel (they have city maps).

Foresteria della Chiesa Valdese is warmly run by a Protestant church offering dorm beds at youth-hostel prices in a handier location (halfway between San Marco and Rialto) in a rundown but charming old palace with elegant paintings on the ceilings (L22,000 dorm beds or L50,000 doubles with sheets and breakfast, more expensive for one-night stays, with some larger "apartments" for small groups; from Campo Santa Maria Formosa walk past the Orologio bar to the end of Calle Lungo and cross the bridge, Castello 5170, tel. 5286797, closed 13:30-18:00).

The **Venice youth hostel** (L22,000 beds with sheets and breakfast in 10- to 18-bed rooms, membership required; on Giudecca Island, tel. 5238211, boat #1 or #82 from station or San Marco to Zittele) is crowded, cheap, and newly remodeled (desk open 7:00-13:00, 14:00-22:00). Their budget cafeteria welcomes non-hostelers.

Eating in Venice

For low-stress, but not necessarily low-price, meals, you'll find plenty of self-service restaurants (*self-service* in Italian). One is right at the Rialto Bridge. Pizzerias are cheap and easy. Those that sell take-out by the slice or gram are cheapest. Menus should clearly explain the *coperto* (cover charge) and *servicio* (service charge).

Any place serving food on the Grand Canal, on St. Mark's, or along the main road connecting the two, may have a pleasant setting but is not a good value.

A key to cheap eating in Venice is bar snacks, especially stand-up mini-meals in out-of-the-way bars. Order by pointing. *Panini* (sandwiches) are sold fast and cheap at bars everywhere. My favorite Venetian dinner is the pub crawl (described above under Sights). Any of the listed bars would make a fine one-stop, sit-down dinner.

The produce market that sprawls for a few blocks just past the Rialto Bridge (best 8:00-13:00) is a great place to assemble a picnic. The nearby street, Ruga Vecchia, has good bakeries and cheese shops. Side lanes in this area are speckled with fine little hole-in-the-wall munchie bars.

The Mensa DLF (to the right of the train station as you face the tracks, 12:30-13:30, 18:00-21:00, closed Saturday, Sunday, and during lunch on Tuesday and Thursday, tel. 716242), the public transportation workers' cafeteria, is cheap and open to the public.

Eating near Campo San Bartolomeo

While these places aren't worth hiking to, they're handy, near the central Campo San Bartolomeo (a block toward San

Marco from the Rialto Bridge). Directions start from the statue in this square's center.

The very local, hustling **Rosticceria San Bartolomeo/ Gislon** (Calle della Bissa 5424, 20 yards behind the statue to its left, under a passageway, tel. 5223569, 9:30-14:30, 17:00-21:00, closed Monday) is a cheap—if confusing—self-service restaurant on the ground floor (L5,000 pasta, prices listed at door, stools along the window). Good but pricier meals are served at the full-service restaurant upstairs. Get a take-out meal to eat on a nearby bridge or campo.

If the statue on the square were to jump off his pedestal, walk ahead 50 yards, and go down a narrow alley to the left, he'd find the **Devil's Forest Pub,** with English decor and self-service Italian food (L7,000 pasta, no cover, open late, closed Monday).

Ristorante Pizzeria da Nane Mora (behind the statue, past PTT, over the bridge, and right at the red Santuario Madonna della Grazie church, on a tiny triangular square, open at 19:00, closed Wednesdays) has good pizza and indoor/outdoor seating.

Train Connections
Venice to: Bern (4/day, change in Milan, 8 hrs), **Brindisi** (3/day, 11 hrs), **Milan** (12/day, 3-4 hrs), **Munich** (5/day, 8 hrs), **Naples** (2/day, 6 hrs), **Paris** (3/day, 11 hrs), **Rome** (5/day, 4-7 hrs, over night possible), **Verona** (12/day, 1½ hrs), **Vienna** (4/day, 9 hrs). **To the Dolomites**: train from Venice to Bolzano (8/day, 4 hrs with one change) and catch a bus into the mountains from there. Train and couchette reservations (L24,000) are easily made at the AmExCo office near San Marco. Venice train info: tel. 041/715555.

Near Venice: Padua, Vicenza, Verona, and Ravenna
While the Italian region of Venetia has much more than Venice to offer, few venture off the lagoon. Five important towns and possible side trips, in addition to the lakes and the Dolomites, make zipping directly from Venice to Milan (3-hr trip, hrly departures) a route strewn with temptation.

Temptations: Venice to Milan

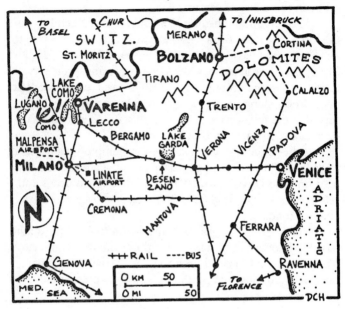

Planning Your Time

The towns of Padua, Vicenza, Verona, and Ravenna are all, for various reasons, reasonable stops. But none are essential parts of the best three weeks Italy has to offer. Of the towns discussed below, only Ravenna (2½ hours from Padua or Florence) is not on the main train line. Each town gives the visitor a low-key slice of Italy compared with Venice/Florence/Rome. While an overnight could be pleasant, only 3 or 4 hours are needed for a quick first visit.

High-speed town-hopping between Venice and Bolzano or Milan (with 3-hr stops at Padova, Vicenza, and Verona) is a good day. Trains run frequently enough to allow flexibility and little wasted time.

Padua (Padova)

Living under Venetian rule for four centuries seemed only to sharpen Padua's independent spirit. Nicknamed "the brain of Veneto," Padua has a prestigious university (founded 1222) and was called home by smart guys like Galileo, Dante, and Petrarch.

The old town is a colonnaded time-tunnel experience, and Padua's museums and churches hold their own in Italy's artistic big league. You'll see Giotto's well-preserved cycle of over thirty frescoes in the Chapel of the Scrovegni (L10,000, daily 9:00-19:00). Don't miss Donatello's *Crucifixion* with statues of Mary and Padua's six patron saints on the high altar of the Basilica di Sant'Antonio, and his great equestrian statue (the first since ancient Roman times) of the Venetian mercenary, General Gattamelata, on Piazza del Santo outside the Basilica. For work by Mantegna, see the important (but devastated by WWII bombs) frescoes in the Church of the Hermits (Chiesa degli Eremitani).

The tourist information office is in the train station (tel. 049/8750655). **Hotel Piccolo Vienna** (D-L43,000, Via Beato Pellegrino 133, tel. 049/8716331) is small and near the station. **Hotel Verdi** (D-L45,000, bus #10 from the station to Teatro Verdi, Via Dondi dell'Orologio 7, tel. 049/875 5744) is in the old center. The well-run **Ostello Citta di Padova** (bus #3, #8 or #12 from the station, Via Aleardi 30, tel. 8752219) packs over 100 L15,000 beds into 13 rooms as comfortably as a hostel can. Many budget travelers enjoy making this hostel a low-stress, low-price home base from which to tour Venice. I'd rather flip-flop it—sleeping in Venice and side-tripping to Padua, 30 minutes away by train.

Vicenza

To many architects, Vicenza is a pilgrimage site. Entire streets look like the back of a nickel. This is the city of Palladio, the 16th-century Renaissance architect who gave us the "Palladian" style, so influential in Britain (countless country homes) and the U.S.A. (Thomas Jefferson's Monticello was inspired by Palladio's Rotonda, a private but sometimes tourable Palladian residence on the edge of Vicenza.)

For the casual visitor, a quick stop offers plenty of Palladio. From the train station, catch nearly any bus (L1,200) to Piazza Matteotti where you can visit the tourist office (Piazza Matteotti 12, tel. 0444/320854, pick up a map). From there, see the Olympic Theater, Palladio's last work (and one of his greatest). This oldest indoor theater in Europe is still used and is considered one of the world's best.

From the Olympic Theater, begin your stroll down Vicenza's main drag, a steady string of Renaissance palaces and Palladian architecture peopled by Vicenzans who keep their noses above the tourist trade and are considered by their neighbors to be as uppity as most of their colonnades.

After a few blocks, you'll see the huge Basilica standing over the Piazza dei Signori, which has been the town center since Roman times. It was young Palladio's proposal to redo the dilapidated Gothic palace of justice in his neo-Greek style that established him as Vicenza's favorite architect. The rest of his career was a one-man construction boom. Notice the 13th-century, 280-foot-tall tower and the Loggia del Capitanio (opposite the basilica), one of Palladio's last works.

If you stay in Vicenza, **Hotel Vicenza** (D-L60,000, DBWC-L80,000, Piazza dei Signori at Stradella dei Nodari, tel. 0444/321512) is a rare, reasonable place in the Palladian center of things.

Finish your Corso Palladio stroll by walking to Piazzale Gasperi (where the PAM supermarket is a handy place to grab a picnic for the train ride) and walk 5 minutes down Viale Roma back to the station. Trains leave about every half-hour toward Milan/Verona and Venice (less than an hour away).

Verona

Romeo and Juliet made Verona a household word. But, alas, a visit here has nothing to do with those two star-crossed lovers. You can pay to visit the house falsely claiming to be Juliet's, with an almost believable (but slathered-with-tour-groups balcony), take part in the tradition of rubbing the breast of Juliet's statue in the courtyard to ensure finding a lover (or picking up the sweat of someone who can't), and even make a pilgrimage to what isn't "La Tomba di Giulietta" (but the town has been an important crossroads for 2,000 years and is therefore packed with genuine history). R and J fans will take some solace in the fact that two real feuding families, the Montecchi and the Capellos, were the models for Shakespeare's Montagues and Capulets. And, if R and J had existed and were alive today, they would recognize much of their "home town."

Verona's main attraction is its wealth of Roman ruins,

the remnants of its 13th- and 14th-century political and cultural boom, and its 20th-century, quiet, pedestrian-only ambience. After Venice's festival of tourism, Veneto's second city (in population and in·artistic importance) is a cool and welcome sip of pure Italy.

Orientation (tel. code: 045)
The most enjoyable core of Verona is along Via Mazzini between Piazza Brå and Piazza Erbe, Verona's medieval market square.

Tourist Information
The TI office is to the right of the Arena on the side of the big yellow building with columns (Via Leoncino 61, tel. 045/592828, open 8:00-20:00, Sunday 8:30-13:30).

Getting Around
To get to Piazza Brå, the town square, from Verona's Porto Nuova train station, catch one of many buses (L1,200, buy ticket at booth across from station). To walk to the piazza, turn right out of the station, then head left about 15 minutes up boring Corso Porta Nuova where you'll see the well-preserved Roman Arena (amphitheater).

Sights—Verona
Verona's Arena, on Piazza Brå, dates from first century A.D. This elliptical, 140-by-120-meter amphitheater, the third largest in the Roman world, is well preserved and looks great in its pink marble. Over the centuries, crowds of up to 25,000 spectators have cheered Roman gladiator battles, medieval executions, and modern plays (including a popular opera/ballet festival every July and August). Climb to the top for a fine city view (L6,000, 8:30-18:30, closed Monday).
Piazza Brå, down Via Mazzini, to Piazza Erbe—For me, the highlight of Verona is the evening *passagiata* (stroll) from the elegant cafés of Piazza Brå, through the old town on Europe's first major pedestrian-only street, to the bustling and colorful medieval market square, Piazza Erbe. (To see the House of Juliet, detour right from Piazza Erbe to Via Cappello #23. Note the amorous graffiti.) Piazza Erbe is a photographer's delight with pastel buildings corralling the

stalls, fountains, pigeons, and people that have come together
here for centuries. Walking under the "arch of the whales
rib" (look up) you'll continue into the Piazza dei Signori
with its statue of a very pensive Dante. Poke around here.
At the far end (through an arch on the right) you'll find the
strange and very Gothic tombs of the Scaligeri family, who
were to Verona what the Medici family was to Florence.

Walking further toward Ponte Pietra (a Roman bridge
that survived until WWII), you'll come to two impressive
churches (the Duomo and Sant' Anastasia) and just across
the river, built into the hill above the Ponte Pietra, is
Verona's Roman Theater, which stages Shakespeare plays
every summer (only a little more difficult to understand in
Italian than in Olde English). You can climb the stairs
behind the theater for a great town view. From the Duomo,
if you hike upstream, you'll pass the well-preserved first-
century Roman gateway, the Porta Borsari. Then, just before
the castle, is the Roman triumphal arch, the Arco dei Gavi
The medieval castle, the Castlevecchio, is now an art
museum (fine 16th- to 18th-century paintings, 8:30-18:30,
closed Monday). Finally, a few blocks farther up the river,
you'll find the 12th-century Church of San Zeno Maggiore.
This offers not only a great example of Italian Romanesque,
but also a set of 48 paneled 11th-century bronze doors that
are nicknamed "the poor man's Bible" (pretend you're an
illiterate medieval peasant and do some reading), and
Mantegna's San Zeno Triptych (usually 7:00-12:30, 16:00-
19:00).

Sleeping in Verona
(L1,600 = about $1, tel. code 045)
Cheap hotels in Verona are drab. **Hotel Catullo** (D-L50,000,
DBWC-L70,000, off Via Mazzini between 1D and 3A at Via
Valerio Catullo 1, tel. 8002786) is also sleepable and right
in the middle of the old town. Tiny **Albergo Ristorante
Ciopeta** (D-L75,000, Vicolo Teatro Filarmonico 2, tel.
8006843, fax 8033722, Sr. Cristofoli speaks *un poco* English)
is barely in business, more *ristorante* than *albergo*, but it's
a cute little place right off Piazza Brà. **Albergo Volto
Cittadella** (D-L42,000, just off Corso Porta Nuova, 2 blocks
toward the station from Piazza Brà, Via Volto Cittadella 8,

tel. 8000077) is very simple but quiet, has an elevator, and is handy to the center and station.

Two classier places just off Piazza Brà toward the river are **Hotel Cavour** (D-L80,000, DBWC-L105,000, air-conditioned, Vicolo Chiodo 4, tel. and fax 590508) and the noisier but newly remodeled **Albergo Al Castello** (DBWC-L90,000, noisy front rooms, Corso Cavour 43, tel. 8004403).

The **Verona youth hostel** (L15,000 beds with breakfast, bus #72 from the station, over the river beyond Ponte Nuovo at Salita Fontana del Ferro 15, tel. 590360) is one of Italy's best hostels.

Train Connections

Town-hopping here couldn't be easier. All three towns (Verona, Padua, Vicenza) are stops (30 minutes apart) on the (hrly, 3 hr) Venice-Milan line. Verona train info: tel. 045/590688.

Ravenna

Ravenna is on the tourist map for one reason—its 1,500-year-old churches decorated with best-in-the-west Byzantine mosaics. Briefly a capital of eastern Rome during its fall, Ravenna was taken by the barbarians. Then in 539, the Byzantine emperor Justinian made the city Byzantium's lieutenant in the west. Ravenna was a light in the Dark Ages. Two hundred years later, the Lombards booted Byzantine out and Ravenna melted into the backwaters of medieval Italy. Apart from being Dante's last home, Ravenna didn't made a history book for a thousand years. Today, the city booms with a big chemical industry, the discovery of off-shore gas deposits, and the construction of a new ship canal. It goes busily on its way, while busloads of tourists slip quietly in and out of town for the best look at the glories of Byzantium this side of Istanbul.

While not worth an overnight, it's only a 90-minute detour from the main Venice-Florence train line, and worth the effort for those interested in old mosaics. While all agree that Ravenna has the finest mosaics in the west, many will find their time better spent taking a careful look at the good but not as sublime Byzantine-style mosaics in Venice.

Orientation (tel. code: 0544)

Central Ravenna is quiet, with more bikes than cars and a
pedestrian-friendly core. For a quick stop, I'd see the basilicas,
mausoleum, covered market, and Piazza del Popolo, then
catch the train.

Trains

Before you leave the station, if you're daytripping to Ravenna,
jot down when the next few trains depart for Ferrara (to go to
Venice) or Bologna (to get to Florence).

Sights—Ravenna

Orientation Walk—A visit to Ravenna can be as short as a
2-hour loop from the train station. From the station, walk
straight down **Viale** Farini to Piazza del Popolo. A right on
Via IV Novembre takes you a block to the colorful covered
market (Marcato Coperto, open for picnic fixings 7:00-13:30,
closed Sunday). Get a map at the tourist office a block away
(daily 9:00-13:00, 15:00-18:00, Via Salara 8, tel. 35404). The
two most important sights, Basilica di San Vitale and the
Mausoleum of Galla Placidia, are 2 blocks away down Via
San Vitale. On the other side of Piazza del Popolo is the
Church of Sant'Apollinare Nuovo, also worth a look. From
there you're about a 5-minute walk back to the station.
(Sights open 9:00-19:00, until 16:30 October-March.)

▲▲**Basilica di San Vitale**—It's impressive enough to see a
1,400-year-old church, but to see one decorated in brilliant
mosaics that still convey the intended feeling that "this
peace and stability was brought to you by your emperor
and God" is rare indeed. Study each of the scenes: the arch
of apostles with a bearded Christ at their head; the lamb on
the twinkly ceiling; the beardless Christ astride a blue earth
behind the altar; and the side panels featuring Emperor
Justinian, his wife Theodora (an aggressive Constantinople
showgirl who used all her charms to gain power with—and
even over—her emperor husband), and their rigid and lavish
courts. San Vitale can be seen as the last of the ancient
Roman art and the first of the Christian era. This church
was the prototype for Constantinople's *Hagia Sophia* built
10 years later, and it inspired Charlemagne to build the first

great church in northern Europe in his capital of Aix-la-Chapelle (present-day Aachen).

▲▲**Mausoleum of Galla Placidia**—Just across the courtyard is the humble-looking little mausoleum with the oldest, and to many, the most impressive mosaics in Ravenna. The little light that sneaks through the thin alabaster panels brings a glow and a twinkle to the very early Christian symbolism (Jesus the good shepherd, Mark's lion, Luke's ox, John's eagle, the golden cross above everything) that fills the little room. Cover the light of the door with your hand to see the beardless Christ as the good shepherd. This was a popular scene with the early church.

▲**Basilica of St. Apollinare Nuovo**—This austere sixth-century church, in the typical early Christian basilica form, has two huge and wonderfully preserved side panels. One is a procession of haloed virgins, each bringing gifts to the Madonna and the Christ Child. Opposite, Christ is on his throne with four angels awaiting a solemn procession of 26 martyrs.

Church of Sant' Apollinare in Classe—Featuring great Byzantine art, this church is generally considered a must among mosaic pilgrims (3 miles out of town, easy bus and train connections, tel. 473004).

Overrated Sights—Skip the nearby beach town of Rimini, an overcrowded and polluted mess.

Sleeping in Ravenna
(L1,600 = about $1, tel. code 0544)
Three cheap hotels near the station are **Al Giaciglio** (Via R. Brancaleone 42, tel. 39403), **Hotel Minerva** (Via Maroncelli 1, tel. 213711), and **Hotel Ravenna** (Via Varoncelli 12, tel. 212204). The **youth hostel** is a 10-minute walk from the station (follow the signs for Ostello Dante, Via Nicolodi 12, tel. 420405).

Train Connections
Ravenna to Venice: 3 hours with a change in Ferrara (Ravenna-Ferrara, every 2 hrs, 60 min; Ferrara-Venice hrly, 100 min). **Ravenna to Florence:** 4 hours with a change in Bologna (Ravenna-Bologna, 8/day, 1½ hrs; Bologna-Florence, hrly, 1½ hrs).

FLORENCE (FIRENZE)

Florence, the home of the Renaissance
and birthplace of our modern world, is a
"supermarket sweep" and the groceries
are the best Renaissance art in Europe.
Get your bearings with a Renaissance walk.
Florentine art goes beyond paintings and statues— there's
food, fashion, and handicrafts. You can lick Italy's best gelato
while enjoying Europe's best people-watching.

Planning Your Time
If you're in Europe for three weeks, Florence deserves a well-
organized day. Siena, an hour away by bus, has none of the
awesome sights but is a more enjoyable home base. For a day
in Florence, see Michelangelo's *David*, tour the Uffizi gallery
(best Italian paintings), tour the underrated Bargello (best
statues), and do the Renaissance ramble (explained below).
Art lovers will want to chisel another day out of their itinerary for the many other cultural treasures Florence offers.
Shoppers and ice-cream lovers may need to do the same.
Watch your sightseeing hours. Get an early start. Mondays
and afternoons can be sparse.

Orientation (tel. code: 055)
The Florence we're interested in lies mostly on the north
bank of the Arno River. Everything is within a 20-minute
walk of the train station, cathedral, or Ponte Vecchio (Old
Bridge). Just over the bridge is the less awesome but more
characteristic Oltrarno (south bank) area. Orient yourself by
the huge red-tiled dome of the cathedral (the Duomo) and
its tall bell tower (Giotto's Tower). This is the center of historic Florence.

Tourist Information
Normally overcrowded, under-informed, and understaffed,
the train station's tourist information office is not worth a
stop if you're a good student of this book. If there's no line,
pick up a map, a current museum-hours listing, and the periodical entertainment guide or tourist magazine (daily in
summer 9:00-21:00, tel. 282893 or 219537). The free

Florence Area

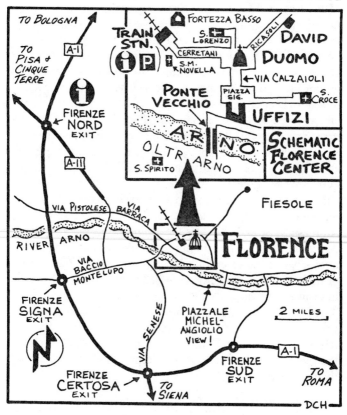

monthly *Florence Concierge Information* magazine lists the latest museum hours and events. It's stocked by the expensive hotels (pick one up, as if you're staying there).

Getting Around

Taxis are expensive. Buses are cheap. A L1,300 ticket lets you ride anywhere for 60 minutes, L1,800 gives you two hours, and L5,000 gets you 24 hours (tickets not sold on bus, buy in tobacco shop, validate on bus). If you organize your sightseeing with some geographic logic you'll do it all on foot.

Helpful Hints

Museums and Churches: See everyone's essential sight, *David*, right off. In Italy, a masterpiece seen and enjoyed is worth two tomorrow; you never know when a place will unexpectedly close for a holiday, strike, or restoration. Late afternoon is the best time to enjoy the popular Uffizi Gallery without its crowds. Many museums close at 14:00 and stop selling tickets 30 minutes before that. Most close Monday and at 13:00 or 14:00 on Sunday. (The *Concierge Information* magazine thoughtfully lists which sights are open on afternoons, Sundays, and Mondays.) Churches usually close 12:30-15:00 or 16:00. Hours can change radically and no one knows exactly what's going on tomorrow. Local guidebooks are cheap and give you a map and a decent commentary on the sights.

Addresses: Street addresses list businesses in red and residences in black or blue (color coded on the actual street number, and indicated by a letter following the number in printed addresses: n=black, r=red). *Pensioni* are usually black, but can be either.

Theft Alert: Florence has particularly hardworking thief gangs. The cheapest central car park is at Fortezza Basso (clearly sign-posted). Your best bet for free parking is along the river on Lungarno Amerigo Vespucci (leave cookies for the thieves).

Sights—Florence

▲▲▲A **Florentine Renaissance Walk**—For a walk through the core of Renaissance Florence, start at the Accademia (home of Michelangelo's *David*) and cut through the heart of the city to the Ponte Vecchio on the Arno River. (A 10-page, self-guided tour of this walk is outlined in *Mona Winks*.) From the Accademia, walk to the Cathedral (Duomo). Check out the famous doors and the interior of the Baptistery. Consider climbing Giotto's Tower. Continue toward the river on Florence's great pedestrian mall, Via de' Calzaioli (or "Via Calz"), which was part of the original grid plan given the city by the ancient Romans. Down a few blocks, notice the statues on the exterior of the Orsanmichele Church. Via Calz connects the cathedral with the central square (Piazza della Signoria), the city palace (Palazzo Vecchio), and the great Uffizi Gallery.

Florence

After you walk past the statues of the great men of the Renaissance in the Uffizi courtyard, you'll reach the Arno River and the Ponte Vecchio. Your introductory walk will be over, and you'll know what sights to concentrate on.

▲▲▲**The Accademia (Galleria dell' Accademia)**—This museum houses Michelangelo's *David* and powerful (unfinished) *Prisoners*. Eavesdrop as tour guides explain these masterpieces. More than any other work of art, when you look into the eyes of *David*, you're looking into the eyes of Renaissance man. This was a radical break with the past. Man was now a confident individual, no longer a plaything of the supernatural. And life was now more than just a preparation for what happens after you die.

The Renaissance was the merging of art and science. In a humanist vein, David is looking at the crude giant of medieval darkness and thinking, "I can take this guy." Back on a religious track (and, speaking of veins), notice how large and overdeveloped David's right hand is. This is symbolic of the hand of God that powered David to slay the giant . . . and, of course, enabled Florence to rise above its crude neighboring city-states.

Beyond the magic marble, there are two floors of interesting pre-Renaissance and Renaissance paintings including a couple of lovely Botticellis (Via Ricasoli 60, L10,000, 9:00-19:00, Sunday 9:00-14:00, closed Monday, may not be open past 14:00, tel. 2388609).

There's a good book-and-poster shop across the street. Behind the Accademia is the Piazza Santissima Annunziata, with its lovely Renaissance harmony, and the Hospital of the Innocents (Spedale degli Innocenti, not worth going inside) by Brunelleschi, with terra-cotta medallions by della Robbia. Built in the 1420s, it is considered the first Renaissance building.

▲▲**Museum of San Marco**—One block north of the Accademia on Piazza San Marco, this museum houses the greatest collection anywhere of dreamy medieval frescoes and paintings by the early Renaissance master, Fra Angelico. You'll see why he thought of painting as a form of prayer and couldn't paint a crucifix without shedding tears. Each of the monks' cells has a Fra Angelico fresco. Don't miss the cell of Savonarola, the charismatic monk who threw out the Medici, turned Florence into a theocracy, sponsored "bonfires of the vanities" (burning books, paintings, and so on), and was finally burned himself when Florence decided to change channels (L6,000, 9:00-14:00, closed Monday).

▲▲**The Duomo**—Florence's mediocre Gothic cathedral has the third-longest nave in Christendom (free, daily, 10:00-17:30, with an occasional lunch break). The church's noisy neo-Gothic facade, from the 1870s, is covered with pink, green, and white Tuscan marble. Since all of its great art is stored in the Museo dell' Opera del Duomo, behind the church, the best thing about the inside is the shade. But it's capped by Brunelleschi's magnificent dome—the first Renaissance dome and the model for domes to follow.

When planning St. Peter's in Rome, Michelangelo said, "I can build a dome bigger, but not more beautiful, than the dome of Florence."

Giotto's Tower—Climbing Giotto's Tower (Campanile, L4,000, daily 9:00-17:30, until 19:30 in summer) beats climbing the neighboring Duomo's dome because it's 50 fewer steps, faster, not so crowded, and offers the same view plus the dome.

▲▲Museo dell' Opera di Santa Maria del Fiore del Duomo—The underrated cathedral museum, behind the church at #9, is great if you like sculpture. It has masterpieces by Donatello (a gruesome wood carving of Mary Magdalene clothed in her matted hair, and the *cantoria*, the delightful choir loft bursting with happy children) and Luca della Robbia (another choir loft, lined with the dreamy faces of musicians praising the Lord), a late Michelangelo Pietà (Nicodemus, on top, is a self-portrait), Brunelleschi's models for his dome, and the original restored panels of Ghiberti's doors to the Baptistery. To get the most out of your sightseeing hours, remember that this is one of the few museums in Florence that stays open late (9:00-17:30, maybe later, closed all Sundays, L4,000, tel. 2302885.)

▲The Baptistery—Michelangelo said its bronze doors were fit to be the gates of Paradise. Check out the gleaming copies of Ghiberti's bronze doors facing the Duomo, and the famous competition doors around to the right. Making a breakthrough in perspective, Ghiberti used mathematical laws to create the illusion of 3-D on a 2-D surface. Go inside Florence's oldest building, and sit and savor the medieval mosaic ceiling. Compare that to the "new, improved" art of the Renaissance (free, 13:00-18:00, Sunday 9:00-13:00, bronze doors always "open"; original panels are in the cathedral museum).

▲Orsanmichele—Mirroring Florentine values, this was a combination church-granary. The best L200 deal in Florence is the machine which lights its glorious tabernacle. Notice the grain spouts on the pillars inside. You can go upstairs through the building behind it and over a sky bridge for the temporary exhibit and a fine city view (free). Also study the sculpture on its outside walls. You can see man stepping out of the literal and figurative shadow of the church in the great

Renaissance sculptor Donatello's *St. George*. (On Via Calzaioli, free, 8:00-12:00, 15:00-18:00.) There are plans for the origi-nal Orsanmichele statues to be stationed upstairs. When this happens, it will be one of the great sights of Florence.

▲**Palazzo Vecchio**—The interior of this fortified palace, which was once the home of the Medici family, is worthwhile only if you're a real Florentine art and history fan. (L8,000, 9:00-19:00, Sunday 8:00-13:00, may be closed Saturday or Thursday, handy public WC inside on ground floor.) Until 1873, Michelangelo's *David* stood at the entrance, where the copy is today. The huge statues in the square are important only as the whipping boys of art critics and as pigeon roosts. The important art is in the nearby Loggia dei Lanzi. Notice Cellini's bronze statue of Perseus (with the head of Medusa). The plaque on the pavement in front of the palace marks the spot where Savonarola was burned.

▲▲▲**Uffizi Gallery**—The greatest collection of Italian painting anywhere is a must, with plenty of works by Giotto, Leonardo, Raphael, Caravaggio, Rubens, Titian, and Michel-angelo, and a roomful of Botticellis, including his *Birth of Venus*. There are no official tours, so buy a book on the street before entering (or follow *Mona Winks*). The museum is nowhere near as big as it is great: few tourists spend more than two hours inside. The paintings are displayed (behind obnoxious reflective glass) on one comfortable floor in chronological order from the 13th through 17th century.

Essential stops are (in this order): the Gothic altarpieces by Giotto and Cimabue (narrative, pre-realism, no real con-cern for believable depth); Uccello's *Battle of San Romano*, an early study in perspective; Fra Lippi's cuddly Madonnas; the Botticelli room, filled with masterpieces including the small *La Calumnia*, showing the glasnost of Renaissance free-thinking being clubbed back into the darker age of Savona-rola; two minor works by Leonardo; the octagonal classical sculpture room with Praxiteles' *Venus de Medici*, considered the epitome of beauty in Elizabethan Europe; a view of the Arno through two dirty panes of glass; Michelangelo's only surviving easel painting, the round Holy Family; Raphael's *Madonna of the Goldfinch*; Titian's *Venus of Urbino*; and an interesting view of the palace and cathedral from the terrace at the end (L10,000, 9:00-19:00, Sunday 9:00-14:00, closed

Monday, last ticket sold 45 minutes before closing, go very late to avoid the crowds and heat).

Enjoy the Uffizi square, full of artists and souvenir stalls. The surrounding statues honor the earthshaking Florentines of 500 years ago. You'll see all the great artists, plus philosophers (Machiavelli), scientists (Galileo), writers (Dante), explorers (Amerigo Vespucci), and the great patron of so much Renaissance thinking, Lorenzo (the Magnificent) de Medici. The Florentine Renaissance involved more than just the visual arts.

▲▲▲**Bargello (Museo Nazionale)**—The city's underrated museum of sculpture is behind the Palazzo Vecchio (4 blocks from the Uffizi) in a former prison that looks like a mini-Palazzo Vecchio. It has Donatello's *David* (the very-influential first male nude to be sculpted in a thousand years), works by Michelangelo, and much more (Via del Proconsolo 4; L6,000, 9:00-14:00, closed Monday). Dante's house, across the street and around the corner, is interesting only to his Italian-speaking fans.

▲**Medici Chapel (Cappelle dei Medici)**—This chapel, containing two Medici tombs, is drenched in incredibly lavish High Renaissance architecture and sculpture by Michelangelo (L8,000, 9:00-14:00, closed Monday). Behind San Lorenzo on Piazza Madonna, it's surrounded by a lively market scene that, for some reason, I find more interesting.

Museo di Storia della Scienza (Science Museum)—This is a fascinating collection of Renaissance and later clocks, telescopes, maps, and ingenious gadgets. A highlight for many is Galileo's finger in a little shrine-like bottle. English guide-booklets are available. It's friendly, comfortably cool, never crowded, and just downstream from the Uffizi (L10,000, Monday, Wednesday, and Friday 9:30-13:00, 14:00-17:00, Tuesday and Thursday 9:30-13:00, closed Sunday, Piazza dei Giudici 1).

▲**Michelangelo's Home, Casa Buonarroti**—Fans enjoy Michelangelo's house at Via Ghibellina 70 (L8,000, 9:30-13:30, closed Tuesday).

▲**The Pitti Palace**—Across the river, it has the giant Galleria Palatina collection with works of the masters (especially Raphael), plus the enjoyable Galleria d'Arte Moderna (upstairs) and the huge semi-landscaped Boboli Gardens—a cool refuge from the city heat (L8,000, five museums, 9:00-14:00, closed Monday).

▲**Brancacci Chapel**—For the best look at the early Renaissance master Masaccio, see his newly restored frescoes here (L5,000, 10:00-17:00, holidays 10:00-13:00, closed Tuesday, across the Ponte Vecchio and turn left a few blocks to Piazza del Carmine).

▲**Piazzale Michelangelo**—Across the river overlooking the city (look for the huge statue of David), this square is worth the half-hour hike or the drive for the view. After dark it's packed with local school kids sharing slices of watermelon with their dates. Just beyond it is the strikingly beautiful, crowd-free, Romanesque San Miniato church. (Bus #13 from the train station.)

Scenic City Bus Ride—For a candid peek at a Florentine suburb, ride bus #7 (from near the station) for about 20 minutes through neighborhood gardens, vineyards, orchards, and large villas. It ends at a plaza with small eateries and good views of Florence and the nearby hills.

▲▲**Gelato**—Gelato is a great Florentine edible art form. Italy's best ice cream is in Florence. Every year I repeat my taste test. And every year Vivoli's (on Via Stinche, see map, closed Mondays and the last three weeks in August) wins. Festival del Gelato and Perche Non!, just off Via Calz, are also good. That's one souvenir that can't break and won't clutter your luggage. Get a free sample of Vivoli's *riso* (rice, my favorite) before ordering.

Siena Evening Side Trip—Connoisseurs of peace and small towns, who aren't into art or shopping (and who won't be seeing Siena otherwise), should consider riding the bus to Siena for the evening. Florence has no after-dark magic. Siena is after-dark magic.

Shopping—Florence is a great shopping town. Busy street scenes and markets abound, especially near San Lorenzo (closed Sunday and Monday), on the Ponte Vecchio, and near Santa Croce. Leather, gold, silver, art prints, and tacky plaster "mini-*Davids*" are most popular.

Sleeping in Florence
(L1,600 = about $1, tel. code: 055)
While Florence is generally crowded and overpriced, the

hotel scene isn't bad. With good information and a phone call ahead, you can find a simple, cheery, and comfortable double for L60,000, with a private shower for L80,000. You get roof-garden elegance for L110,000. Do not use the Tourist Information room-finding service. The prices listed here are guaranteed through 1995 only if you call direct. Involving the tourist office costs your host and jacks up the price. Also, since credit cards cost your host about 5 percent, many of these prices are for cash only. Except for Easter and Christmas, there are plenty of rooms in Florence and budget travelers can call around and find soft prices. If your limit is L55,000 for a double, call four places and stick to it. If you're staying for three or more nights, ask for a discount. The technically optional and overpriced breakfast can be used as a bargaining chip. Call ahead. I repeat, call ahead. Places will happily hold a room until early afternoon. If they say they're full, mention you're using this book. Accept only the prices I've listed through 1995.

Sleep code: **S**=Single, **D**=Double/Twin, **T**=Triple, **Q**=Quad, **B**=Bath/Shower, **WC**=Toilet, **CC**=Credit Card (**V**isa, **M**astercard, **A**mex). English is generally spoken.

Sleeping East of the Train Station

Casa Rabatti (D-L55,000, DB-L60,000-L70,000, L25,000 per bed in shared quad or quint, no breakfast, 6 blocks from station, Via San Zanobi 48 black, doorbell left of door, 50129 Florence, tel. 212393) is the ultimate if you always wanted to be a part of a Florentine family. Simple, clean, friendly, and run by Marcella and Celestino (who don't speak English), this is my best rock-bottom listing.

Hotel Enza (S-L50,000, SB-L60,000, D-L70,000, DB-L85,000, ask about a discount for three nights, no breakfast, 6 blocks from station, Via San Zanobi 45 black, 50129 Florence, tel. 490990) has 16 clean and cheery rooms, run by English-speaking Eugenia who clearly enjoys her work.

Sra. Piera Grossi rents five clean and homey rooms one block from the station (D-L60,000, no breakfast, corner of Via Nationale and Via Fiume, at Via Fiume 1, up lots of stairs, away from the traffic noise, tel. 293040).

Soggiorno Magliani (S-L39,000, D-L54,000, no breakfast, first floor up, 4 blocks from the station on the corner of

Via Guelfa and Via S. Reparata, at Via S. Reparata 1, tel. 287378, little English spoken) is a well-located, untouristy, very simple, local-style inn.

Other guidebooks rave about the same places 2 blocks from the station on Via Faenza. The street is filled with English-speaking tourists and sleepable L60,000 doubles. No. 56 is an English-speaking slumber mill: **Albergo Azzi** (L60,000 doubles, L30,000 per bed in shared quads and quints, L5,000 for breakfast, Via Faenza 56, tel. 213806). Not quite as good are **Merlini** (tel. 212848), **Paola** (tel. 213682), and **Armonia** (tel. 211146).

Hotel Loggiato dei Serviti (L235,000 doubles with everything, Piazza SS. Annunziata 3, Firenze, tel. 289592, fax 289595) has about the most prestigious address in Florence, on the most Renaissance (traffic-free) square in town. It gives you Renaissance romance with a place to plug in your hair dryer. Stone stairways lead you under open beam ceilings through this 16th-century monastery's elegantly appointed public rooms. The cells, with air-conditioning, TVs, mini-bars, and telephones, wouldn't be recognized by their original inhabitants.

Sleeping South of the Station near Piazza Santa Maria Novella

From the station, follow the underground tunnel to Piazza Santa Maria Novella, a pleasant square by day that's filled with drunks and police after dark. It's handy: 3 blocks from the cathedral, near a good laundromat (La Serena, 8:30-20:00, closed Sunday, Via della Scala 30 red, fast, L18,000 for 11 pounds), cheap restaurants (on Via della Scala and via Palazzuolo, see below), the bus and train station, and with a great Massaccio fresco (*The Trinity*) in the church on the square (free).

Hotel Universo (D-L80,000, DB-L100,000, including breakfast, these discounted prices promised with this book through 1995, CC:VM, elevator, English spoken, right on Piazza S. M. Novella at #20, 50123 Florence, tel. 281951, fax 292335), a big group-friendly hotel with stark concrete hallways but fine rooms, is warmly run by a group of gentle men.

Hotel Visconti (D-L56,000, DB-L70,000, optional L12,000 breakfast, elevator, TV room, peaceful and sunny roof garden, 20 meters off the square opposite the church at Piazza Degli Ottaviani 1, tel. 213877) artfully decorated by English-speaking and very mellow Manara, is like living in a relaxing blue-and-white cameo. In the same building, up one floor, the simple, threadbare, a little bit musty but tidy **Pensione Ottaviani** rattles in its spaciousness (D-L60,000, DB-L75,000 including breakfast, tel. 2396223, fax 293355, English spoken).

Hotel Pensione Elite (SB-L60,000, SBWC-L65,000, DB-L80,000, DBWC-L95,000, optional L10,000 breakfast, at end of square with back to church, go right to Via della Scala 12, second floor, tel. 215395) has eight comfortable rooms. With none of the backpacking flavor of Via Faenze, it's a good basic value; run warmly by Maurizio and Nadia.

Pensione Sole (S-L43,000, D-L64,000, DB-L75,000-L80,000, TB-L105,000, no breakfast, lots of stairs, Via del Sole 8, third floor, no lift, tel. 2396094, Anna speaks no English), a clean, cozy, family-run place with seven bright rooms, is well located just off S.M. Novella toward the river.

Pensione Centrale (D-L105,000, DBWC-L125,000 with breakfast, near the Duomo at Via dei Conti 3, 50123 Florence, tel. 215216) is run by Marie Therese Blot, who is a wealth of information and makes you feel right at home.

Sleeping on the River Arno
Pensione Bretagna (S-L50,000, SB-L65,000, D-L95,000, DB-L105,000, including breakfast, west of the Ponte Vecchio, just past Ponte San Trinita, at Lungarno Corsini 6, 50123 Firenze, tel. 289618, fax 289619), a classy, Old World elegant place with thoughtfully appointed rooms, is run by English-speaking Antonio. Imagine breakfast under a painted, chandeliered ceiling over-looking the Arno river.

Sleeping in Oltrarno, South of the River
Across the river in the Oltrarno area, between the Pitti Palace and the Ponte Vecchio, you'll still find small traditional crafts shops; neighborly piazzas hiding a few offbeat art treasures; family eateries; two distinctive, moderately priced hotels; two student dorms; and a youth hostel. Each of these places is only a few minutes' walk from the Ponte Vecchio.

Hotel La Scaletta (D-L100,000, DB-L135,000, T-L140,000, TB-L170,000, breakfast included, 8% discount for cash, 10% for cash and flowers, elevator, English spoken, Via Guicciardini 13 black, 50125 Firenze, straight up the street from the Ponte Vecchio, next to the AmExCo, tel. 283028, fax 289562, easy telephone reservations, call first) is elegant, friendly, clean, with a dark, cool, labyrinthine floor plan and lots of Old World lounges. Owner Barbara and her children, Manfredo, Bianca, and Diana, elevate this well-worn place with brute charm. Your journal becomes poetry when written on the highest terrace of La Scaletta's panoramic roof garden (cheap drinks). If Manfredo is cooking dinner, eat here.

Pensione Sorelle Bandini (D-L100,000, DB-L125,000, including breakfast, Piazza Santo Spirito 9, 50125 Firenze, tel. 215308, fax 282761) is a ramshackle 500-year-old palace on a perfectly Florentine square, with cavernous rooms, museum warehouse interiors, a musty youthfulness, a balcony lounge-loggia with a view, and an ambience that, for romantic bohemians, can be a highlight of Florence. Mimmo or Sr. Romeo will hold a room until 16:00 with a phone call.

Institute Gould (D-L50,000, DB-L54,000, L21,000 beds in shared doubles and quads, 49 Via dei Serragli, tel. 212576, office open Monday-Friday 9:00-13:00, 15:00-19:00, Saturday 9:00-12:00) is a Protestant Church-run place with 72 beds in 27 rooms and clean, modern facilities. Since you must arrive during their office hours, you can't check in on Sunday.

The Catholic-run **Pensionato Pio X-Artigianelli** (L18,000 beds in doubles and quads, L3,000 extra if you want a single or a private shower, Via dei Serragli 106, tel. 225044) is more free-wheeling and ramshackle, with 44 beds in 20 rooms.

Ostello Santa Monaca (L18,000 beds with sheets, membership required, no breakfast, 6 Via Santa Monaca, a few blocks past Ponte Alla Carraia, tel. 268338, fax 280185), with 146 beds in crowded 8- to 20-bed dorms, takes no reservations. Sign up for available beds from 9:30-13:00 or when the hostel reopens after 16:00. You can leave bags (without valuables) there until it opens after siesta. This and the classy **Villa Camerata IYHF hostel** (tel. 6014151), on the outskirts of Florence, should be last alternatives.

Eating in Florence

Eating South of the River
There are several good and colorful restaurants in Oltrarno near Piazza Santo Spirito. **Trattoria Casalinga** (from Pitti Palace follow via Michelozzi to Santo Spirito, just off Piazza Santo Spirito at 9 Via dei Michelozzi, tel. 218624, closed Sunday) is an inexpensive and popular standby, famous for its home cooking. Good values but more expensive are **Trattoria Sabitino** on Borgo S. Frediano and **Osteria del Cinghiale Bianco** at Borgo S. Jacopo 43 (closed Tuesday and Wednesday). **Trattoria Oreste** (on Piazza S. Spirito at #16), with a renowned cook and on-the-piazza ambience, may have the best L35,000 dinner in the area. The **Ricchi** bar on the same square has some of the best homemade gelati in Firenze and a particularly pleasant interior. The best places change, so I'd just wander in a colorful neighborhood and eat where I see locals eating.

Eating near Santa Maria Novella
Trattoria il Contadino (Via Palazzuolo 69 red, a few blocks south of the train station, 12:00-14:30, 18:00-21:30, closed Sunday, tel. 2382673) and **Trattoria da Giorgio** (Via Palazzuolo 100 red, 12:00-15:00, 18:30-22:00, closed Sunday) each offer a L14,000 hearty family-style, fixed-price menu with a bustling working-class/budget-Yankee-traveler atmosphere. Get there early or be ready to wait. **La Grotta di Leo** (Via della Scala 41 red, tel. 219265, closed Wednesday) has a cheap, straightforward menu and decent food.

Il **Latini** is an internationally famous but popular-with-the-locals traditional Florentine eatery. You'll share a large table under hanging hams. There's no menu. The wine's already on the table. Just order as you go. This isn't cheap but it can provide a memorable evening's experience, not to mention a wonderful dinner (Via del Palchetti 6, just off Moro between S.M. Novella and the river, tel. 210916, closed Monday).

A Quick Lunch near the Sights
I keep lunch in Florence fast and simple, eating in one of countless self-service places, Pizza Rusticas (holes-in-walls

selling cheap, delicious pizza by weight), or just picnicking (juice, yogurt, cheese, roll: L8,000). For mountains of picnic produce or just a cheap sandwich and piles of people-watching, visit the huge multi-storied **Mercato Centrale** (7:00-14:00, closed Sunday) in the middle of the San Lorenzo street market. Behind the Duomo, **Snack** (15 Pronconsolo) serves decent cheap lunches. For a reasonably priced pizza with a Medici-style view, try one of the pizzerias on Piazza della Signori.

Eating in Fiesole
Many locals enjoy catching the bus to the breezy hill town of Fiesole for dinner, a sprawling Florence view, and a break from the city heat. **Ristorante La Romagnola** (Via A. Gramsci 43, closed Monday) serves fine meals and inexpensive pizza. City buses make the 20-minute trip regularly.

Train Connections
Florence to: Assisi (6/day, 2½ to 3 hrs), **Brindisi** (3/day, 11 hrs with change in Bologna), **Frankfurt** (3/day, 12 hrs), **La Spezia** (for the Cinque Terre, 2/day direct, 2 hrs, or change in Pisa), **Milan** (12/day, 3 hrs), **Naples** (5/day, 5 hrs, possible overnight), **Orvieto** (6/day, 2 hrs), Paris (1/day, 12 hrs overnight), **Pisa** (2/hr, 1 hr), **Rome** (12/day, 2 hrs), **Venice** (7/day, 3 hrs), **Vienna** (4/day, 9-10 hrs). **Siena:** SITA buses go from near the Florence train station nearly hourly (L18,000 round-trip, 75 minutes each way, much better than the train, bus info tel. 483651, the schedule's in Florence's Concierge magazine).

Driving Florentine
Arriving in Florence, follow signs to Centro and Fortezza di Basso. After driving and trying to park in Florence, you'll understand why Leonardo never invented the car. Cars flatten the charm of Florence. Get near the centro and park where you can. Garages are expensive. Most charge around L30,000 a day. The big underground lot at the train station charges L2,000/hour. The cheapest and biggest garage is at Fortezza di Basso (L18,000/day). Borgo Ognissanti 96, near the Amerigo Vespucci bridge, is reasonable and closer to the center. You can try Piazza del Carmine for a free spot if you're staying

across the river. White lines are free, blue are not. I got towed once in the town of Michelangelo—an expensive lesson.

Pisa

Pisa was a regional superpower in her medieval heyday (11th, 12th, and 13th centuries), rivaling Florence and Genoa. Its Mediterranean empire, which included Corsica and Sardinia, helped make it a wealthy republic. But the Pisa fleet was beaten (1284, by Genoa) and its port silted up, leaving the city high and dry with only its Piazza of Miracles (and its university) keeping it on the map.

Planning Your Time

Pisa is basically a clichéd quickie. By car it's a 45-minute detour from the freeway. Train travelers may be changing trains in Pisa anyway. Hop on the bus and see the tower. Since you can't climb the tower, a look doesn't take very long. Sophisticated sightseers stop more for the art in the cathedral and baptistery than for a look at the tipsy tower. There's nothing wrong with the town, but I'd stop only to see the "field of miracles" and get out.

Orientation (tel. code: 050)

Pisa's three important sights (the cathedral, baptistery, and bell tower) float regally on a lush, picnic-perfect lawn—the best grass in Italy, with the most expensive public toilets (L1,000) to match. Even as the church was being built, the Piazza del Duomo was nicknamed the Campo dei Miracoli, or "Field of Miracles," for the grandness of the undertaking. The style throughout is Pisa's very own "Pisan Romanesque" (surrounded by what may be Italy's tackiest ring of souvenir stands).

Tourist Information

Tourist Info is at the train station and open daily, 9:00-18:00, Sunday, 9:00-12:00 Sundays, tel. 050/560464.

Trains

Some milk-run trains stop at San Rossore station and some buses stop at Piazza Manin (each just a short walk from the Leaning Tower)

Getting Around

Getting from the central train station to the tower is easy. Bus #1 leaves from the bus circle to the right of the station every 10 minutes. Buy your ticket from the magazine kiosk in the station's main hall or from the yellow machine just outside to the left (push *corsa semplice*) outside the Tourist Information door.

Sights—Pisa

▲▲**Leaning Tower**—This is the most famous textbook example of the town's unique Pisan Romanesque architecture. The 294 tilted steps to the top are now closed. The tower was leaning even before its completion. Notice how the architect, for lack of a better solution, kinked up the top section.

▲▲**Cathedral**—The huge "Pisan Romanesque" cathedral (free, 7:45-12:45, 15:00-18:45), with its richly carved pulpit by Giovanni Pisano, is artistically more important than the more famous tipsy bell tower.

Baptistery—The baptistery (biggest in Italy, in front of the cathedral, L5,000, 8:00-20:00), with a pulpit by Nicolo Pisano (1260), which inspired Renaissance art to follow, is interesting for its great acoustics. If you ask nicely and leave a tip, the doorman uses its echo power to sing haunting harmonies with himself. Notice that even the baptistery leans about 5 feet.

Other Sights—Pisa, of course, is much more than the Campo dei Miracoli. The cemetery bordering the cathedral square is not worth the L5,000 admission, even if its "Holy Land dirt" does turn a body into a skeleton in a day. Pisa's untouristed and interesting old town centers along the Arno between the Duomo and the station. But for most, Pisa is just a cliché that needs to be seen and a chance to see the Pisano pulpits. For more Pisan art, see the Museo dell' Opera del Duomo (behind the tower) and the Museo Nazionale di San Matteo (on the river near Piazza Mazzini).

Train Connections

Pisa to: Florence (hrly, 90 min), **La Spezia** (hrly, 60 min, milk-run from there into coastal villages), **Siena** (change at Empoli: Pisa-Empoli, hrly, 40 min; Empoli-Siena, hrly, 60 min). Even the fastest trains stop in Pisa, and you'll very likely be changing trains here whether you plan to stop or not.

Driving in Pisa

Cinque Terre to Pisa to Florence (90 miles): The white stuff you'll see in the mountains as you leave La Spezia for Pisa isn't snow. It's Carrara marble, Michelangelo's choice for his great art.

Drivers will see the Leaning Tower as they approach Pisa from the north. There's a large parking lot right at the sights, just outside the wall on the north end of town, so those coming in by freeway don't actually have to drive into Pisa.

The drive from Pisa to Florence is a rare case when the non-autostrada highway (free, more direct, and at least as fast) is a better deal than the autostrada.

HILL TOWNS
OF CENTRAL ITALY

Break out of the Venice-Florence-Rome syndrome. There's more to Italy! Experience the slumber of Umbria, the texture of Tuscany, and the lazy towns of Lazio.

For starters, here are a few of my favorites.

Siena seems to be every Italy connoisseur's pet town. In my office whenever Siena is mentioned, someone moans, "Siena? I luuuv Siena!" San Gimignano is the quintessential hill town, with Italy's best surviving medieval skyline. Popular-but-still-powerful Assisi is known for its hometown boy, St. Francis, who made very good. Orvieto, one of the most famous hill towns, is best used as a springboard for trip to tiny Cività. Stranded alone on its pinnacle in a vast canyon, Cività's the most lovable.

Planning Your Time

The hill towns are itinerary wreckers. Don't mess with the mediocre towns. Streamline. By train, keep things simple if you're short on time. By car, this is one of the most charming areas of Italy. If you're traveling with a rail/drive pass, this is definitely a place for cashing in a car day or two and exploring.

Siena, the must-see town, has the easiest train and bus connections. With three weeks for Italy, I'd spend three nights in Siena (with a whole-day side trip into Florence and a day to relax and enjoy Siena). Whatever you do, enjoy a sleepy medieval evening in Siena. After an evening in Siena, its major sights can be seen in half a day.

Cività di Bagnoregio is the awesome pinnacle town. A night in Bagnoregio (via Orvieto bus) with time to hike to the town and spend three hours makes the visit worthwhile. Two nights and an entire day is a good way to keep your pain/pleasure ratio in order.

Assisi is the third most visit-worthy town. It has half a day of sightseeing and another half a day of wonder. While a zoo by day, it's magic at night.

Siena

Seven hundred years ago, Siena was a major military power in a class with Florence, Venice, and Genoa. The town was weakened by a disastrous plague in 1348. In the 1550s her bitter rival Florence really salted her, making Siena forever a non-threatening backwater. Siena's loss became our sightseeing gain, as its political and economic irrelevance pickled it purely Gothic.

Siena is the hill-town equivalent of Venice. Traffic-free red-brick lanes cascade every which way. Siena's thriving historic center offers Italy's best Gothic city experience. While most people do Siena, just 30 miles south of Florence, as a day trip, it's best experienced after dark. In fact, it makes more sense to do Florence as a day trip from Siena. While Florence has the blockbuster museums, Siena has an easy-to-enjoy soul. You'll feel like old friends as soon as you're introduced.

For those who dream of a Fiat-free Italy, this is it. Sit at a café on the red-bricked main square. Take time to savor the first European city to eliminate automobile traffic (1966), and then, just to be silly, wonder what would happen if they did it in your city.

Hill Towns of Central Italy

Orientation (tel code: 0577)

Siena lounges atop a hill, stretching its three legs out from Il Campo. This main square is the historic meeting point of Siena's neighborhoods. The entire center is pedestrians-only, no buses and no cars. Everything I mention is within a 15-minute walk of the square. Navigate by landmarks, following the excellent system of signs on every street corner. Landmarks are clearly signposted. The average visitor sticks to the San Domenico–Il Campo axis. There's a handy public WC just off Il Campo at Via Citta (see map).

Tourist Information

Use the main TI on Il Campo (#56, look for the yellow Change sign, 8:30-19:30, less off season, closed Sunday, tel. 280551, get the excellent and free topographical town map). The small hotel information office at San Domenico is in cahoots with local hotels and charges for maps.

Getting Around

From Siena's train station, buy a bus ticket from the yellow machine near the exit, cross the street, and board any orange city bus heading for Piazza Gramsci or via Tozzi. Your hotel is probably within a 5-minute walk of Piazza Gramsci. If you arrive in Siena by intercity bus, you'll be dropped off at Siena's San Domenico church, a 10-minute walk from the center square (go left of the church following yellow signs to Il Campo).

Sights—Siena

Siena is one big sight. Its essential individual sights come in two little clusters: the square, with the museum in the city hall and its tower; and the cathedral, its baptistery, and the cathedral's museum with its surprise viewpoint. Check these sights off, and you're free to wander.

▲▲▲Il Campo—Siena's great central piazza is urban harmony at its best. Like a stage set, its gently tilted floor fans out from the tower and city hall backdrop. Notice how beautiful the square is in spite of the complete absence of landscaping. It's the perfect invitation to loiter. Built in 1347, Il Campo was located at the historic junction of Siena's various competing districts, or *contrada*, on the old marketplace. The

Siena

PINACOTECA -PICTURE GALL.-

PIAZZA MERCATO MARKET

PALAZZO PUBLICCO -CITY HALL-

V. S. PIETRO

DI SOTTO

CASATO DI SOTTO

STALLOREGGI

TORRE MANGIA -TOWER- CLIMB FOR A GREAT VIEW!

CITTA

CASTORO

CAPITANO

❹ OPERA METRO-POLITANA -CATHEDRAL MUSEUM-

CAMPO

G DI

VIA TELL.

WC

PIAZZA DUOMO

PIAZZA TOLOMEI

DI SOPRA

TERMINI

DIACCETO

DUOMO BAPTISTRY

BANCHI

TERME

V. GALLUZZA

V. ROSSI

❸

SANCT. S. CAT.

❼

VIA D. CAMPOREGIO

VIA B. SAPIENZA

❽

ESTERNA FONT.

PIAZZA SALIMBENI

❺

VIA PARADISO

POST

SAN DOMENICO

PIAZZA MATTEOTTI

VIA CURTATONE

WC

*MOST CITY-ORANGE BUSES STOP HERE

VIALE TOZZI

VIALE DEI MILLE

SITA BUSES TO FLORENCE & REST OF TUSCANY

PIAZZA GRAMSCI

STADIO P

❾ ❿

100 YDS.

VIALE MACCARI

25 APRILE

TO PARKING & AUTOSTRADA

LA LIZZA

VIALE FRANCHI

VIALE

FORTEZZA ENOTECA ITALIA

TO TRAIN STATION & CAMPING

❶ LOCANDA GARIBALDI
❷ PICCOLO HOTEL ETRURIA
❸ PENSIONE LA PERLA
❹ HOTEL DUOMO
❺ HOTEL CANNON
❼ PENSION BERNINI
❽ ALMA DOMUS
❾❿ LEA+LIBERTY

DCH

brick surface is divided into nine sections, representing the council of nine merchants and city bigwigs who ruled medieval Siena. Don't miss the Fountain of Joy at the square's high point, with its pigeons gingerly tightroping down slippery snouts to slurp a drink. At the base of the tower, the Piazza's chapel was built in 1348 as a thanks to God for ending the Black Plague (after it killed over a third of the population).

▲**Museo Civico**—The Palazzo *Pubblico* (City Hall at the base of the tower) has a fine and manageable museum housing a good sample of Sienese art. You'll see, in the following order, the Sala Risorgimento with dramatic scenes of Victor Emmanuel's unification of Italy, the chapel with impressive inlaid wood chairs in the choir, and the Sala del Mappamondo with Simone Martini's *Maesta* (Enthroned Virgin) facing the faded Guidoriccio da Fogliano (a mercenary providing a more concrete form of protection). Next is the Sala della Pace, which has two interesting frescoes showing "The Effects of Good and Bad Government." Notice the whistle-while-you-work happiness of the utopian community ruled by the utopian government (in the best-preserved fresco) and the fate of a community ruled by politicians with more typical values (in a terrible state of repair). Later you'll see the gruesome *Slaughter of the Innocents* (L6,000, daily 9:00-19:00, winter closing at 13:45, tel. 292111).

▲**Torre del Mangia (the city tower)**—Siena gathers around its city hall, not its church. It was a proud republic and its "declaration of independence" is the tallest secular medieval tower in Italy, the tall-as-a-football-field Torre del Mangia (named after a watchman who did more eating than watching; his statue is in the courtyard, to the left as you enter). Its 300 steps get pretty skinny at the top, but the reward is one of Italy's best views (L4,000, 10:00-18:00 or 19:00, limit of 30 towerists at a time, go early or late to minimize your time in line).

The Palio—The feisty spirit of each of Siena's 17 *contrada*, or districts, lives on. These neighborhoods celebrate, worship, and compete together. Each even has its own historical museum. Contrada pride is evident any time of year in the colorful neighborhood banners, but most evident twice a year (around July 2 and August 16) when they have their world-famous Palio di Siena. Ten of the seventeen neighborhoods compete (chosen by lot), hurling themselves with medieval abandon into several days of trial races and traditional revelry. On the big day, Il Campo is stuffed to the brim with locals and tourists as the horses charge wildly around the square in this literally no-holds-barred race. Of course, the winning neighborhood is the scene of grand celebrations afterward. The grand prize: simply proving your *contrada* is numero uno. You'll see sketches and posters all over town depicting the Palio. The TI has a free scrapbook-quality Palio brochure with English explanations.

▲▲**The Duomo**—Siena's cathedral is as Baroque as Gothic gets. The striped facade is piled with statues and ornamentation, and the interior is decorated from top to bottom. Even the floors are covered with fine inlaid art. In this *panforte* of Italian churches, your special treats are a Donatello statue of St. John the Baptist (in a chapel on the left side) and a couple of Michelangelo statues (on each side of the Piccolomini altar). Above it all peer the heads of 172 popes. This is one busy interior, the antithesis of San Domenico. The artistic highlight is Pisano's pulpit. The library (L2,000) has a Roman copy of the Greek *Three Graces* statue, fine frescoes, and illustrated medieval books (free, 7:30-19:30, until 18:30 off-season, modest dress required).

▲**Baptistery**—Siena is so hilly that there wasn't enough flat ground to build a big church on. What to do? Build a big church and prop up the overhanging edge with the baptistery. This dark and quietly tucked away cave of art is worth a look (and L2,000) for the bronze carvings of Donatello and Ghiberti on the baptismal font (Della Quercia, pay to light it) and for its cool tranquility.

▲▲**The Opera Metropolitana (cathedral museum)**—Siena's most enjoyable museum, on the Campo side of the church (look for the yellow signs), was built to house the cathedral's art. The ground floor is filled with the cathedral's original Gothic sculpture by Pisano. Upstairs to the left awaits a private audience with Duccio's *Maesta* (Enthroned Virgin). Pull up a chair and study this medieval masterpiece. Opposite is what was the flip side of the *Maesta*, with 26 panels, the medieval equivalent of pages, showing scenes from the passion of Christ. After more art, you'll find a little sign directing you to the "panorama." It's a long spiral climb. From the first landing, take the skinnier second spiral for Siena's surprise view. Look back over the Duomo, then consider this: when rival republic Florence began its grand cathedral, Siena decided to outdo it by building a church that would be the biggest in all Christendom. The existing cathedral would be used as a transept. You're atop what would have been the entry. The wall below you that connects the Duomo with the museum of the cathedral was as far as Siena got before the terrible plague killed the city's ability to finish the project. Were it completed, you'd be looking straight down the nave. (L5,000, 9:00-19:30, closing at 18:30 in shoulder months, and 13:30 off-season, tel. 283048.)

Church of San Domenico—This huge brick church, a landmark for those arriving by bus, is worth a quick look. The simple, bland interior fits the austere philosophy of the Dominicans. Walk up the steps in the rear of the church for a look at various paintings from the life of Saint Catherine, patron saint of Siena and, since 1939, of all Italy. Halfway up the church on the right, you'll find her head. (free, 7:00-13:00, 15:00-17:30, less in winter.)

Sanctuary of Saint Catherine—A few downhill blocks toward the center from San Domenico you'll see signs to the Santuario di Santa Caterina. Step into this cool and peaceful place, the site of Catherine's home. Siena remembers its favorite hometown girl, a simple, unschooled, but almost mystically devout girl who, in the mid-1300s, helped get the pope to return from France to Rome. Pilgrims have come here since 1464. Wander around to enjoy art depicting scenes from her life. Her room is downstairs. (free, 9:00-12:30, 15:30-18:00.)

▲The Pinacoteca (National Picture Gallery)—Siena was a power in Gothic art. But the average tourist, wrapped up in a love affair with the Renaissance, hardly notices. This museum takes you on a walk through Siena's art, chronologically from the 12th through 15th centuries. For the casual sightseer, the Sienese art in the city hall and cathedral museums is adequate. But art fans enjoy this opportunity to trace the evolution of Siena's delicate and elegant art. (From the Campo, walk out the Via Citta to the Piazza di Postieria and make a left on San Pietro, L8,000, 8:30-19:00 June-September, closes at 14:00 on Monday, 13:00 on Sunday, 13:45 off-season; tel. 281161.)

Sleeping in Siena
(L1,600 = about $1, tel code: 0577, zip code: 53100)
Since most visitors day-trip in from Florence, finding a room is not tough (unless you arrive during Easter or for the Palio

in early July and mid-August). While tour groups turn the town into a Gothic amusement park in midsummer, Siena is basically yours in the evenings and off-season, with your pick of the following hotels.

Nearly all listed hotels lie between Il Campo and the church of San Domenico (the intercity bus stop) and Piazza Gramsci (where the bus from the train station drops you). Call ahead, as it seems Siena's few budget places are listed in all the budget guidebooks. Most places serve no breakfast and are accustomed to holding telephone reservations until 17:00, if you can get the message across in Italian.

Sleep code: **S**=Single, **D**=Double/Twin, **T**=Triple, **Q**=Quad, **B**=Bath/Shower, **WC**=Toilet, **CC**=Credit Card (**V**isa, **M**astercard, **A**mex), **SE**=Speaks English (graded **A-F**).

Sleeping near Il Campo

Each of these first listings is just a horse wreck away from one of Italy's most wonderful civic spaces.

Locanda Garibaldi (D-L60,000-L65,000, half a block downhill off the square to the right of the tower at Via Giovanni Dupre 18, tel. 284204, fax . . . what's that? SE-D) is a dying breed. In this modest, very Sienese restaurant-*albergo*, Marcello wears two hats, running a busy restaurant with seven doubles upstairs. This is a fine place for dinner.

Piccolo Hotel Etruria (SB-L58,000, DB-L85,000, TB-L115,000, QB-L144,000, breakfast L5,000, CC:VMA; with back to the tower, leave Il Campo to the right, Via Donzelle 1-3, tel. and fax 288088, SE-D) is a good bet for a real hotel with all the comforts just off the square. Cheaper rooms (DB-L65,000, QB-L111,000) are in an annex (*dependenza*) across the street.

Albergo Tre Donzelle (S-L32,000, D-L53,000, DB-L67,000, no breakfast, Via Donzelle 5, tel. 280358, SE-F) is a plain, institutional, but decent place next door that makes sense only if you think of Il Campo as your terrace.

Pension La Perla (D-L63,000, DB-L78,000, no breakfast, tiny box showers in the DB rooms, a block off the square opposite the tower on Piazza Independenza at Via della Terme 25, tel. 47114) is a funky, jumbled place with a narrow maze of hallways, forgettable rooms, and a laissez-faire environment, run by English-speaking Paolo.

Hotel Duomo (DB-L150,000, TB-L195,000, including breakfast; CC:VMA; facing the tower, trot right from Il Campo, follow Via Citta, which becomes Via Stalloreggi, to #34 Via Stalloreggi; tel. 289088, fax 43043, SE-B) is the best-in-the-old-town splurge, a truly classy place with spacious, elegant rooms. Don't ask for room #62.

A few blocks up Via Banchi di Sopra, a block off Piazza Matteotti, is the spacious, group-friendly **Hotel Cannon d'Oro** (about SB-L65,000, D-L73,000, DB-L95,000, skip the L9,000 breakfast, CC:VM, Via Montanini 28, tel. 44321, fax 280868, SE-B).

Sleeping Closer to the Bus Stop and San Domenico Church

These hotels are still only a 10-minute walk from Il Campo, but ideal for those arriving by car or wanting to minimize luggage-lugging. Most enjoy fine views of the old town and cathedral (which sits floodlit before me as I type).

Pension Bernini (S-L60,000, D-L60,000-L80,000, L7,500 breakfast on the terrace, from San Domenico follow signs to Il Campo, you'll pass Via Sapienza 15, tel. 289047, SE-F) is the place to stay if you want to join a Sienese family in a modest, clean home with a few immaculate and comfortable rooms. The bathrooms are down the hall, the upholstery is lively, and the welcome is warm. Even if you normally require private plumbing, the spectacular view from the garden terrace and the friendly owner, Nadia, will make the inconvenience seem petty. Picnic on the terrace for dinner.

Alma Domus (S-L34,000, SB-L47,000, DB-L68,000, TB-L90,000, QB-L114,000, from San Domenico, walk downhill toward the view, turn left down Via Camporegio; make a U-turn at the little chapel down the brick steps and you'll see the sign, Via Camporegio 37, tel. 44177, fax 47601, SE-F) is ideal, unless nuns make you nervous or you plan on staying out past the 23:00 curfew. This quasi-hotel (not a convent) is run with firm but angelic smiles by sisters who offer clean, quiet, rooms for a steal and save the best views for the foreigners. Bright lamps, quaint balconies, fine views, grand public rooms, top security, and a friendly atmosphere make this the best deal in town for the lire. The checkout time is a strict 10:00, but they have a *deposito* for luggage

For a Sienese villa experience in a classy residential neighborhood a few blocks away from the center (past San Domenico), with easy parking on the street, consider **Albergo Lea** (D-L80,000, DB-L95,000 with breakfast, CC:VMA, Viale XXIV Maggio 10, tel. and fax 283207, SE-C), **Hotel Chiusarelli** (S-L46,000, SB-L68,000, DB-L105,000 without breakfast, across from the stadium at Viale Curtone 9, tel. 280562, SE-C), and if you're traveling with rich relatives who want sterility near the action, the **Hotel Villa Liberty** (DB-L180,000 with breakfast, CC:VMA, facing the fortress at Viale V. Veneto 11, tel. 44966, fax 44770, SE-B).

The tourist office has a list of private homes that rent rooms for around L25,000 per person. Many are filled with long-term students, and others require a stay of several days, but some are central and a fine value. Siena's **Guidoriccio Youth Hostel** (L19,000 beds in doubles or triples with breakfast, cheap meals, bus #15 or #10 from Piazza Gramsci or the train station to Via Fiorentina 89 in the Stellino neighborhood, open 7:00-9:00, 15:00-23:30, tel. 52212, SE-B) has 120 cheap beds, but given the hassle of the bus ride and the charm of downtown Siena at night, I'd skip it.

Eating in Siena

Restaurants are reasonable by Florentine and Venetian standards. Don't hesitate to pay a bit more to eat pizza on Il Campo (**Pizzeria Spadaforte**, tel. 281123, mediocre pizza, great setting, the tables are steeper than the price). The ambience is a classic European experience. For authentic Sienese dining at a fair price, eat at the **Locanda Garibaldi** (down Via Giovanni Dupre a few steps from the square [see Sleeping, above], closed Saturday, open at 19:00, arrive early to get a table, L22,000 menu). For a peasant's dessert, take your last glass of Chianti (borrow the *bicchiere for dieci minuti*) with a chunk of bread to the square, lean against a pillar, and sip Siena Classico. Picnics any time of day are royal on the Campo.

Trattoria Tellina (52 via della Terme) is a cozy and reasonable place to eat. **Osteria della Artista** (1 via Stalloreggi) is popular with locals for a cheap meal. **Rosticceria 4 Cantoni** (near Hotel Duomo at Piazza di Postierla 5, tel. 281067, closed Wednesday) is cheap, easy, and away from the tourism.

And **Pizza Rustica** places, scattered throughout Siena, serve up cheap pizza sold by the gram to go.

For a chance to enjoy a snack on a balcony overlooking the Campo, stop by the Gelateria Artigiana or the Bar Barbero (*panforte* and cappuccino), each just off the square at via di Citta.

Siena's claim to caloric fame is its *panforte*, a rich, chewy concoction of nuts, honey, and candied fruits that impresses even fruitcake-haters (although locals I met prefer a white cookie called *Ricciarelli*). All over town *Prodotti Tipici* shops sell Sienese specialties. A handy one is on Il Campo (right of tower). Don't miss the evening *passagiata* (peak time is 19:00) along Via Banchi di Sopra with gelato in hand (**Nannini's** at Piazza Salimbeni has fine gelato).

Transportation Connections

Sienna to Florence: While most trains take longer and require a change (in Empoli), rapido SITA buses go regularly between downtown Florence and Siena's San Domenico church, nonstop by autostrada (L8,300, 70 minutes, info tel. 221221, buy ticket before boarding at the *biglietteria* or ticket office). **Rome trains:** 8/day, 3½ hrs including 20-minute connection in Chiusi.

Arriving by car: Follow the Centro, then Stadio, signs (stadium, soccer ball). The soccer-ball signs take you to the tour-bus lot. Park at any white-striped car stall on the nearby streets or pay L15,000 a day to park down in the stadium, just across from the huge brick San Domenico church.

San Gimignano

The epitome of a Tuscan hill town with 14 medieval towers still standing (out of an original 72!), San Gimignano is a perfectly preserved tourist trap so easy to visit and visually pleasing that it's a good stop. Remember, in the 13th century, back in the days of Romeo and Juliet, towns were run by feuding noble families. And they'd periodically battle things out from the protective bases of their respective family towers. Skylines like San Gimignano's were the norm in medieval Tuscany, and Florence had literally hundreds of towers.

Tourist Information: Get a map at the Tourist Information office in the old center on the Piazza Duomo (daily, 9:30-12:30, 15:00-19:00 tel. 940008).

Sights: While the basic three-star sight here is the town itself, the **Collegiata** (on Piazza del Duomo), a Romanesque church filled with fine Renaissance frescoes, and the **Rocco** (castle, free entry, a short climb behind the church, with a fine view and a great picnic perch, especially at sunset) are important stops. You can also climb San Gimignano's tallest tower, the 180-foot-tall **Torre Grossa** above the Palazzo del Popolo. Market day is Thursday (8:00-13:00), but for local merchants, every day is a sales frenzy. Minimize the rusticated-shopping-mall feeling of downtown San Gimignano by walking around the outside of the wall and nipping in through the wall at various points.

San Gimignano streets are clogged mainly by day-trippers, but its hotels are expensive. The tourist office has a list of private homes that rent rooms. The Convento di Sant' Agostino (S-L25,000, D-L35,000, Piazza Sant' Agostino, tel. 940383) has good cheap beds.

Transportation Connections

San Gimignano to Florence: From Florence, take a bus to San Gimignano (regular departures, 75 min, change in Poggibonsi) or catch the train to Poggibonsi, where buses make the frequent 20-minute ride into San Gimignano. Buses also connect San Gimignano with **Siena** and **Volterra**.

You can't drive within the walled town of San Gimignano, but a car park awaits just a few steps from the town gate which leads straight up the traffic-free town's cobbled main drag to the Piazza del Cisterna (with its 13th-century well) and the Piazza del Duomo.

Assisi

Around the year 1200, a simple monk from Assisi challenged the decadence of church government and society in general with a powerful message of nonmaterialism, simplicity, and a "slow down and smell God's roses" lifestyle. Like Jesus, Francis taught by example. A huge monastic order grew out of his teachings, which were gradually embraced (some would say co-opted) by the church. Catholicism's purest example of Christ-like simplicity is now glorified in beautiful churches. In 1939, Italy made Francis its patron saint.

Any pilgrimage site will be commercialized, and the legacy of St. Francis is Assisi's basic industry. In summer, the town bursts with splash-in-the-pan Francis fans and Franciscan knickknacks. Those able to see past the tacky monk mementos can actually have a "travel on purpose" experience. Francis's message of love and simplicity and sensitivity to the environment has a broad appeal. Assisi recently hosted an ecumenical summit attended by leaders of nearly every major religion on earth.

Orientation (tel code: 075)
Assisi, crowned by a ruined castle, is beautifully preserved and has a basilica nearly wallpapered by Giotto. Most visitors are day-trippers. Assisi after dark is closer to a place Francis could call home.

Tourist Information
On Piazza della Comune (open 8:00-14:00, 15:30-18:30, Saturday 9:00-13:00, 15:30-18:30, Sunday 9:00-13:00, tel. 812534). Buses connect Assisi's train station with the old town center (2/hr, 5 km).

Sights—Assisi
▲▲The Basilica of St. Francis—At Francis's request, he was buried outside of his town with the sinners on the "hill of the damned." This once-humble place is now one of the artistic highlights of medieval Europe. The basilica is actually two churches built over the tomb of St. Francis. Start at the beginning and the bottom by hiking down into the crypt (enter halfway down the nave of the lower church). The lower church is more appropriately Franciscan, subdued and Romanesque, offering a great look at Romanesque painting or fresco. Most important is the Cappella di San Martino (first chapel on the left as you enter the lower nave), which was designed and decorated completely by the Sienese master Simone Martini. Also important are the Madonna, Child, angels, and St. Francis by Cimabue in the south transept.

The upper church, Gothic and therefore lighter, is designed to glorify the saint. It's basically a gallery of frescoes by Giotto and his assistants showing 28 scenes from the life of St. Francis. Follow the great events of Francis's life, starting at the altar and working around clockwise. The cycle culminates in the scene of St. Francis receiving the stigmata (the wounds of the Crucifixion, awarded to only the most pious). Giotto was considered the first modern painter. Note the realism and depth for which he strives as Italy is about to bring Europe out of the Dark Ages. Don't miss Cimabue's powerful *Crucifixion* in the north transept of the upper church. (The church is free, open 7:00-19:00, sometimes closed for lunch or mass, strictly enforced modest dress code; call 813491 and ask for an English tour or to join a scheduled English tour, or tag quietly along with an English-speaking pilgrimage group, which will invariably have an English-speaking Franciscan explaining the basilica.)

Visit the bookshop in the courtyard. A short biography of St. Francis makes a walk through the back streets of Assisi, up to the ruined castle, or through the nearby countryside more of a walk with the saint.

Piazza della Comune—This square is the center of town. You'll find a Roman forum, the temple of Minerva, a Romanesque tower, banks, the post office, the Pinacoteca (art gallery), and the tourist information office. (The square is straight up Via San Francesco from the basilica.)

Views—The Rocca Maggiore (big castle) offers a good look at a 14th-century fortification and a fine view of Assisi and the Umbrian countryside. For a picnic with the same birds and views that inspired St. Francis, leave all the tourists and hike to the smaller castle above St. Clare's church. (The Church of St. Clare, or Basilica de Santa Chiara, is interesting mostly for pilgrims, but her tomb, downstairs, impresses all.)

Santa Maria degli Angeli—Towering above the buildings below Assisi, near the train station, is this huge Baroque church, St. Mary of the Angels. It was built around the tiny chapel, Porziuncola. As you enter, notice the sketch on the door showing the original little chapel with the monk huts around it, and Assisi before it had its huge basilica. Francis lived here after he founded the Franciscan Order in 1208. And this was where he consecrated St. Clare as the Bride of Christ. Clare, St. Francis's partner in poverty, founded the Order of the Poor Clares.

Sleeping in Assisi
(L1,600 = about $1, tel code: 075, zip code: 06081)
The town accommodates large numbers of pilgrims on religious holidays. Finding a room any other time should be easy.

Albergo Italia (D-L42,000, DBWC-L65,000, just off the Piazza del Comune's fountain at Vicolo della Fortezza, tel. 812625) is clean and simple with great beds. Some of its 13 rooms overlook the town square.

Hotel Belvedere (D-L60,000, DBWC-L90,000, 2 blocks from Piazza Santa Chiara and St. Clare's church at Via Borgo Aretino 13, tel. 812460, fax 816812) offers comfortable rooms, good views, and a friendly, English-speaking management.

St. Anthony's Guest House (S-L32,000, SBWC-L38,000, DBWC-L68,000, TBWC-L96,000, with breakfast, two night minimum, between San Rufino and Saint Clare's church, at 10 Via Galeazzo, tel. and fax 812542), run by Franciscan Sisters of the Atonement from New York, offers reasonable beds, easy communications, and a fine view.

Francis probably would have bunked with the peasants in Assisi's **Ostello della Pace** (L17,000 beds with breakfast, in 4- to 6-bed rooms, a 15-minute walk below town at via di Valethye, at the San Pietro stop on the station-town bus, tel. 816767).

Train Connections
Assisi to: Rome (7/day, 2½ hrs with a change in Foligno), **Florence** (6/day, 2½ hrs, sometimes changing at Terontola-Cortona).

Orvieto
Umbria's grand hill town is no secret but still worth a quick look. Just off the freeway, with three popular gimmicks (its ceramics, cathedral, and Classico wine), it's loaded with tourists by day—quiet by night. The TI has a good free map (#24 Piazza Duomo, tel. 0763/41772, 8:00-14:00, 16:00-19:00).

Orientation
Check your bag and your connection at the train station, then hop on the funicular (4/hr, L1,400 ticket includes connecting Piazza Cahen-Piazza Duomo mini-bus transfer, where you'll find the TI and everything that matters). If

you have a car, don't drive it up. Park it at the huge, safe, and cheap parking lot behind the Orvieto train station. Take the pedestrian tunnel under the train tracks to the funicular that zips you to the old town.

Sights

The Orvieto Duomo (cathedral) has Italy's most striking facade. Grab a gelato from the gelateria to the left of the church and study this fascinating mass of mosaics and sculpture. In a chapel to the right of the altar, you'll find some great Signorelli frescoes (7:00-13:00, 15:00-20:00, earlier off-season).

Surrounding the striped cathedral are a fine **Etruscan Museum** (L3,000, 9:00-13:30, 15:00-19:00, Sunday 9:00-13:00), a great gelati shop, and unusually clean public toilets (down the stairs). Drinking a shot of wine in a ceramic cup as you gaze up at the cathedral lets you experience all of Orvieto's claims to fame at once.

Orvieto Area

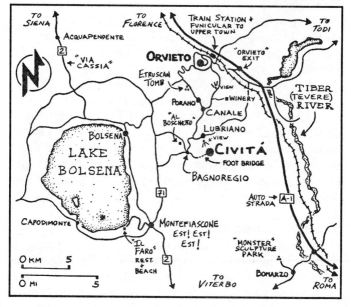

Ask at the TI about English walking tours (L10,000, most days at 10:00). Ride the back streets into the Middle Ages. The town sits majestically on tufa rock. Streets lined with buildings made of the dark volcanic stuff seem to grumble Dark Ages. Piazza Cahen is only a transportation hub at the entry to the hilltop town. It has a ruined fortress with a garden, a commanding view, and a popular well which is an impressive (but overpriced) double helix carved into tufa rock.

Sleeping in Orvieto
(L1,600 = about $1, tel. code: 0763, zip code: 05018)
Here are four places in the old town and one in a more modern neighborhood near the station.

Hotel Corso (DBWC-L80,000, on the main street up from the funicular toward the Duomo at Via Cavour 343, tel. 42020) is small, clean, and friendly, with comfy modern rooms.

Hotel Duomo (D-L48,000, DBWC-L76,000, from the Duomo, turn left past the Gelati to Via di Maurizio 7, tel. 41887) is a funky, brightly colored, Old World place with simple, ugly rooms and a great location.

Albergo Posta (D-L55,000, DBWC-L75,000, Via Luca Signorelli 18, tel. 41909) is in the center of the hill town, a 2-minute walk from the cathedral. It's a big, old, formerly elegant, but well-cared-for-in-its-decline building with a breezy garden, a grand old lobby, and spacious, clean, plain rooms.

Bar Ricci (D-L40,000, via Magalotti 22, tel. 41119) serves up cheap rooms as well as cheap tasty pasta.

Albergo Picchio (D-L40,000, DBWC-L60,000, Via G. Salvatori 17, 05019 Orvieto Scalo, tel. 90246) is a shiny, modern, concrete-and-marble place, more comfortable and family run, but with less character. It's in the lower, ugly part of town, 300 yards from the train station. They have a cheaper annex across the street.

Train Connections
Orvieto to: Rome (8/day, 70 min, take only trains going to Rome's Termini Station where the subway takes day-trippers conveniently to the major sights; consider leaving your car at the large car park behind the Orvieto station), **Siena** (5/day,

2-3 hrs, with change in Chiusi), **Bagnoregio** is a cheap 40-minute bus ride (6:25, 7:50, 9:10, 12:40, 13:55, 14:30, 15:45, and 18:35 from Orvieto's Piazza Cahen and from its train station daily except Sunday, buy tickets on the bus, get return times from the conductor).

Città di Bagnoregio

Perched on a pinnacle in a grand canyon, this is Italy's ultimate hill town. Immerse yourself in the traffic-free village of Città. Curl your toes around its Etruscan roots.

Città is terminally ill. Only 15 residents remain, as bit by bit it's being purchased by rich big-city Italians who will escape to their villas here. Apart from its permanent (and aging) residents and those who have weekend villas here, there is a group of Americans (mostly Seattle-ites), introduced to the town through a small University of Washington architecture program, who have bought into the rare magic of Città. When the program is in session, 15 students live with residents and study Italian culture and architecture.

Città is connected to the world and the town of Bagnoregio by a long donkey path. While Bagnoregio lacks the pinnacle-town romance of Città, it rings true as a pure bit of small-town Italy. It's actually a healthy, vibrant community (unlike Città, the suburb it calls "the dead city"). Get

a haircut, sip a coffee on the square, walk down to the old laundry (ask, *Dové la lavandaria vecchia?*). From Bagnoregio, yellow signs direct you along its long and skinny spine to its older neighbor, Cività. Enjoy the view as you head up the long donkey (and now, Vespa) path to Cività and its main (and only) square. A shuttle bus runs from Cività to Bagnoregio to Al Boschetto about hourly in season (L800).

Al Forno (green door on main square, open daily, June–October only, tel. 0761/793586), run by the Paolucci family, is the only restaurant in town and serves up a good reasonable pasta and wine lunch or dinner.

At the church on the main square, Anna will give you a tour (tip her and buy your postcards from her). Around the corner, on the main street, is a cool and friendly wine cellar with a dirt floor and stump chairs, where Domenica serves local wine—L1,000 a glass and worth it, if only for the atmosphere. Step down into her cellar and note the traditional wine-making gear and the provisions for rolling huge kegs up the stairs. Tap on the kegs in the cool bottom level to see which are full. Most village houses are connected to cellars like this which often date from Etruscan times.

Down the street is Victoria's **Antico Mulino** (L1,000), an atmospheric room of old olive-presses. Just down the way, Maria (for a tip) will show you through her garden with a fine view (**Maria's Giardino**). Continuing through the town, the main drag peters out and a trail leads you down and around to the right to a tunnel that has cut through the hill under the town since Etruscan times. Slowly the town is being bought up by wealthy, big-city Italians. The "Marchesa," who married into the Fiat family, owns the house at the town gate—complete with Cività's only (for now) hot-tub.

Evenings on the town square are a bite of Italy. The same people sit on the same church steps under the same moon, night after night, year after year. I love my cool late evenings in Cività. Listen to the midnight sounds of the valley from the donkey path.

Whenever you visit, stop halfway up the donkey path and listen to the sounds of rural Italy. Reach out and touch one of the monopoly houses. If you know how to turn the volume up on the crickets, do so If you visit in the cool of the early morning, have cappuccino and rolls at the small café on the town square.

Sleeping and Eating near Civitá
(L1,600 = about $1, tel. code: 0761)

When you leave the tourist crush, life as a traveler in Italy becomes easy and prices tumble. Room-finding is easy in small-town Italy.

Just outside Bagnoregio is **Al Boschetto**. The Catarcia family speaks no English; they don't need to. Have an English-speaking Italian call for you from Venice or Florence (D-L60,000, DB-L70,000, breakfast L5,000, Strada Monterado, Bagnoregio [Viterbo], Italy, tel. 792369, walking and driving instructions below). Most rooms have private showers (no curtains; slippery floors, be careful not to flood the place; sing in search of your shower's resonant frequency).

The Catarcia family (Angelino, his wife Perina, sons Gianfranco and Dominico, daughter-in-law Giuseppina, and the grandchildren) is wonderful, and if you so desire, the boys will take you down deep into the gooey, fragrant bowels of the cantina. Music and vino melt the language barrier in the wine cellar. Maybe Angelino or his sons will teach you their theme song, "Trinka, Trinka, Trinka." The lyrics are easy (see previous sentence). Warning: Angelino is Bacchus squared, and he's taught his boys well. Descend at your own risk. There are no rules unless the female participants set them. (For every three happy reports I get, I receive one angry postcard requesting I drop these guys from my book.) If you are lucky enough to eat dinner at Al Boschetto (L30,000, bunny is the house specialty), ask to try the *dolce* (sweet) dessert wine. Everything at Angelino's is deliciously home-grown—figs, fruit, wine, rabbit, pasta. This is traditional rural Italian cuisine at its best If you're interested in savoring small-town Italy, it doesn't get any better than Bagnoregio, Civitá, and Al Boschetto.

The Orvieto bus drops you at the town gate. From there, walk out of town past the old arch (follow Viterbo signs), turn left at the pyramid monument and right at the first fork (follow Montefiascone sign) to get to hotel Al Boschetto. Civitá is a pleasant 45-minute walk (back through Bagnoregio) from Al Boschetto. If you plan to leave Al Boschetto early in the morning, get them to leave the *chiave* (kee-ah-vee) in the front door or you're locked in.

Hotel Fidanza (DB-L78,000, Via Fidanza 25, Bagnoregio [Viterbo], tel. and fax 793444), comfortable, normal, and right in Bagnoregio town, is the only other hotel in town. Rooms 206 and 207 have views of Civitá.

Transportation Connections

Civitá is a 30-minute walk from **Bagnoregio**. A shuttle bus zips back and forth every hour or so. Public buses connect Bagnoregio to the rest of the world via Orvieto (for connections, see Orvieto, above).

Driving from Orvieto to Bagnoregio: Orvieto overlooks the autostrada (and has its own exit). The shortest way to Civitá from the freeway exit is to turn left (away from Orvieto) and follow signs to Lubriano and Bagnoregio. The more winding and scenic route takes 20 minutes longer: From the freeway, pass under hill-capping Orvieto (on your right, signs to Lago di Bolsena, on Viale I Maggio), take the first left (direction: Bagnoregio), winding up past great Orvieto views, the Orvieto Classico vineyard (see below), through Canale, and through farms and fields of giant shredded wheat to Bagnoregio, where the locals (or rusty old signs) will direct you to Angelino Catarcia's Al Boschetto, just outside town. Either way, just before Bagnoregio, follow the signs left to Lubriano and pull into the first little square by the church on your right for a breathtaking view of Civitá. Then return to the Bagnoregio road. Drive through Bagnoregio (following yellow "Civitá" signs) and park at the base of the steep donkey path up to the traffic-free, 2,500-year-old, canyon-swamped pinnacle town of Civitá di Bagnoregio.

Sights—Near Orvieto, Bagnoregio, and Civitá

If you have a car (and a good local map), it's easy to go to Lake Bolsena for a swim, to Canale for a winery tour, to Porano for a tour of an Etruscan tomb, or to the Bomarzo monster park. None of these places are worth the trouble by public transportation.

▲**Etruscan Tomb**–Driving from Bagnoregio toward Orvieto, stop just past Porano to tour an Etruscan tomb. Follow the yellow road signs, reading *Tomba Etrusca*, to Giuseppe's farm. Walk behind the farm and down into the lantern-lit, 2,500-year-old Hescanos family tomb discovered 100 years ago by Giuseppe's grandfather. New excavations on the site may turn it into the usual turnstile-type visit (open 9:00-12:00, 14:00-17:00, tel. 65242).

Swimming—For a fun and refreshing side trip, take a dip in Lake Bolsena, which is nestled within an extinct volcano, 30 minutes by car from Bagnoregio. Ristorante Il Faro, on the lake below the town of Montefiascone, offers good meals on a leafy terrace overlooking the beach.

Monsters—Nearby Bomarzo has the gimmicky monster park (Parco di Mostri), filled with stone giants and dragons. Built about two centuries ago, it proves that Italy has a long and distinguished tradition of tacky.

Winery—Orvieto Classico wine is justly famous. For a homey peek into a local winery, visit Tanuta Le Velette, where Julia Bottai and her English-speaking son, Corrado, welcome those who'd like a look at their winery and a taste of the final product (daily 8:00-12:00, 14:00-17:00, closed Sunday, tel. 0763/29090 or 29144). You'll see their sign 5 minutes past Orvieto at the top of the switchbacks on the Bagnoregio road.

Still Not Satisfied?

Italy is spiked with hill towns. Perugia is big and reeks with history. Cortona is smaller with a fine youth hostel (tel. 0575/601765). Todi is nearly untouristed. Pienza (Renaissance planned town) and Montepulciano (dramatic setting) are also worth the hill-town lover's energy and time. Sorano and Pitigliano have almost no tourism. Train travelers often use the town of Chuisi as a home base for the hill towns. The region's trains (to Siena, Orvieto, Assisi) go through or change at this hub, and there are several reasonable *pensioni* near the station.

THE CINQUE TERRE

The Cinque Terre, a remote chunk of the Italian Riviera, is the traffic-free, low-brow, underappreciated alternative to the French Riviera. There's not a museum in sight. Just sun, sea, sand (well, pebbles), wine, and pure unadulterated Italy. Give yourself a vacation to enjoy the villages, swimming, hiking, and evening romance of one of God's great gifts to tourism, the Cinque Terre. For a home base, choose among five villages, each filling a ravine with a lazy hive of human activity. Vernazza is my favorite.

Planning Your Time

The Cinque Terre is served by the milk-run train from Genoa and La Spezia. Speed demons arrive in the morning, check their bag in La Spezia, take the 5-hour hike through all five towns, laze away the afternoon on the beach or rock of their choice, and zoom away on the overnight train to somewhere back in the real world. The ideal minimum stay is two nights and a completely uninterrupted day. Each town has its own character, and all are a few minutes apart by an hourly train. There's no checklist of sights or experiences. Just the hike, the towns, and your fondest vacation desires.

For a good Cinque Terre day consider this: Pack your beach and swim gear, wear your walking shoes, and catch the train to Riomaggiore (town #1). Walk the cliff-hanging Via dell' Amore to Manarola (#2) and buy food for a picnic, then hike to Corniglia (#3) for a rocky but pleasant beach. Swim here or in Monterosso (#5). From #5, hike or catch the boat home to Vernazza (#4).

If you're into *la dolce far niente* (the sweetness of doing nada) and don't want to hike, you could enjoy the blast of cool train-tunnel air that announces the arrival of every Cinque Terre train and go directly to Corniglia or Monterosso to maximize beach time.

If you're a hiker, hike from Riomaggiore all the way to Monterosso al Mare, where a sandy "front door"-style beach awaits.

Getting Around

The town of La Spezia is the gateway to the Cinque Terre. In La Spezia's train station, the milk-run Cinque Terre train schedule is posted at window #5. Take the L1,800 half-hour train ride into the Cinque Terre town of your choice.

Cinque Terre Train Schedule: The schedule changes with the seasons. Since the train is the 5-Terre lifeline, any shop or restaurant posts the current schedule (La Spezia train info tel. 0187/714960).

Trains leaving La Spezia for the Cinque Terre villages (last year's June-September schedule): 6:25, 7:14, 8:30, 10:04, 11:00, 12:20, 13:12, 13:47, 14:17, 14:46, 15:22, 16:28, 17:48, 18:17, 19:06, 19:49, 21:10, 22:36, and 23:55.

Within the Cinque Terre: While you can hike or catch the irregular boats, the easy way to zip from town to town is by train. These *locale* trains (that's Italian for "milk-run") are so tiny they don't even register on the Thomas Cook train time-table. But they go nearly hourly and are cheap. To orient yourself, remember that directions are "*per* (to) *Genoa*" or "*per La Spezia*," and virtually any train that stops at one of the five villages will stop at all five. The five towns are just minutes apart by train. Know your stop. After leaving the town before your destination, move down to the door. Since the stations are small and the trains are long, you may need to get off the train deep in a tunnel and you may need to open the door yourself.

Helpful Hints

Taking Trains: Since a one-town hop costs the same as a five-town hop (L1,500), and every ticket is good all day with stopovers, save money by exploring the region in one direction on one ticket.

Hiking and Swimming: Wear your walking shoes and pack your swim gear. Each beach has showers that may work better than your hotel's. (Bring soap and shampoo.)

Wine: If you like sweet, sherry-like wine, the local *Sciachetra* (shock-ee-TRA) wine is expensive, but delicious. While ten kilos of grapes will give you seven liters of local wine, it yields only 1.5 liters of *Sciachetra*. The local white wine flows cheap and easy throughout the region. In the cool, calm evening, sit on the Vernazza breakwater with a glass of wine, and get mushy.

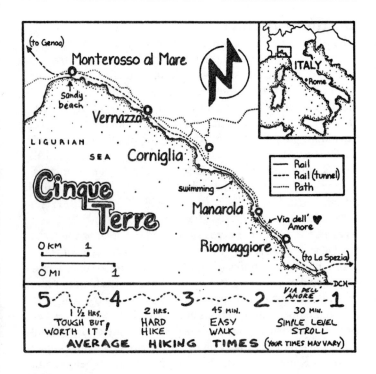

Sights—Cinque Terre

The best way to see the area is to hike from one end to the other. After fifteen years of visits, I still get the names confused. But it's easy to think of the towns by number. Here's a rundown on towns one through five.

Riomaggiore–town #1: The most substantial non-resort town of the group, Riomaggiore is a disappointment from the train station. But walk through the tunnel next to the train tracks (or take the high road, straight up and to the right), and you land in a fascinating tangle of pastel homes leaning on each other as if someone stole their crutches. There is homemade gelati at the Bar Central.

From the Riomaggiore station, the Via del' Amore affords a film-gobbling 15-minute promenade (wide enough for baby strollers) down the coast to Manarola. While there's no beach here, a stairway leads the way for sunbathing on the rocks.

Manarola–town #2: Like town #1, #2 is attached to its station by a 200-yard-long tunnel. Manarola is tiny and rugged, a tumble of buildings bunny-hopping down its ravine to the tiny harbor. This is a good place to buy your picnic (stores close from 13:00-17:00) before walking to the beaches of town #3, Corniglia. To reach town #3 (from the waterfront), it's easiest to take the high trail out of town. The broad and scenic low trail ends with steep stairs leading to the high road. The walk from #2 to #3 is a little longer, and a little more rugged, than from #1 to #2. If it's closed (as it has been for several years) you can climb around one fence, take the narrow trail across a washed-out section, and climb over the other fence. Any cat burglar can handle it. If you're concerned, ask other travelers about its current status.

Corniglia–town #3: A zigzag series of stairs that looks worse than it is leads up to the only town of the five not on the water. Remote and rarely visited, Corniglia has a windy belvedere, a few restaurants, and a handful of often-empty private rooms for rent. (Ask for Sra. Silvani.) Villa Ceccio serves a great and filling L8,000 pasta, and has a house Tiramasu as impressive as its view.

I do my 5-Terre swimming on the pathetic but peaceful manmade beach below the Corniglia station. Unfortunately, much of it has washed away and it's almost nonexistent when the surf's up. It has a couple of buoys to swim to, and is clean and less crowded than the beach at town #5. The beach bar has showers, drinks, and snacks. Between the station and the beach you'll pass "Albergo Europa," a bungalow village filled with Italians doing the Cinque Terre in 14 days.

Vernazza–town #4: With the closest thing to a natural harbor, overseen by a ruined castle and an old church, and only the occasional noisy slurping up of the train by the mountain to remind you these are the 1990s, Vernazza is my 5-Terre home base.

The action is at the harbor, where you'll find a kids' beach, plenty of sunning rocks, outdoor restaurants, a bar hanging on the edge of the castle (great for evening drinks), the tiny town soccer field, the busiest *foosball* game in Italy, and fresh fish filling wheelbarrows each morning.

The hike from #3 to #4 is rewarding, the wildest and greenest of the coast (with the nude Guvano beach about 30 minutes out of Vernazza). The trail from Vernazza to #5 is a scenic, up-and-down-a-lot 90 minutes. Trails are rough, but

Vernazza

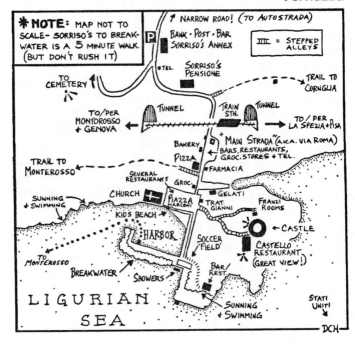

these are the best hikes of the 5-Terre. An hourly boat service connects #4 and #5 (L4,000 one way, L6,000 round-trip). A 5-minute hike in either direction from Vernazza gives you a classic village photo stop. There's a bar with a panoramic terrace at the tower on the trail towards Corniglia.

In the evening, stroll Vernazza's main (and only) street to the harbor to join the visiting Italians in a sing-along. Have a gelato, cappuccino, or glass of the local Cinque Terre wine at a waterfront café or on the bar's patio that overlooks the breakwater (follow the rope railing above the tiny soccer field, notice the photo of rough seas just above the door inside).

Vernazza restaurants are good but expensive. The Castello (Castle) restaurant serves good food just under the castle. Trattoria Franzi (on the waterfront) and Trattoria da Sandro (often with an entertaining musical flair) are better values. The town's only gelateria is good, and most harborside bars will let you take your glass on a breakwater stroll. You can get good pizza by the L3,500 slice on the main

street. Grocery store hours are 7:30-13:00, 17:00-19:30.
Monterosso al Mare–town #5: This is a resort with cars,
hotels, rentable beach umbrellas, and crowds. Still, if you
walk east of the station through the tunnel, you'll find some
charm. If you want a sandy beach, this is it. Adventurers may
want to rent a rowboat or paddleboat and find their own private cove. There are several coves between #4 and #5, one
with its own little waterfall. (Tourist office, 10:00-12:00,
17:00-20:00, closed Sunday afternoon, tel. 817506.)

Sleeping and Eating in the Cinque Terre
(L1,600 = about $1, zip code: 19018, tel. code: 0187)
While the Cinque Terre is too rugged for the mobs that rav-
age the Spanish and French coasts, it's popular with Italians.
Room-finding can be tricky. Easter, July, August, and summer Fridays and Saturdays are tight. August weekends are
miserable. If you're trying to avoid my readers, stay away
from Vernazza and Mama Rosa's.

Real hotels, which enjoy a demand that exceeds the local
supply, are expensive, lazy, and require dinner in the summer.
The budget alternative, a room in a private home, often gets
you a more comfortable room for about half the price. With
any luck, you'll get a smashing view to boot. Any bar has a
line on local rooms for rent. If you arrive without a room,
ask on the street or in the local bars for *affitta camere* (rooms
in private homes). Going direct cuts out a middleman and
softens prices. Off season there are plenty of rooms.

Sleep code: **S**=Single, **D**=Double/Twin, **T**=Triple,
Q=Quad, **B**=Bath/Shower, **WC**=Toilet, **CC**=Credit Card
(Visa, Mastercard, Amex), **SE**=Speaks English (graded **A-F**),
breakfast is included only in real hotels.

Sleeping in Vernazza
Vernazza, the essence of the Cinque Terre, is my favorite
town. (Have I mentioned that before?) There is just one real
pension, but two restaurants have about a dozen simple rooms
each, and a gaggle of locals rent extra rooms. Anywhere you
stay here will require some climbing.

Trattoria Gianni (S-L50,000, D-L75,000, DB-L85,000,
TB-L110,000, no breakfast, CC: VMA, Piazza Marconi 5,
19018 Vernazza, tel. and fax 812228, tel. 821003, closed

January 6-March 6, SE-D) is the best value in town. They
have 14 small, simple, comfortable doubles, artfully decorated
à la shipwreck, up lots of tight, winding, spiral stairs near the
castle, where the views are Mediterranean blue and the only
sounds you'll hear are the surf and the hourly ringing of the
church bells (through the night). The restaurant/reception is
right on the harbor square. The Franzi family (Dea, Marisa,
and Gianni) run their pension simply, but with a smile.

   Pension Sorriso is the only real pension in town, and
Sr. Sorriso knows it. Don't expect an exuberant welcome.
Sr. Sorriso and his nephew, Giovanni, will hold a room for
you without a deposit (D-L80,000, DB-L90,000, including
breakfast, summertime dinner is required and a room with
dinner and breakfast costs L65,000 per person; CC: VM;
19018 Vernazza, Cinque Terre, La Spezia, 50 yards up the
street from the train station, tel. 812224; while train sounds
rumble through the front rooms of the main building, the
annex up the street is quieter; closed January and February,
SE-C). Call well in advance and reconfirm a few days before
your arrival with another call. If you like sweet wine, you'll
love his *Sciachetra*. Sciache-price (after much negotiation,
with this book only), L3,000.

   Locanda Barbara is run spittoon-style by Giacomo
at the Taverna da Capitano (tiny loft D-L65,000, bigger
D-L70,000, no breakfast, Piazza Marconi 20, tel. 812201,
closed December-January, SE-F). On the harbor square,
many of his nine quiet, basic doubles (in the top floors of
what seems like a vacant city hall) have harbor views.

   Affitta Camere: Vernazza is honeycombed with private
rooms and apartments for rent. No English is spoken at
these places, and each offers 6 or 8 cheap rooms year-round.
Affitta Camere da Nicolina (3 apartments with kitchens
and 3 rooms, L30,000 per person, great views, right over the
harbor but close to the noisy church bell tower, ask at the
Vulnetia restaurant/pizzeria, tel. 821193). **Affitta Camere
da Filippo** (8 rooms, D-L60,000, T-L70,000, Q-L80,000,
no views, less noise, ask at Trattoria da Sandro, tel. 812244).
Affitta Camere da Franco (4 quiet rooms, D-L55,000, DB
with view-L60,000, going down the main street, turn right at
the pharmacy, climb via Carattino to #64, tel. 821082, Franco
runs the "Bar la Torre" at the top of via Carattino at the ivy-

covered tower. Franco speaks German; his wife, Anna Maria, speaks a little English; his cigar-chomping cousin Mike lived in New York and rents an apartment next door (tel. 812374). **Affitta Camere da Giuseppina Villa** (3 rooms including a gorgeous 5-bed apartment with kitchen, D-L60,000, TB-L80,000, QB-L100,000, QuintB-L120,000, Via S. Giovanni Battista 5, tel. 812026, SE-F).

Sleeping in Riomaggiore

Youth Hostel Mama Rosa is run with a splash of John Belushi and a pinch of Mother Theresa by Rosa Ricci (an almost-too-effervescent and friendly character who welcomes backpackers at the train station), her husband, Carmine, and their English-speaking son Silvio. This informal hostel is a chaotic but manageable jumble with the ambiance of a YMCA locker room (with a cat-pee aroma and nearly outdoor toilets and showers behind scanty curtains) filled with bunk beds. (L20,000 beds, price guaranteed through 1995, Piazza Unita 2, 20 yards in front of the station on the right past the "sporting club" in an unmarked building; tel. 920173, rarely answered, most just show up without a reservation, no curfew.) It's the only cheap dorm on the Cinque Terre. The 10 co-ed rooms, with 4-10 beds each, are plain and basic with only roof vents. But a family atmosphere rages with a popular self-serve kitchen, free laundry facilities, showers, and Silvio's five unnamed cats (available as bed partners upon request). This is one of those rare places where perfect strangers become good friends with the slurp of a spaghetti, and wine supersedes the concept of ownership. The Mama Rosa spaghetti-and-wine festa gives you all you can eat for L10,000. Mama Rosa also rents five doubles (*affitta camere*) in nearby homes for L50,000 each. You can eat reasonably next door at the **Vecchio Rio** restaurant (tel. 920173, closed Wednesday except in summer). While the station and hostel are in a bland, concrete part of Riomaggiore, a short walk through the tunnel puts you into its colorful center. For *affitta camere* in Riomaggiore try Michielini Anna (5 D-L60,000 with kitchens, via Colombo 65, tel 920411) and Soggiorno Alle Cinque Terre (Luciano Fazioli, near the castle on the top of the town, Via de Gasperi 1, tel. 920587).

Sleeping in Manarola

Marina Piccola has decent rooms right on the water, so they figure a personal touch is unnecessary (DB-L95,000, breakfast-L8,000, dinner never required, tel. 920103, fax 920966).

Just up the hill, **Albergo ca' d'Andrean** (DB-L91,000, breakfast-L8,000, Via A. Discovolo 25, tel. 920040, fax 920452, closed November) is quiet, comfortable, modern, and very hotel-esque, with ten rooms and a cool garden complete with orange trees.

Farther up the street, **Casa Capellini** (D-L50,000, the *alta camera*, on the top with a kitchen, private terrace and a knockout view-L60,000, no breakfast; take a hard right just off the church square, then two doors down the hill on your right, Via Antonio Discovolo 6, tel. 920823, run by an elderly couple who speak no English) is a private home renting four rooms.

Eating in Manarola

Il Porticiolo (closed Wednesday) near the water on the main street, or **Trattoria da Billy**, with the best view in town up in the residential area, are both reasonable for the over-priced area.

Sleeping Elsewhere in or near the Cinque Terre

Some enjoy staying in Monterosso al Mare, the most beach-resorty and least friendly of the five Cinque Terre towns. There are plenty of hotels, rentable beach umbrellas, shops, and cars. **Albergo Marina** (D-L75,000, DB-L85,000, Via Buranco 40, tel. and fax 817242 or 817613, open March-October); the big, fancy, and a little more expensive **Albergo degli Amici** (next door at via Buranco 36, tel./fax 817544 or 817424); and **Pensione al Carugio** (DL-80,000, DB-L90,000, tel. 817453) all require dinner in the summer.

Nearby Lerici is a pleasant town with several reasonable harborside hotels and a daily boat connection to Vernazza. The **youth hostel** in Finale Ligure (L16,000 per bed with sheets and breakfast, members only, 019/690515), down the coast a ways, is a friendly, deluxe castle.

When all else fails, you can stay in a noisy bigger town like La Spezia: **Hotel Terminus** (D-L55,000, DB-L65,000, no breakfast, Via Paleocapa 21, just down from the station, tel. 37204) has filthy rooms with worn-out carpets, yellow walls, and old plumbing. **Albergo Parma** (D-L56,000, DB-L66,000, no breakfast, Via Fiume 143, 19100 La Spezia, tel. 743010) brighter but without the character, is located just below the station, down the stairs.

The nearby town of Santa Margherita Ligure (a short train-ride south of the Cinque Terre) offers a nice base for those who want to drive right to their hotel's doorstep and not suffer too much Riviera glitz. The friendly Sabini family runs the stately old **Hotel Nuova Riviera** (D-L75,000, DB-L75,000-L85,000 with a big breakfast, 16038 S. Margherita Ligure, tel. 0185/287403).

Train Connections

The five towns of the Cinque Terre are on a milk-run train line so small it doesn't even register on the Cooks Train Timetable. Hourly trains connect each town with the others, La Spezia and Genova. About ten little beach towns (including the 5-Terre) lie on the line from La Spezia to Genova (a trip which takes about two hours). While a few of the milk run trains go to more distant points (Milan or Pisa), it's faster to change in La Spezia to a bigger train. **From La Spezia trains go to: Rome** (10/day, 4 hrs), **Pisa** (hrly, 60 min), **Florence** (hrly, 2½ hrs, change at Viareggio), **Milan** (hrly, 3 hrs., change in Genova).

Transportation

Milan to the Cinque Terre (130 miles): Drivers will speed south by autostrada from Milan, skirt Genoa, and drive along some of Italy's most scenic and impressive freeway toward the port of La Spezia. The road via Parma is faster but less scenic.

It's now possible to snake your car down the treacherous little road into the Cinque Terre and park above the town. This is risky in August and on Saturday or Sunday, when Italian day-trippers clog and jam the region. Vernazza has several parking lots above the town. To drive into the Cinque Terre, leave the autostrada at Uscita Brugnato just west of La Spezia.

You can also park your car near the train station in La Spezia. Any spot with white lines and no sign should be okay. Look for diagonal parking spots in front of the station or on the streets below. Be patient, spots do open up. Confirm that parking is okay and leave nothing inside to steal.

MILAN (MILANO)

They say that for every church in Rome, there's a bank in Milan. Italy's second city and the capital of Lombardy, Milan is a city of 2 million mostly hard-working, fashion-conscious, time-is-money people.

Milan is a melting pot of people and history. Its industriousness may come from the Teutonic blood of the Lombards or from the region's Austrian heritage. Milan is Italy's industrial, banking, TV, publishing, and convention capital. The economic success of modern Italy can be blamed on this city of publicists and power lunches.

It's an ugly city with a recently-bombed-out feeling (WWII). Its huge financial buildings are as manicured as its parks are shaggy. As if to make up for its harsh concrete shell, the people and the windows are works of art. Milan is an international fashion capital, the city that gave us the term "millinery." Even the cheese comes gift-wrapped.

Three hundred years before Christ, the Romans called this place Mediolanum or "the central place." By the fourth century A.D. it was the capital of the western half of the Roman Empire. It was from here that Emperor Constantine issued the Edict of Milan, legalizing Christianity. After some barbarian darkness, medieval Milan rose to regional prominence under the Visconti and Sforza families. By the time of the Renaissance it was called "the New Athens" and was enough of a cultural leader for Leonardo to call it home. Then came 400 years of foreign domination (Spain, Austria, France, more Austria). Milan was a center of the 1848 revolution against Austria and helped lead Italy to unification in 1870.

Mussolini left a heavy Fascist touch on the city's architecture (such as the central train station). His excesses also led to the WWII bombing of Milan. But Milan rose again. The 1959 Pirelli Tower (the skinny, sleek skyscraper in front of the station) was a trend-setter in its day. Today the city has a pedestrian-friendly center, a great transit system, banks everywhere, and enough police to keep those not looking for trouble out of trouble.

While many tourists come to Italy for the past, Milan is today's Italy, and no Italian trip is complete without seeing it.

While Milan's public-relations expertise has made it a fashion and finance winner, it's not big on the tourist circuit. But it has plenty to see, it's no more expensive than other Italian cities, and it's well organized and completely manageable. Our motto for Milan: don't worry, be clever.

Planning Your Time

Okay, it's a big city. So you probably won't linger. But if you give it two nights and a full day you can gain an appreciation for the town and see the major sights. With 36 hours, I'd sleep in, and focus on, the center. Tour the Duomo, the La Scala museum, hit what art you like (Brera Gallery, Michelangelo's *Pietà*, Leonardo's *Last Supper*), browse through the elegant shopping area and the Gallery, and try to see an opera. Technology buffs could spend a day in the Science and Technology museum, while medieval art buffs could spend a day touring the city's very old churches. People-watchers and pigeon-feeders could spend an entire vacation never leaving sight of the Duomo.

Since Milan is a cold Italian plunge, and most flights to the U.S.A. leave Milan early in the morning, you may want to start your Italian trip softly by going directly from the Milan airport to Lake Como (Varenna) or the Cinque Terre (Vernazza) and seeing Milan at the end of your trip before flying home.

Orientation (tel. code: 02)

In Milan, I'm constantly disoriented. Go slow, use the map. Before exiting the subway, note the street markings. You'll notice the street plan is a series of rings that used to be medieval walls.

Tourist Information

There are two offices (in the central train station and on Piazza Duomo, to the right as you face the church, 8:00-20:00, Sunday 9:00-17:00, tel. 809662). Stop by to confirm your sightseeing plans and pick up a map (the overall map is handy with sketches of sights, but ask for one listing more streets), the classy *Museums in Milan* booklet (an extensive survey of the top sights), a listing of museum hours, and the *Milano Mese* monthly listing of events and entertainment.

Milan

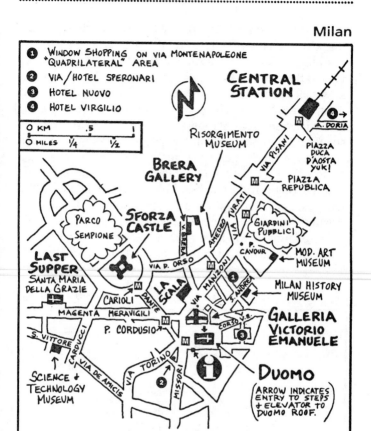

① WINDOW SHOPPING ON VIA MONTENAPOLEONE "QUADRILATERAL" AREA
② VIA/HOTEL SPERONARI
③ HOTEL NUOVO
④ HOTEL VIRGILIO

CENTRAL STATION

RISORGIMENTO MUSEUM

BRERA GALLERY

SFORZA CASTLE

PARCO SEMPIONE

LAST SUPPER
SANTA MARIA DELLA GRAZIE

VIA P. ORSO

LA SCALA

CARIOLI

MAGENTA

MERAVIGLI

P. CORDUSIO

S. VITTORE

SCIENCE & TECHNOLOGY MUSEUM

PIAZZA DUCA D'AOSTA yuk!

PIAZZA REPUBLICA

GIARDINI PUBBLICI

MOD. ART MUSEUM

MILAN HISTORY MUSEUM

GALLERIA VICTORIO EMANUELE

DUOMO
(ARROW INDICATES ENTRY TO STEPS & ELEVATOR TO DUOMO ROOF.)

— DCH —

Trains

Avoid the long lines at the station ticket office. The handiest Milan travel agency is CIT in Galleria Vittorio Emanuele (open until 19:00, great for buying train tickets or *couchettes*, tel. 866661) or American Express (up Via Verdi from La Scala, Via Brera 3, tel. 876674 or 72003694).

Getting Around

Use Milan's great subway system. The clean, spacious, fast and easy three-line Metro zips you anywhere you may want to go. Transit tickets (L1,200 at newsstands, normally in the subway station) are good for one subway ride followed by 75 minutes of bus or tram travel. The L4,000 all-day, or *diurno*, pass is a handy option (sold at major stations and some newsstands, two days for L7,000). I've keyed all of the sightseeing with the subway system. While most sights are within a few blocks of each other, Milan is an exhausting city to walk in, and the well-marked buses can be useful. (While the kiosks all sell the L5,000 Milan city transit map, the City Transit information offices next to the TI in the station and at the Duomo Metro station often have free ATM maps showing all bus lines.) Small groups go cheap and fast by taxi (metered, drop charge L6,000 and L1,300 per km, often easiest to walk to a taxi stand rather than try to hail one).

Driving is bad enough in Milan to make the L35,000 a day you'll pay in a downtown garage a blessing. If you're driving, do Milan (and maybe even Lake Como) before or after you rent. If you have a car, ask about the city's suburban Parcheggi, affordable and safe suburban parking lots.

Milan Metro

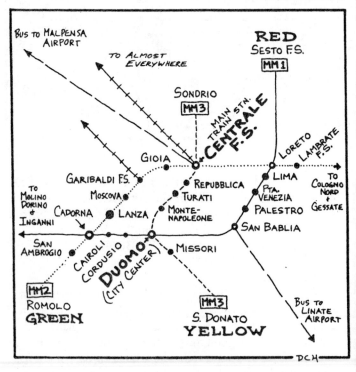

Helpful Hints

Theft Alert: Be on guard. Milan's thieves target tourists. At the station and around the Duomo, beggars—actually thieves—roam, usually in gangs of three too-young-to-arrest children.

Museums: Museums are closed on Mondays (except La Scala). The museums that are good for you (city-run museums covering obscure history and matters of local pride) are free. The famous things that all tourists do are generally expensive (L5,000-L10,000).

Weather: August is rudely hot and muggy. Locals who can, vacate, leaving the city just about dead. Those visiting in August will find many shops closed and nightlife pretty quiet.

Sights—Milan

Compared to Rome and Florence, Milan's art is relatively mediocre, but the city does have unique and noteworthy sights. To maximize your time, use the Metro and note which places stay open through the siesta. I've listed sights in a logical geographical order.

There's much more to see in Milan than I've listed here. Its many thousand-year-old churches make it clear that Milan was an important beacon in the Dark Ages. Local guidebooks and the tourist information office can point you in the right direction if you have more time.

▲▲**Duomo**—Milan's cathedral, the city's centerpiece, is the third-largest church in Europe (after the Vatican's and Sevilla's). At 480 feet long and 280 feet wide, with 52 150-foot-tall sequoia pillars inside and over 2,000 statues, the place can seat 12,000 worshipers. If you do two laps, you've done your daily walk. Built from 1386 until 1810, it started Gothic (notice the fine Gothic apse behind the altar) and was finished under Napoleon. It's an example of the flamboyant, or "flamelike," overripe final stage of Gothic, but architectural harmony is not its forte. Note the giant stained-glass windows that try to light the cavernous interior (open daily 7:00-19:00; enforced dress code: no shorts or bare shoulders; Metro: Duomo).

The rooftop is a fancy forest of spires with great views of the city, the square, and on clear days, even the Swiss Alps. Overlooking everything is the 13-foot-tall gilt Virgin Mary, 300 feet above the ground (climb the stairs for L4,000 or ride the elevator for L6,000, 9:00-17:00, enter outside from the north, clue: in Europe old churches face roughly east).

Museo del Duomo—The cathedral's museum is a scrapbook of 600 years of cathedral history offering a close look at the stained glass, statues, and gargoyles (14 Piazza Duomo, L7,000, open 9:30-12:30, 15:00-18:00, closed Monday, Metro: Duomo).

▲**Piazza Duomo and nearby**—Piazza Duomo is a classic European scene. Professionals scurry, label-conscious kids loiter, young thieves peruse. For that creepy-crawly pigeons-all-over-you experience, buy a bag of seed. Behind the Duomo is a pedestrian shopping zone. Within a block of the piazza are a few interesting glimpses of old Milan. The center of medieval Milan was Piazza Mercanti, a small square just opposite the Duomo. It's a strangely peaceful place today. The church of **Santa Maria presso San Satiro** (just off Via Torino, a few yards past Via Speronari) was the scene of a temper tantrum in 1242, when a losing gambler vented his anger by hitting the baby Jesus in the Madonna-and-Child altarpiece. Blood "miraculously" spouted out and the beautiful little church has been on the pilgrimage trail ever since. For the 750th anniversary the pope has offered special indulgences to those who worshipped here. Even though the offer expired in March of 1993, it's worth a visit to see the illusion of depth (*trompe l'oeil*), designed by Bramante, behind the basically flat altar.

▲▲**Galleria Vittorio Emanuele**—Milan is symbolized by its great four-story-high, glass-domed arcade. This is the place to turn an expensive cup of coffee into a good value with some of Europe's best people-watching. Stand under the central dome and enjoy the art above. For good luck, locals step on the testicles of the mosaic Taurus on the floor's zodiac design. Two local girls explained that it works better if you actually do a spin. (Metro: Duomo; under the dome is the CIT travel agency and the SIP bank of unvandalized public phone booths; the "comune di Milan" office at the La Scala end has tourist information.)

▲▲**La Scala Opera House and Museum**—From the Galleria, you'll see a statue of Leonardo. He's looking at a plain but famous neoclassical building, possibly the world's most prestigious opera house, Milan's Teatrale alla Scala. La

Scala opened in 1778 with an opera by Antonio Salieri (of *Amadeus* fame). While tickets are as hard to get as they are expensive, anyone can get a peek into the grand theater from a box connected to the museum. Opera buffs will love the museum's extensive collection of things that would mean absolutely nothing to the MTV crowd: Verdi's top hat, Rossini's eyeglasses, Toscanini's baton, Fettucini's pesto, and original scores, busts, portraits, and death masks of great composers and musicians (L5,000, daily 9:00-12:00, 14:00-18:00, erratic hours due to performances, Metro: Duomo).

The opera season is December-July. September-November is for classical concerts. La Scala is closed in August. Ask about the sky-high but affordable gallery seats that are often available two hours before the performance on the day of the show, or L10,000 standing room which can be purchased in advance (tel. 7200 3744, showtime usually 20:00).

▲**World Class Window-shopping**—The "Quadrilateral," as the elegant, high-fashion shopping area around Via Montenapoleone is called, is worth a wander. In this land where cigarettes are still chic, the people-watching is as fun as the window-shopping. Via Montenapoleone and Via Spiga are the best streets. From La Scala, walk up Via Manzoni to the Metro stop: Montenapoleone, browse down Montenapoleone (with a possible side stroll up to Spiga) to Piazza San Babila and then down the pedestrians-only Corso Vittorio Emanuele II to the Duomo.

Museums of Milan and of Contemporary History—These museums (both at Via Sant'Andrea 6) are free and offer a quick walk through wall-sized pages of Milan's past, including the especially interesting 1914 to 1945 period (9:30-17:30, often with a lunch break, closed Monday). Metro: Montenapoleone.

▲**The Brera Art Gallery**—Milan's top collection of paintings is without a doubt world class, but it can't top Rome or Florence. Established in 1809 to house Napoleon's looted art, the gallery's highlights include works by the Bellini brothers, Caravaggio (*Supper at Emmaus*), Raphael (*Wedding of the Madonna*), and Mantegna's textbook example of feet-first foreshortening (*The Dead Christ*). Even if you don't go into the gallery, see Napoleon nude (by Canova) in the courtyard and wander through the art school on the ground floor (cheapest cup of coffee in town from the machine down the hall, L8,000, open 9:00-17:30, Sunday 9:00-12:30, closed Monday, Metro: Lanza).

▲**Risorgimento Museum**—This tells the interesting story (if you speak Italian or luck out as I did with a bored and talkative English-speaking guard) of Italy's rocky road to unity: from Napoleon (1796) to the victory in Rome (1870). Just around the corner from the Brera Gallery at Via Borgonuovo 23 (free, 9:30-17:30, closed Monday).

▲**Sforza Castle (Castello Sforzesco)**—This immense, much bombed and rebuilt brick fortress is exhausting at first sight. It can only be described as heavy. But its courtyard has a great lawn for picnics and siestas, and its free museum is filled with interesting medieval armor, furniture, early Lombard art, and, most important, Michelangelo's unfinished *Rondanini Pietà*. Michelangelo died while still working on this piece, which hints at the elongation of the mannerist style that would follow. This is a rare opportunity to enjoy a Michelangelo with no crowds (9:30-17:30, closed Monday, free; Metro: Cadorna, enter from Ricasoli).

▲**Leonardo da Vinci's Last Supper (Cenacolo)**—This Renaissance masterpiece is in the refectory of the church of Santa Maria delle Grazie. It captures the emotional moment when Jesus says to his disciples, "One of you will betray me," and each of the twelve wonders nervously, "Lord, is it I?" Notice Judas with his 30 pieces of silver, looking pretty guilty. This ill-fated masterpiece suffers from Leonardo's experimental use of oil rather than the normal fresco technique. Deterioration began within six years of its completion. The church was bombed in WWII, but the *Last Supper* survived. Now undergoing extensive restoration, it's a faded mess with most of the original paint gone and most of the rest behind scaffolding (L6,000, 8:15-13:45, closed Monday).

▲**National Leonardo da Vinci Science and Technology Museum (Museo Nazionale della Scienze e della Tecnica)**—The spirit of Leonardo lives here in Italy's top science-and-technology museum. Most tourists visit for the hall of Leonardo designs illustrated in wooden models, but Leonardo's mind is just as easy to appreciate by paging through a coffee-table edition of his notebooks in any bookstore. The rest of this immense collection of industrial cleverness is fascinating, with plenty of pushbutton action (unfortunately, no English descriptions): trains, the evolution of radios, old musical instruments, computers, batteries, telephones, chunks of the first transatlantic cable, and on and on. (Via San Vittore 21, bus #50 from the Duomo, 9:30-16:50, closed Monday, L10,000.)

Nightlife—For evening action, check out the arty, student-oriented Brera area in the old center and Milan's formerly Bohemian, now gentrified "Little Venice," the Navigli neighborhood. Specifics change so quickly that it's best to rely on the entertainment information in periodicals from the TI.

Sleeping in Milan
(L1,600 = about $1, tel. code: 02)

Milan has plenty of simple, central, and reasonable accommodations. Prices are the same throughout the year. None includes breakfast, which, if available, is a lousy value (eat down the street in a café). I have listed only places that should have no traffic noise problems. All are within a few minutes' walk of Milan's fine subway system. Anytime but summer, the city can be completely jammed by conventions; summer is usually wide open. Hotels cater more to business travelers than to tourists. I've limited recommendations to two areas: in the center near the Duomo and near the train station.

Sleep code: **S**=Single, **D**=Double/Twin, **T**=Triple, **Q**=Quad, **B**=Bath/Shower, **WC**=Toilet, **CC**=Credit Card (Visa, Mastercard, Amex).

Sleeping in the City Center

The Duomo (cathedral) area is my favorite place to feel the pulse of Milano. It's an area thick with people-watching, reasonable eateries, and the major sightseeing attractions, but just four stops on the Metro from the central train station.

Hotel Speronari (S-L50,000, SB-L66,000, D-L70,000, DB-L70,000, DBWC-L100,000-L110,000, hallway showers-L5,000, CC:VM; ideally located on a pedestrian street off Via Torino, one block off the far left end of the Piazza Duomo with back to church, at Via Speronari 4, 20123 Milano, tel. 86461125, fax 72003178) is my home in Milan. It's perfectly located, safe and quiet, on a great pedestrian street full of fun delis and food shops, run by genteel and helpful Paolo Isoni and his family. Bright, clean, no views and no traffic noise, but thin walls. Phones in the rooms (but programmed not to work for U.S.A. direct calls).

Hotel Nuovo (40 rooms, S-L47,000, D-L67,000, DB-L110,000, T-L90,000, through 2 blocks of shopping arcades immediately behind the Duomo on the quiet, ugly Piazza Beccaria 6, 20122 Milano, tel. 86464444, fax 72001752) is a rare one-star hotel in the center. The price and locale are great. The interior is quiet and clean, but borderline dank and depressing yellow paint throughout.

Other one-star hotels in the center with rooms in the L70,000 range include: **Hotel Alcione** (Via G. Mora 2, tel. 8322050), **Hotel Manzoni** (Via Senato 45, tel. 76021002, fax 798834), **Hotel Cesare Correnti** (Via C Correnti 14, tel. 8057609), and **Hotel Kent** (Via F. Corridoni 2, tel. 55187635). Nicer, but farther out is **Hotel Del Sud** (at the Brenta Metro stop, Corso Lodi 74, tel. 5693457).

Sleeping near the Train Station

With Milan's fine Metro, you can get anywhere in town in a flash. For pure convenience and price, this is a handy, if dreary, area. The area between the station and Corso Buenos Aires has a seedy, frumpy, prostitutes-after-dark problem. Most of these listings are on the fringe of decency. Corso Buenos Aires is a bustling main shopping and people-watching drag. All listings below are within two subway stops or a 10-minute walk of the station. The last is near the less seedy but noisier main drag, Corso Buenos Aires.

"The Best" Hotel (DBWC-L80,000, walk down Via Scarlatti from the station, near the Lima Metro stop at Via B. Marcello 83, 20124 Milano, tel. 29404757, fax 201966, elevator, phones in the room, free parking on square) actually is the best in its price range. Run by friendly, English-speaking Luciana and Peter with a homey lounge and rooms overlooking either a garden or an ugly car-filled square that becomes an open-air market on Tuesdays and Saturdays. Request a *tranquillo giardino* room. In a sad battle of self-congratulatory names, the Hotel Paradiso next door (D-L60,000, DBWC-L80,000, Via B. Marcello 85, tel. 2049448) is sleepable, but fails miserably to live up to its name.

Hotel Due Giardini (S-L45,000, D-L65,000, T-L90,000, these are special prices for cash with this book; from the station walk 5 blocks down via Vitruvia, right to via Settala 46, 20124 Milano, tel. 29521093, fax 29516933, family Salis), plain, simple, and friendly, is a popular *Let's Go* listing but plenty big and offers a peaceful garden.

Hotel Virgilio (S-L48,000, SB-L73,000, D-L75,000, DBWC-L110,000, breakfast-L10,000, CC:VMA; leave station, backtrack along via Aporti, right after 2 blocks to Via P.L. da Palestrina 30, 20124 Milano, tel. 6691337, fax 66982587) is dark and designed for smoking businessmen, but a reasonable value for someone looking for a real hotel near the station.

Hotel Serena (DBWC-L120,000, CC:VM, 30 yards off Corso Buenos Aires near the Lima Metro stop, Via Boscovich 59, tel. 29522152, fax 29404958) is plain, quiet, and handy.

Hotel Cristoforo Colombo (DBWC-L160,000, if no convention is going, ask for Friday, Saturday, or Sunday rates: DBWC-L100,000, CC:VM; at Metro: Porta Venezia, Corso Buenos Aires 3, 20124 Milano, tel. 29406214, fax 29516096) is my token normal hotel recommendation complete with uniformed bellhops, TVs, and the works.

Hotel Casa Mia (S-L40,000, SBWC-L50,000, D-L60,000, DBWC-L80,000, T-L90,000, TBWC-L110,000, a stone's throw from the Piazza della Repubblica Metro stop, Viale Vittorio Veneto 30, tel. 6575249) is a simple, quiet, hardworking family affair, rare in downtown Milan.

Eating in Milan

This is a fast-food city. But fast food in a fashion capital isn't a burger and fries. The bars, delis, *rosticceria*, and self-services cater to people with plenty of taste and more money than time.

You'll find delightful eateries all over town. Notice the fine (and free) munchies that appear late in the afternoon in many bars. A L3,000 beer can (if you're either likable or discreet) become a light meal.

Eating near the Duomo
and Recommended Hotel Speronari

For a low-stress affordable lunch facing the Duomo square, eat at **Ciao**, a shiny, modern, second-floor self-serve (daily 11:30-15:00, 18:00-23:00, view tables from top "terrace" floor). For a more challenging adventure in eating Milanese, and a classy hotel room dinner, hit the colorful shops on Via Speronari (off Via Torino, a block southwest of Piazza Duomo: *rosticceria*, classy cheese, bread, and produce shops). **Peck**, nearby on Via G. Cantu, off Via Dante, is an elegant *rosticceria*. The **Peck Snack Bar** (nearby just off via Orefici at via Victor Hugo 4, 7:30-21:00) is a classy cafeteria.

Other self-serve restaurants near the Duomo are **Brek** (Corso Italia 3, closed Sunday) and **Amico** (where via Torino hits the Duomo square, closed Monday). Also near the Duomo, the **Pizzeria Dogana** at via Dogana 3, serves up cheap, hearty, and tasty pizzas (closed Monday).

Eating near the Train Station and Recommended "Best" Hotel

Ristaurante Salernitano (Via Vitruvio 8), **Trattoria Leo**, and several places on via Tadino are reasonable, friendly, and relaxed. To eat classy in this area, try the bright and elegant **Ristorante Mediterranea Di Valerio e Maurizio** (Piazza Cincinnato 4, tel. 29522076, closed Sunday).

Breakfast is a bad value in hotels and fun in bars. It's okay to quasi-picnic. Bring in a box of juice (*plastic bicchiere* = plastic cups) and some bananas (or whatever) and order a toasted ham and cheese *panino* (*calda* = hot) or croissant with your cappuccino.

Train Connections

Milan Central Station to: Venice (hrly, 3 hrs), **Florence** (hrly, 3 hrs), **Genoa** (hrly, 2 hrs), **Rome** (hrly, 5 hrs), **Brindisi** (4/day, 10-12 hrs), **Cinque Terre** (hrly, 3-4 hrs to La Spezia, sometimes changing in Genoa, trains from La Spezia to the villages go hourly), **Varenna** on Lago di Como (the small line to Lecco/Tirano leaves from Milan's central station every 2 hours for the 1-hour trip to Varenna; note that some Varenna trains leave from the Milano Porta Garibaldi station). The city of **Como** on Lago di Como (hrly from Milano Nord station, 1 hr, ferries go from Como to Varenna).

International destinations: **Amsterdam** (4/day, 14 hrs), **Barcelona** (2 changes, 17 hrs), **Bern** (7/day, 4 hrs), **Frank-**

furt (5/day, 9 hrs), **London** (2/day, 18 hrs), **Munich** (5/day, 8 hrs), **Nice** (5 day, 7-10 hrs), **Paris** (4/day, 8 hrs), **Vienna** (4/day, 14 hrs). Milan train info tel. 67500.

Milan's Airports

Most international flights land at Milan's surprisingly cozy **Malpensa** airport, 30 miles northwest of the city. Malpensa airport seems to be designed to help you overcome your fears of Italy. Customs guards fan you through, and even the sniffing dog seems friendly. The airport bank has fine rates (Banco di Milano, 8:00-20:00, no limit). Visit the bus/train information and ticket office (convenient chance to buy train tickets and check departure times for train trips from Milan, buy a L10,000 telephone card, and confirm your hotel). A shuttle bus connects Malpensa and the Central train station (2/hr, 45-minute ride, L12,000, tel. 40099280). Taxis into Milan cost $80. If you're picking up a rental car, the country-side is an ideal place to get used to driving in a new car in a new country.

Milan's second airport is **Linate** (5 miles to the east, linked by regular shuttle buses with Piazza Luigi di Savoia at the central train station, 3/hr, 5:40-21:00, L4,000 tickets from driver, tel. 66984509).

For flight information for either airport, call 02/74852200. (British Air, tel. 7382028; American Airlines, tel. 290 04919; Alitalia, tel. 26852.)

LAKE COMO (LAGO DI COMO)

Commune with nature where Italy is welded to the Alps, in the lovely Italian Lakes District. The million-lire question is: Which lake? For the best mix of accessibility, scenery, offbeatness, and a complete dose of Italian-lakes wonder and aristocratic-old-days romance, Lake Como is my choice. And the sleepy town of Varenna, at midlake, is my home base. Bustling Milan, just an hour away, doesn't even exist. You're on vacation.

Lake Como, lined with elegant 19th-century villas, crowned by snowcapped mountains, and buzzing with ferries, hydrofoils, and little passenger ships, is a good place to take a break from the intensity and obligatory turnstile culture of central Italy. It seems half the travelers you'll meet have tossed their itineraries into the lake and are actually relaxing.

Today, the lake's only serious industry is tourism. Thousands of lakeside residents travel daily to nearby Lugano, in Switzerland, to find work. The area's isolation and flat economy have left it pretty much the way the 19th-century romantic poets described it.

Planning Your Time

Don't come to Lago di Como unless you're planning to relax. Even though there are no essential activities, plan for at least two nights so you'll have an uninterrupted day to see how slow you can get your pulse. The scenic approach is by train from Milan to Como (hrly, 50 min) where you'll catch the 2-hour boat ride up the lake to Varenna. Knowing how great Varenna is, I zip there directly by train (1 hour from Milan), get set up, and limit my activities to midlake (Varenna, Bellagio, and Menaggio).

Getting Around

Lago di Como is well served by boats and hydrofoils. The lake service is divided into three parts: north-south from Como to Colico; midlake between Varenna, Bellagio, Menaggio, and Cadenabbia (Villa Carlotta); and the southeastern arm to Lecco. Unless you're going through Como, you'll probably

Lake Como

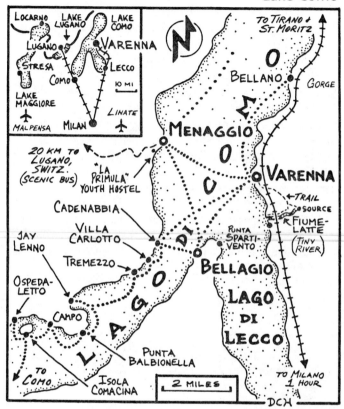

limit your cruising to the midlake service (info tel. 031/273324).
Boats go about hourly between Varenna, Menaggio and
Bellagio (15 min, L4,200).

Passengers pay the same for car or passenger ferries, but
50 percent more for the enclosed, stuffy, less scenic, but very
quick hydrofoil. The free schedule (at tourist office, hotel, or
boat dock) lists times and prices. Stopovers aren't allowed
and there's no break for round-trips, so buy a ticket for each
ride. All-day passes make sense only if you're taking more
than four rides. (Boat-schedule literacy tips: *Feriale* = workdays,
Monday-Saturday. *Festivo* = Sunday and holidays. *Partenze
da* = departing from.)

While you can easily drive around the lake, the road is
narrow, congested, and lined by privacy-seeking walls, hedges,

and tall fences. It costs L12,000 to take your car onto a ferry. And parking is rarely easy where you need it, especially in Bellagio. Park in Varenna (free on the main road south of town) and cruise.

Sights—Lake Como

▲▲▲**Varenna**—This town is the best of all lake worlds. Easily accessible by train, on the less driven side of the lake, Varenna has a romantic promenade, a tiny harbor, narrow lanes, and its own villa. It's the right place to savor a lakeside cappuccino or *aperitivo*. The town is quiet at night. The *passerella* (lakeside walk) is adorned with caryatid lovers pressing silently against each other in the shadows.

There's wonderfully little to do in Varenna. A tiny public beach is just past the ferry dock, and a tiny private one (L2,000 entry, showers, rentable chairs and cabins, bar) is just beyond that. Varenna's TI is on the main square (Pro Local, tel. 0341/830367).

Varenna

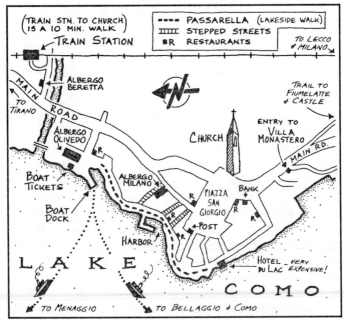

For a reasonable meal in Varenna, try the *pizzeria* (#1, Piazza San Giorgio, below Hotel Royal Victoria, across from the church) or **Ristorante del Sole** (tasty meals, especially Naples-style pizzas, at Piazza San Giorgio 17, tel. 830206). For a splurge, the **Vecchia Varenna** restaurant, with its romantic loggia on the old harborfront, is great (L50,000 meals, tel. 830793, closed Monday). For the same great view but much cheaper eating, the two harbor-front bars (next to Vecchia Varenna) serve salads and hot sandwiches. For cold, sweet, and fruity treats, check out the haborfront *frapperia*. The grocery stores on the main square have all you need for a classy balcony or breakwater picnic dinner. (For accommodations, see Sleeping, below.)

Three mediocre sights are nearby: north, south, and up. A steep trail leads to Varenna's ruined castle capping the hill above. It's as intriguing as a locked-up castle can be. While you can't get in, there's a fine view and a peaceful, traffic-free, one-chapel, no-coffee town behind it. The nearby town of Bellano, to the north, harbors the Orrido, an impressive gorge cutting into the mountainside (9:00-12:30, 14:00-18:00). Just south of Varenna, the town of Fiumelatte is named for its milky river, which is only 800 feet long. (It runs only during the tourist season, and it's a pleasant walk from Varenna via the cemetery to Fiumelatte.)

▲**Bellagio**—The self-proclaimed "Pearl of the Lake" is a classy combination of tidiness and Old World elegance. If you don't mind that "tramp in a palace" feeling, it's a fine place to surround yourself with the more adventurous of the posh travelers and shop for umbrellas and ties. The heavy curtains between the arcades keep the visitors from sweating. Steep-stepped lanes rise from the harborfront, and the shady prom-enade leads to the Lido (beach). The town has a tourist office (on Piazza Chiesa next to the church, tel. 031/950204, loosely open 9:00-12:00, 15:00-18:00, closed Sunday and Tuesday), a worth-a-look church, and some surprisingly affordable funky old hotels (listed below). For something off-beat to do in Bellagio, look up Tony, the wine king. He runs a wild little cantina just up the street behind the camera shop near the ferry dock (Salita Genazzini 3, tel. 950935).

Bellagio, the administrative capital of the midlake region, is located where the two southern legs split off. For an easy break in a park with a great view, wander right on out to the crotch. Meander past the rich and famous Hotel Villa Servelloni, past the little Ortofrutta market (fruit and juice for the viewpoint, 8:00-12:30, 14:30-18:30, closed Monday), and walk 5 minutes to the Punta Spartivento, literally "the point that divides the wind." You'll find a Renoir atmosphere complete with a bar, a tiny harbor, and a chance to sit on a bench and gaze north past Menaggio and Varenna to the Swiss Alps and the end of the lake.

▲**Menaggio**—Just 8 miles from Lugano in Switzerland, Menaggio has more urban bulk than its neighbors. Since the lake is getting a bit dirty for swimming, consider its fine public pool. This is the starting point for a few hikes. Only 25 years ago, these trails were used by cigarette smugglers. As many as 180 people a night would sneak through the darkness from Switzerland back into Italy with tax-free cigarettes. The hostel (see Sleeping, below) has information about catching the bus to trailheads on nearby Mount Grona or to the top of the pass on the Lugano road. Also the hostel rents bikes for a great 40-kilometer, 4-hour bike trip: pedal 15 level kilometers from the hostel to Argeno, catch the lift to 2,500 foot high Pigra (L5,000 with bike), and coast scenically back to Menaggio.

Villa Carlotta—This is the best of Lake Como's famed villas. I see the lakes as a break from Italy's art, but if you're in need of a place that charges admission (L8,000, 9:00-18:00 daily in season), Villa Carlotta offers an elegant Neoclassical interior, a famous Canova statue, and a garden (its highlight, best in spring). If you're touring one villa on the lake, this is probably the best. Nearby Tremezzo and Cadenabbia are pleasant lakeside resorts an easy walk away. Boats serve all three places.

Isola Comacina—To the south of Villa Carlotta, Isola Comacina is Como's only island. It's filled with ruins and connected by ferry from scenic little Ospedaletto. As you cruise around the peninsula just north of the island, check out the lovely Villa Balbianello. As WWII was winding up, Mussolini tried to flee to Switzerland. He was caught at Dongo, a town on the north end of the lake, and shot in Azzano with his mistress on April 28, 1945.

Como—On the southwest tip of the lake, Como has a good, traffic-free old town; an interesting Gothic/Renaissance cathedral; and a pleasant lakefront with a promenade. It's an easy walk from the boat dock to the train station (Milan, hrly, 40 min). Boats leave Como about hourly for midlake (ferries, 2 hrs; hydrofoils, 1hr; tel. 031/273324)

Sleeping on Lake Como
(L1,600 = about $1)

The area is tight in August, snug in July, and wide open most of the rest of the year. All places listed are family-run, have lake-view rooms, and some English is spoken. (Request "*con vista.*") View rooms are given (usually for no extra cost) to those who telephone reservations and request "*camera con vista.*" If ever I were to kill, it would be here . . . for the view. Prices go soft in the off-season. Shop around by phone to confirm the view and price. If you fail, ask to get a view balcony for your second night.

Sleep code: **S**=Single, **D**=Double/Twin, **T**=Triple, **Q**=Quad, **B**=Bath/Shower, **WC**=Toilet, **CC**=Credit Card (Visa, Mastercard, Amex), **SE**=Speaks English (graded **A-F**).

Sleeping in Varenna
(tel. code: 0341, postal code: 22050)

Albergo Olivedo (prices vary with season and views: S-L50,000-L65,000, D-L60,000-L85,000, DBWC-L85,000-L110,000, including breakfast, plenty of sit-down tub showers and toilets across the hall, tel. 830115, Laura SE and takes easy telephone reservations), right at the ferry dock, is a neat and tidy old hotel. Each room has squeaky hardwood floors, World War II furniture, and lumpy beds. Many have glorious little lake-view balconies. It's a fine place to hang out and watch the children, boats, and sun come and go.

Albergo Milano (DBWC-L110,000, a little more in July and August, discounted for two nights in off-season or with a side view; optional breakfast on the terrace with cheese, meat, a trolley of sweets, and Amelia's charm is worth the L10,000, CC:VM; Via XX Settembre 29, 22050 Varenna/Como, tel. and fax 830298, ideally reserve with a fax and credit-card number), located right in the old town, is your best splurge. Friendly but non-English-speaking Amelia obviously loves serving people. Her son, Giovanni, speaks English. Each of the nine rooms is comfortable and comes with great plumbing. Rooms 1 and 2 have the royal balconies. Rooms 5 and 6 have small balconies, but even bigger views. This place screams *luna di miele* (honeymoon).

Albergo del Sol (D-L40,000, Piazza San Giorgio 17, tel. 830206) is a 6-room, 1-tub place on the main square offering the best cheap beds in town.

Albergo Beretta (D-L60,000, DBWC-L80,000, room 9 without a shower has a view balcony for only L60,000, tel. 830132), off the water on the main road below the station, with more mustiness than character, has good beds.

Sleeping in Bellagio

Hotel du Lac (DBWC-L160,000 with breakfast, CC:VM, Leoni family, 22021 Bellagio/Como, tel. 031/950320, fax 951624) is your best splurge. Right on the harbor with a roof garden, it's completely remodeled (air-conditioning, TVs, mini-bars) and gives you the old flavor with absolutely no loss of comfort. **Hotel Suisse** (DBWC-L70,000, optional L10,000 breakfast, Piazza Mazzini 8, 22021 Bellagio, tel. 031/950335, fax 951755, CC:VM) somehow landed right on the harbor next to the stuffy places. It's frumpy with simple rooms, hardwood floors, fine bathrooms, terrible beds, and some great views and balconies. The similar one-star **Hotel Roma** (D-L50,000, DBWC-L65,000, L6,000 breakfast, CC:VMA, elevator, decent restaurant, tel. 031/950424, fax 951906) cranes its neck behind and above Hotel Suisse. The fifth floor has the cheapest rooms (shower down the hall) with great view balconies. **Hotel Giardinetto** (D-L50,000, DBWC-L65,000, L8,000 breakfast, Via Roncati 12, tel. 031/950168, SE-A), near the tourist office and about 100 steps above the waterfront, offers squeaky-clean, cool, and quiet rooms, above a breezy and peaceful garden. It's warmly run by the Ticozzi family.

Sleeping in Menaggio

La Primula Youth Hostel is a rare hostel. Family-run for ten years by Ty and Paola, it caters to a quiet, savor-the-lakes crowd and offers the only cheap beds in the area. Located just south of the Menaggio dock (you'll see the sign from the boat), it has a view terrace, lots of games, a members' kitchen, a washing machine, bike rentals (L15,000 a day,

L30,000 for non-hostelers), discount tickets to Villa Carlotta, discount boat passes, easy parking, and a creative and hard-working staff. (Closed 10:00-17:00 daily and from mid-November–mid-March, L14,000 per night in a 4- to 6-bed room with sheets and breakfast, L15,000 with private plumbing, hearty dinners with a local flair and wine are only L13,000.) Ty and Paola print a newsletter to advertise their activities programs (inexpensive 14-day Italian language, 3- to 7-day hikes, bike trips, cooking classes). The bike ride described under Sights—Menaggio is a favorite with hostelers. Show your copy of this book and receive a free La Primula recipe book. Ostello La Primula, Via 4 Novembre 86, 22017 Menaggio, tel. and fax 0344/32356.

Train Connections

The quickest Milan connection to any point at midlake (Bellagio, Menaggio, or Varenna) is via the train to Varenna. Trains run between Milan Centrale and Varenna (10 day, 60 min, L6,000). Note: some Milan trains depart to Varenna from the Garibaldi station, an easy Metro connection from the Central station. Milan train schedules list Sondria and Lecco, but often not Varenna; Varenna is a small stop. Some cars on long trains don't even get a platform. Ask for help so you don't miss the stop. You may have to open the door yourself. (Look for the button.) Trains leave Varenna for Milan at 5:30, 6:19, 7:27, 8:27, 10:27, and every two hours until 22:27. This makes a comfy last stop before catching the shuttle from Milan's station to the airport.

Como and Milan: Trains zip between Milan's North station and Como (hrly, 40 min), where you can catch the 2-hour ferry or faster hydrofoil to midlake (Varenna).

Drivers should park in Varenna and use the boat. Cars are costly on the ferries. Consider doing Milan and Lake Como before or after you rent a car.

THE DOLOMITES

Italy's dramatic limestone rooftop, the Dolomites, offers some of the best and certainly unique mountain thrills in Europe. Bolzano is the gateway to the Dolomites, and Castelrotto is a good home base for your exploration of Alpe di Siusi, Europe's largest alpine meadow. The weather forecast is great, and the staggering peaks can't wait. Take a hike!

Planning Your Time

Drivers can get the best one-day look at the Dolomites by traveling from Venice to Bolzano via the Great Dolomite Road. Train travelers should side trip in from Bolzano (an hour north of Verona). To get a feel for the Alpine culture here, spend a night in Castelrotto. With two nights in Castelrotto you can actually get out and hike. But for the real experience, avid hikers will want to spend a night in a mountain hut above Castelrotto. This means two nights in Castelrotto straddling a night in a hut.

Orientation

The Dolomites are well developed, and the region's famous valleys and towns suffer from après-ski fever. But the bold limestone pillars, flecked with snow over green meadows under a blue sky, offer a worthwhile mountain experience. The cost for the comfort of reliably good weather is a drained-reservoir feeling. Lovers of the Alps may miss the lushness that comes with the unpredictable weather farther north.

A hard-fought history has left the region bicultural, with an emphasis on the German. Locals speak German first, and some wish they were still part of Austria. In the Middle Ages, the region faced north, part of the Holy Roman Empire. Later, they were firmly in the Austrian Hapsburg realm. By losing WWI, Austria's South Tirol became Italy's Alto Adige. Mussolini did what he could to Italianize the region, including giving each town an Italian name. Even in the last decade, secessionist groups have agitated violently for more autonomy. The government has wooed locals with economic breaks that make it one of Italy's richest areas

The Dolomites

(as local prices attest) and today all signs and literature in the autonomous province of Alto Adige/Süd Tirol are in both languages. Many include a third language, Ladin, the ancient Latin-type language still spoken in a few traditional areas. (I have listed both the Italian and German so the confusion caused by this guidebook will match that caused by your travels.)

In spite of all the glamorous ski resorts and busy construction cranes, the local color survives in a warm, blue-aproned, ruddy-faced, long-white-bearded way. There's yogurt and yodeling for breakfast. Culturally as much as geographically, the area reminds me of Austria. The Austrian Tirol is named for a village that is now part of Italy.

This is one region that understands the importance of tourist information. Each town has an excellent tourist office that can find you rooms in private homes and give you all the details you'll need to choose the right hike. They have excellent free maps and even entire books (in English) on local hikes available for free.

Lifts, trails, outdoor activity-oriented tourist offices, and a decent bus system make the region especially accessible. Before choosing a hike, get advice at the TI. Ideally, pick a hike with an overnight in a mountain hut.

Sleeping in the Dolomites

Most towns have no alternative to hotels, which charge at least L30,000 per person, or private homes, which offer beds for as low as L20,000 but are often a fair walk from the town centers. Beds nearly always come with a hearty breakfast. Those traveling in peak season or staying for only one night are often penalized. Local TIs can always find budget travelers a bed in a private home (*Zimmer*). Hikers find that most mountain huts, called *rifugios*, offer reasonable doubles, cheaper dorm (*Lager*) beds, and good inexpensive meals. Telephone any hut to secure a spot before hiking there. Most huts are open only mid-June-September.

In local restaurants, there is no cover charge and tipping is not expected. If you're low on both money and scruples, Süd Tirolian breakfasts are the only ones in Italy big enough to steal lunch from. A *Jausenstation* is a place that serves cheap, hearty, and traditional mountain-style food to hikers.

The seasons are brutal. Everything is open, booming, full price, and normally crowded from July 20 to September 20. Shoulder seasons are June 20-July 20 and September 20 until the end of October. After about a month off, the snow hits and it's busy again until April. May and early June are dead, with no lifts running and the most exciting trails still under snow. And most huts and budget accommodations are closed, as locals are more concerned with preparing for another boom season than catering to the stray off-season tourist.

Bolzano/Bozen

Willkommen to the Italian Tirol! If it weren't so sunny, you could be in Innsbruck. This enjoyable old town of 100,000 is the most convenient gateway to the Dolomites, especially if you're relying on public transportation. It's just the place to gather Dolomite information and take a Tirolean stroll. From the train station, walk 5 minutes to Piazza Walther. Follow arcaded Via dei Portici to the Piazza Erbe with its ancient and still thriving open-air produce market.

Tourist Info (TI): City tourist information is on Piazza Walther (tel. 0471/993808). The excellent Dolomites information office is just down the street (Monday-Friday 9:00-12:30, 15:00-17:30, Parrocchia 11, tel. 0471/993809).

Buses: The bus station with an information office is between the train station and Piazza Walther.

Side Trip: Many are tempted to wimp out on the Dolomites and see them from a distance by making the popular quick trip into the hills above Bolzano (cable car from near the Bolzano station to the cute but touristy village of Oberbozen where you'll take a long, pastoral walk to the Pemmern chairlift; ride to Schwarzseespitze; and walk 45 more minutes to the Rittner Horn). You'll be atop a 7,000-foot peak with distant but often hazy Dolomite views.

Sleeping in Bolzano
(zip: 39100)

While the cool, scenic, and nearby Dolomites make sleeping in hot and humid Bolzano a last resort, the town does have substantial charm.

Sleep code: **S**=Single, **D**=Double/Twin, **T**=Triple, **Q**=Quad, **B**=Bath/Shower, **WC**=Toilet, **CC**=Credit Card (Visa, Mastercard, Amex), **SE**=Speaks English (graded **A-F**).

Gasthof Weisses Kreuz (D-L52,000, DBWC-L70,000, a block off Piazza Walther in the old town at Kornplatz 3, tel. 0471/977552, SE-D) is your best bet. It couldn't be better located or more German. The modern, clean, institutional **Kolpinghaus Bozen** (SBWC-L49,000, DBWC-L82,000,

TBWC-L123,000 with breakfast, in the center also at
Spitalgasse 3, tel. 0471/971170, fax 973917, SE-B) has more
rooms and less character. Each room has all the comforts
and twin beds. Its cheap cafeteria (L10,000 dinners, 18:30-
19:30 Monday-Friday) is open to all.

Transportation Connections
Trains from Bolanzo to **Milan** (2/day, 4 hrs), **Verona** (hrly,
1½ hrs), **Trento** (hrly, 40 min), **Innsbruck** (hrly, 2½ hrs),
Merano (hrly, 40 min), and **Venice** and **Florence** (via
Verona, 3-4 hrs), train info tel. 974292.

Buses into **the Dolomites:** Frequent scenic buses connect Bolzano to most western Dolomite valleys. **Castelrotto**
(8/day, 1 hr), continuing to **Saltria** in the alpine meadow of
Alpe di Siusi (4-8/day, info tel. 971259). **Val di Fassa, Vigo
di Fassa,** and **Canazei** (2/day, 4/day in summer, 2 hrs). **Val
Gardena, Ortisei/St. Ulrich, St. Cristina, Selva,** and **Plan**
(4/day, 1 hr).

Alpe di Siusi (Seiser Alpe)
Europe's largest high alpine meadow, Alpe di Siusi, is less
than an hour by bus from Bolzano. This area of the Dolomites
is a natural preserve, and in the summer it's car-free. Only
the park bus service shuttles hikers closer to the base of the
postcard-dramatic Sasso peaks (Sassolunga, 3,180 meters).
Trails are well marked, and the brightly painted numbers are
keyed into local maps. Pick up the blue #05 Val Gardena/Alpe
di Suisi 1:25,000 "Tobacco" map at the TI or a bookstore.

Castelrotto (Kastelruth)
(zip: 39040)
Castelrotto, the ideal homebase for exploring the Alpe di
Siusi, has more village character than any town I saw in the
region. It's full of real people (be in town as the moms bring
home the grade-schoolers) and it isn't a full-blown resort
(TI, 9:00-12:30, 14:00-18:00, closed Sunday afternoon,
tel. 0471/706333).

Sleeping in Castelrotto
Good reasonable beds are at **Gasthof Zum Turm** (DBWC-
L90,000 with breakfast, behind the TI at Kofelgasse 8, tel.

The Western Dolomites

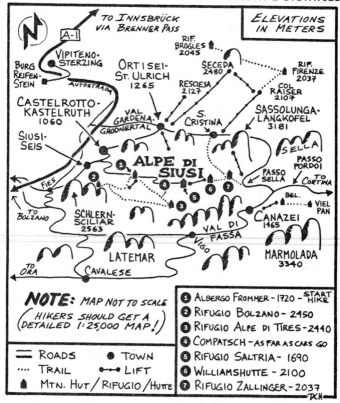

TO INNSBRÜCK VIA BRENNER PASS

ELEVATIONS IN METERS

A-1

VIPITENO·STERZING

BURG REIFEN-STEIN

AUTOSTRADA

CASTELROTTO-KASTELRUTH 1060

SIUSI-SEIS

FIE?

TO BOLZANO

ORTISEI-ST. ULRICH 1265

RIF. BROGLES 2045

SECEDA 2480

RESCIESA 2127

VAL GARDENA·GRÖDNERTAL

S. CRISTINA

❶ ALPE DI SIUSI

❷

SCHLERN-SCILIAR 2563

❸

❹

❺

❻ ❼

RIF. FIRENZE 2037

COL RAISER 2107

SASSOLUNGA-LANGKOFEL 3181

SELLA

PASSO PORDOI

PASSO SELLA

TO CORTINA

BEL.

VIEL PAN

CANAZEI 1465

VAL DI FASSA

VIGO

LATEMAR

TO ORA

CAVALESE

MARMOLADA 3340

NOTE: MAP NOT TO SCALE
(HIKERS SHOULD GET A)
DETAILED 1:25,000 MAP!)

ROADS   ● TOWN
···· TRAIL   ●—●—● LIFT
▲ MTN. HUT / RIFUGIO / HÜTTE

❶ ALBERGO FROMMER – 1720 – START HIKE
❷ RIFUGIO BOLZANO – 2450
❸ RIFUGIO ALPE DI TIRES – 2440
❹ COMPATSCH – AS FAR AS CARS GO
❺ RIFUGIO SALTRIA – 1690
❻ WILLIAMSHUTTE – 2100
❼ RIFUGIO ZALLINGER – 2037

DCH

0471/706349, fax 707268, SE-D) and **Gasthof Zum Wolf** (L70,000-L90,000 per person for bed, breakfast, and dinner, depending on the season, 100 meters below the square at Wolkenstein strasse 5, tel. 0471/706332, fax 706699, SE-D). **Hotel Alpenflora** (L72,000-L102,000 per person for room, breakfast and dinner depending on the season, CC:VMA, a 5-minute walk south of town at Oswald von Wolkenstein strasse 32, tel. 706326, fax 707173, SE-A) is a classy three-star option. Ask the TI for the latest on L20,000 beds with break-fast in private homes (**Pramstrahler Martha** at Grondlboden-weg 23, tel. 706775, is inexpensive, open all year and located to the right of the square as you face the M, SE-F) or for a dor-mitory bed in a mountain hut (around L15,000) There are several lagers with dorm beds near Saltria in the Alpe di Siusi

Eating in Castelrotto

Gasthofs Zum Turm and Zum Wolf both have fine restaurants (L20,000 dinners). For a picnic, go to the supermarket at 10 Wolkenstein strasse (scenic benches on hill above town). The supermarket's **Café Stella** has cheap meals with great mountain views.

Transportation Connections

Shuttle buses go nearly hourly (8:00-17:00) from Castelrotto into Alpe di Siusi. In the summertime, this park is closed to cars, so the bus goes even more often.

Hikes in the Alpe di Siusi

Easy meadow walks abound, giving tenderfeet classic Dolomite views from baby-carriage trails. Experienced hikers should consider two tough and exciting treks from the Alpe di Siusi. Before attempting these hikes, confirm your understanding of the time and skills required through the local tourist office.

Summit hike of Sciliar/Schlern—For a challenging 12-mile, 2-day hike with an overnight in a traditional mountain refuge, consider hiking to the summit of Sciliar/Schlern and spending a night in Rifugio Bolzano. From the bus stop at Albergo Frommer, catch the chairlift, hike 4 hours across the meadow, and climb steeply to the plateau of the tabletop Sciliar/Schlern. From the Rifugio Bolzano/Schlernhaus (2,450 meters, D-L52,000, L15,000 dorm beds, tel. 0471/612024, call for a reservation), hike 2 hours (12 km) along a rugged ridge past Rifugio Alpe di Tires (smaller than Bolzano, also with doubles and dorm beds, tel. 0471/727958), drop 1,000 steep meters back down to the Alpe di Siusi and the long, easy-going meadow-walk back.

Loop around Sassolunga—More difficult is the long day's hike around Sassolunga. Ride the bus to Saltria (end of the line), ride the chairlift to Williamshutte, walk to Rifugio Zallinger (overnight possible), and circle the Sasso group.

More Sights and Hikes in the Dolomites

▲▲**Reifenstein Castle**—For one of Europe's most intimate looks at medieval castle life, let the lady of Reifenstein (Frau

Blanc) show you around her wonderfully preserved castle. She leads tours on the hour, in Italian and German. She's friendly and will squeeze in what English she can.

Just before the Austrian border, leave the autostrada at Vipiteno/Sterzing; follow signs toward Bolzano, then over the freeway to the base of the castle's rock. It's the castle on the west. While this is easy by car, it's probably not worth the trouble by train (from Bolzano, 6/day, 70 min). Telephone 0472/765879 in advance to confirm your tour. The pleasant mini-park beside the drawbridge is a good spot for a picnic. (Pack out your litter.) Tours normally Easter-November at 9:30, 10:30, 14:00, and 15:00, closed Friday, L4,000.

▲**Glurns**—Drivers deciding to connect the Dolomites and Lake Como by the high road via Meran and Bormio or the southwest of Switzerland should spend the night in the amazing little fortified town of Glurns (45 minutes west of touristy Meran between Schluderns and Taufers). Glurns still lives within its square wall on the Adige River, with a church bell-tower that has a thing about ringing, and real farms, rather than boutiques, filling the town courtyards. This is a refreshing break after so many cute and wealthy tourist towns. There are several small hotels in the town, but I'd stay in a private home 100 yards from the town square, near the church, just outside the wall on the river (Family Hofer, DBWC-L60,000 with breakfast, less for two nights, tel. 0473/81597, well marked).

Val di Fassa—This valley is Alberto Tomba country. Free postcards featuring Italy's most famous Olympian are everywhere. In the summer, the whole place reminds me of a ski resort without the snow, but there are plenty of lifts, accommodations, and spectacular high-country hikes.

The town of Canazei, at the head of the valley and the end of the bus line, has the most ambience and altitude (4,600 feet). From there a lift takes you to Col dei Rossi Belvedere, where you can hike past the Rifugio Belvedere along an easy but breathtaking ridge to the Rifugio Viel del Pan. This is a 3-hour round-trip hike with views of the highest mountain in the Dolomites, the Marmolada, and the quintessentially Dolo-mighty Sella group along the way.

Val Gardena/Grodner Tal—This valley, famous for its woodcarvers (ANRI is from a town in Val Gardena called St

Cristina), its traditional Ladin culture, and now its skiing and hiking resorts, is a bit overrated. Even if its culture has been suffocated by the big bucks of hedonistic European fun-seekers, it remains a good jumping-off point for trips into the mountains.

Ortisei/St. Ulrich is the main town and best base. From here, you can ride the lifts into the high country for some fine hikes. Consider hikes from the top of either the Resciesa or the Seceda lifts, hiking to Rifugio Brogles and/or Rifugio Firenze, and riding the Col Raiser lift into St. Cristina for some of the most dramatic views within easy striking distance. (TI tel. 0471/796328, open 8:30-18:30, Sunday 10:00-12:00). The best reasonable sleep is at the **Aurelia Guesthouse**, Streda Rezia 236, tel. 0471/796258, open all year, DBWC-L75,000 with breakfast and a pass to the swimming pool.)

▲▲**Great Dolomite Road**—This is the road to drive by car (Belluno/Cortina/Pordoi Pass/Sella Pass/Val di Fassa/Bolzano). There is no direct public route covering this road, but the Goller-Reisen tour company in Castelrotto (Paniderstrasse, tel. 0471/706315) offers a 1-day small-bus tour making the scenic loop from Castelrotto to Cortina and back (L35,000, 9:30-18:00 with about 4 hours of stops, including 2 hours in Cortina, Thursdays summers only. The Castelrotto TI has specifics). The drive from Cortina to Bolzano is 130 breathtaking miles over the Pordoi Pass, the Sella Pass, and through the Val di Fassa. Remember, in the spring and early summer, passes labeled "closed" are often bare, dry, and, as far as local drivers are concerned, wide open.

NAPLES, POMPEII, AND THE AMALFI COAST

If you like Italy as far south as Rome, go farther south. It gets better. If Italy is getting on your nerves, think twice about going farther. Italy intensifies as you plunge deeper south. Naples is a barrel of cultural monkeys, Italy in the extreme—its best (birthplace of pizza and Sophia Loren) and its worst (home of the Camorra, Naples' "family" of organized crime). Serene Sorrento, just an hour to the south and without a hint of Naples, makes a great home base. It's the gateway to the much-loved Amalfi Coast. From the jet-setting island of Capri to the stunning scenery of the Amalfi Coast, from ancient Pompeii to even more ancient Paestum, this is Italy's Coast with the Most.

Planning Your Time

On a quick trip, give the area three days. With Sorrento as your sunny springboard, spend a day in Naples, a day on the Amalfi coast, and a day split between Pompeii and the town of Sorrento. While Paestum, the crater of Vesuvius, Herculaneum, and the island of Capri are decent options, these are worthwhile only if you give the area more time. Consider a night train in or out of the area.

For a blitz tour, you could catch the very early (2-hour) train from Rome, do Naples and Pompeii in a day, and be back in Rome in time for Letterman. That's exhausting, but more interesting than a third day in Rome.

For a small-town vacation from your vacation, spend a few more days on the Amalfi coast, sleeping in Positano or Atrani.

Naples (Napoli)

Italy's third-largest city (more than 2 million people) has almost no open spaces or parks, which makes its position as Europe's most densely populated city plenty evident. Watching the police try to enforce traffic sanity is almost comical in Italy's grittiest, most polluted, and crime-ridden city. But Naples surprises the observant traveler with an impressive knack for living, eating, and raising children in the streets with good humor and decency. Overcome your fear of being run down or ripped off enough to talk with people—enjoy a few smiles and jokes with the man running the cobblestone tripe shop or the lady taking her day-care class on a walk through the traffic.

Twenty-five hundred years ago, Neapolis ("new city") was a thriving Greek commercial center. It remains southern Italy's leading city, offering a fascinating collection of museums, churches, eclectic architecture, and volunteers needing blood for dying babies. The pulse of Italy throbs in Naples. Like Cairo or Bombay, it's appalling and captivating at the same

Naples

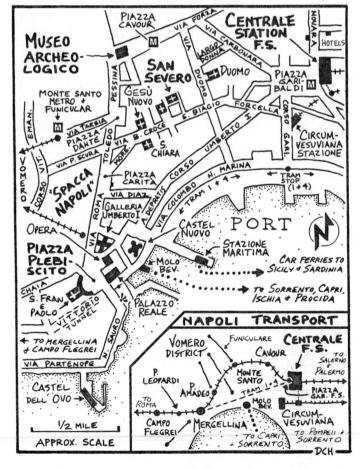

time, the closest thing to "reality travel" you'll find in Europe. But this tangled mess still somehow manages to breath, laugh, and sing—with a captivating Italian accent.

Orientation (tel. code: 081)

For a quick visit, start with the museum, do the walk from there, and celebrate your survival with pizza. Of course, Naples is huge. But with limited time, if you stick to the described route and grab a cab when you're lost or tired, it's fun. Treat yourself well in Naples; this city is cheap by Italian standards.

Tourist Information

At the TI in the central train station, pick up a map and the *Qui Napoli* booklet (if they say they're "finished" ask for an old one), 9:00-20:00, Sunday 9:00-13:00, tel. 268779. (Ignore the toupee-topped con man.)

Trains

There are several Naples stations. Naples Centrale is the main one (facing Piazza Garibaldi, baggage check, Circumvesuviana stop for commuter trains to Sorrento and Pompeii, TI). Since Centrale is a dead-end station, through-trains often stop at Piazza Garibaldi (actually a subway station just downstairs from Centrale) or Napoli Mergellina (equipped with a TI, across town, a direct 10-minute subway ride to Centrale, train tickets to Napoli Centrale and train passes cover you for the connecting ride to Centrale, subway trains depart about every 10 minutes). As you're coming in, ask someone which stations your train stops at.

Getting Around

Naples' simple one-line subway, the Metropolitana, runs basically from the Mergellina station to the Centrale station through the center of town, stopping at Montesanto (top of Spanish Quarter and Spaccanapoli) and Piazza Cavour (Archaeology Museum). Especially if you can afford a taxi, I wouldn't mess with the buses. Taxis are easy to hail, and a short ride costs L4,000-L6,000 (insist on the meter).

Helpful Hints

Traffic and Crime: In Naples, red lights are discretionary, and mopeds can mow you over from any place at any time Don't venture into neighborhoods that make you uncomfortable, walk with confidence as if you know where you're going and what you're doing, and assume able-bodied beggars are thieves. Give your money belt an extra half-hitch and keep it completely hidden. Stick to busy streets, and beware of gangs of young street hoodlums. Remember, a third of the city is unemployed, and the local government sets an example the Mafia would be proud of. Assume con artists are more clever than you. Any jostle or commotion is probably a thief team's smoke screen. Lately Naples has been occupied by an army of police, which has made it feel safer. Still, err on the side of caution.

Baggage Check: If you're doing Naples as a day trip, check your bags at the central train station (Deposito Bagagli in front of track #24, L1,500). In the afternoon, Naples' street life slows and many sights close as the temperature soars.

Sights—Naples

▲▲▲**Museo Archeologico**—For lovers of antiquity, this museum alone makes Naples a worthwhile stop. This museum offers the only peek possible into the artistic jewelry boxes of Pompeii and Herculaneum. The actual sights are vast and impressive but rather barren. Somehow, their best art ended up here.

Climb the grand stairs to the top floor and go left into a Pompeiian art gallery lined with paintings, bronze statues, artifacts, and an impressive model of the town of Pompeii, all of which make the relative darkness of medieval Europe obvious and clearly show the source of inspiration for the Renaissance greats. From the same staircase, one floor down, on the opposite side, you'll find a smaller but exquisite collection of Pompeiian mosaics (especially the fourth-century B.C. Battle of Alexander showing the Macedonians defeating the Persians). The ground floor (on the far left as you leave the stairs) has enough Greek, Roman, and Etruscan art to put any museum on the map, but its highlight is the Farnese Collection of huge, bright, and wonderfully restored statues excavated from Rome's Baths of Caracalla. You can almost hear the *Toro Farnese* snorting. This largest intact statue from antiquity was carved out of one piece of marble and restored by Michelangelo.

Amazingly for Italy, much of the museum is thoughtfully explained in English, making the L10,000 museum guidebook unnecessary (L8,000, 9:00-19:00, Sunday until 13:00, closed first and third Mondays, tel. 081/440166, call to confirm times if visiting in the afternoon). From the Centrale train station, follow signs to Metropolitana (tickets from window on left, ask which track—"*che binario?*"—to Piazza Cavour, and ride the train one stop). As you exit, turn right. At the end, of cluttered Piazza Cavour, you'll see the museum, a huge pink brick building. The WC below and behind the main stairway is uncharacteristically pleasant.

▲▲▲The Slice-of-Neapolitan-Life Walk—Walk from the museum through the heart of town and back to the station (allow at least 2 hours plus lunch and sightseeing stops). Sights are listed in the order you'll see them on this walk.

Naples, a living medieval city, is its own best sight. Couples artfully make love on Vespas surrounded by more fights and smiles per cobble here than anywhere else in Italy. Rather than see Naples as a list of sights, see the one great museum, then capture its essence by taking this walk through the core of the city. Should you become overwhelmed or lost, step into a store and ask for help (for example "*Dové il stazione centrale?*") or hop in a taxi and point in this book to the next sight.

Via Toledo and the Spanish Quarter (city walk, first half): Leaving the Archaeological Museum at the top of Piazza Cavour (Metro: Piazza Cavour), cross the street, veer right, and dip into the ornate galleria on your way to Via Pessina. The first part of this walk is a long, straight ramble down the straight boulevard to Galleria Umberto I near the Royal Palace. Coffee will be waiting.

Busy Via Pessina leads downhill to Piazza Dante. (For a quick lunch, the bar with seating on the tiny square, on the right, before the tobacco shop, halfway to Piazza Dante, is pleasant and can whip you up a cheap salad or sandwich.)

At Piazza Dante, notice poor old Dante in the center, stuck on his graffiti-streaked pedestal, looking out over the chaos with a hopeless gesture. Past the square, Via Pessina becomes Via Toledo, Naples's principal shopping street. About five blocks below Piazza Dante, at Via Maddaloni, you cross the long straight "Spaccanapoli" (literally, "split Naples"). Look left and right. Since ancient times, this street (which changes names several times) has bisected the city. (To abbreviate this walk, turn left here, follow Via Maddaloni to the Gesu church, and skip down to the Spaccanapoli section.)

Via Toledo runs through Piazza Carita. You may meet a Fascist here eager to point out the Mussolini photo in his wallet and the Fascist architecture overlooking the square. Wander down Via Toledo a few blocks past the Fascist architecture of two banks (both on the left). Try robbing the second one (Banco di Napoli, 178 Via Toledo, 8:30-13:00, 14:45-16:00).

Up the hill to your right is the Spanish Quarter, Naples at its rawest, poorest, and most historic. Thrill-seekers (or someone in need of a $20 prostitute) will take a stroll up one of these streets and loop back to Via Toledo. The only thing predictable about this Neapolitan tidepool is the ancient grid plan of the streets, the friendliness of its shopkeepers, and the boldness of the mopeds. Concerned locals will tug on their lower eyelid, warning you to be wary.

Continue down Via Toledo to the Piazza Plebiscito. From here you'll see the church of **San Francesco di Paola** with its Pantheon-inspired dome and broad arcing colonnades. Opposite is the **Royal Palace**, which has housed Spanish, French, and even Italian royalty. The lavish interior is open for tours (L6,000, 9:00-14:00, Sunday until 13:00, closed Monday). Next door, peek inside the Neoclassical **Teatro San Carlo**, Italy's second most respected opera house (after Milan's La Scala). The huge castle on the harborfront just beyond the palace houses government bureaucrats and is closed to tourists.

Before doubling back to the station, enjoy a coffee break under the Victorian iron and glass of the 100-year-old Galleria Umberto I; go through the tall yellow arch at the end of Via Toledo or across from the opera house. Gawk up.

Spaccanapoli to the Birth of Pizza (city walk, second half): To continue your walk, double back up Via Toledo past Piazza Carita to Via Maddaloni. Look east and west to survey the straight-as-a-Roman-arrow Spaccanapoli. Formerly the main thoroughfare of the Greek city of Neapolis, it starts up the hill near the Montesanto funicular (a colorful and safer Spanish Quarter neighborhood, from which you can see how strictly Spaccanapoli splits Naples' historic center).

Turn right off Via Toledo and walk to two bulky old churches on Piazza Gesu Nuovo. Check out the austere, fortress-like church of **Gesu Nuovo** with its peaceful but brilliant Baroque interior. Across the street, the simpler Gothic church of **Santa Chiara** offers a stark contrast complete with WWII scars and friendly friars who, for a tip, may take you into the monastery grounds for a fragrant and fruit-tree-filled respite from the turbulence outside (churches usually close 12:00-16:30).

The rest of this walk is basically a straight line (all of which locals call Spaccanapoli). Continue down Via B. Croce to the Piazza S. Domenico Maggiore. The castle-like **San Domenico Maggiore** church (closed 12:30-16:30), dominating the square, has a surprisingly lavish Baroque high altar. Walk behind San Domenico Maggiore (to the right as you face the church, take the first right after that), following yellow signs to the **Capella di Sansevero** (Via de Sanctis 19). This small chapel is a Baroque explosion mourning the body of Christ laying on a soft pillow under an incredibly realistic veil—all carved out of marble. It's like no statue I've seen (by Giuseppe "howdeedoodat" Sammartino, 1750). Lovely statues, carved from a single piece of marble, adorn the altar. *Despair* struggles with a marble rope net (on the right, opposite *Chastity*). Then, for the ghoul in all of us, walk down the stairway to the right for a creepy look at two 200-year-old studies in varicose veins (L6,000, 10:00-17:00, Sunday and Tuesday 10:00-13:00). Was one decapitated? Was one pregnant?

Back on Via B. Croce, turn left and continue the Spaccanapoli cultural scavenger hunt back to the train station. Across from San Domenico Maggiore is Scaturcho, a *café* filled with local ambiance and a unique Neapolitan pastry called *sfoigliatella* (sweet ricotta cheese with nuggets of candied fruit in a pastry). As Via B. Croce becomes Via S. Biagio dei Librai, notice the gold and silver shops.

Cross the busy Via Duomo, and the street scenes along Via Vicaria intensify. Paint a picture with these thoughts: Naples has the most intact street plan of any ancient Roman city. Imagine life here as in a Roman city (retain these images as you visit Pompeii) with street-side shop fronts that close up to form private homes after dark. Today is just one more page in a 2,000-year-old story of city activity: all kinds of meetings, beatings, and cheatings; kisses, near misses, and little-boy pisses. You name it, it occurs right on the streets today, as it has since Roman times. For a peek behind the scenes in the shade of wet laundry, venture down a few side streets. Buy two carrots and get a lady on the fifth floor to haul them up in her bucket to wash them for you. A few streets after crossing Via Duomo, veer right (avoiding a more dangerous area straight ahead) onto Via Forcella, which brings you to Corso Umberto.

For a tasty and typically Neapolitan finale, drop by the quintessential Naples pizzeria. From Via Forcella, you'll hit Corso Umberto near the **Antica Pizzeria da Michele** (cheap, filled with locals, 50 yards before you hit Corso Umberto on Via Cesare Sersale, look for the vertical red Antica Pizzeria sign, 8:00-22:00, closed Sunday). Here's your chance to taste pure pizza in its birthplace. Naples, baking just the right combination of fresh dough, mozzarella, and tomatoes in traditional wood-burning ovens, is famous for its pizzas. This place, serving only two kinds: Margherita (tomato sauce and mozzarella) or Marinara (tomato sauce, oregano, and garlic with no cheese), is for purists. A pizza with beer costs L8,000. **Pizzeria Trianon** (across the street at via Pietro Colletta 42, tel. 5539426, open daily), da Michele's arch-rival, offers more choices and a cozier atmosphere.

Turn left on the grand-boulevardian Corso Umberto, which leads through all kinds of riffraff to the vast and ugly Piazza Garibaldi. On the far side is the Central Station. Run for it!

Naples has many more museums, churches, and sights that some consider important. For a rundown on these, refer to the TI's free *Qui Napoli* publication.

Sleeping in Naples
(L1,600 = about $1, tel. code: 081)
With Sorrento just an hour away, I can't imagine why you'd sleep in Naples. But if needed, here are two safe, clean places 200 yards from the station and a more out-of-the-way hostel.

For the hotels, turn right out of the station and walk 2 minutes up Corso Novara. It's a thoroughly ugly but reasonably safe area. Be careful after dark.

Hotel Eden (DBWC-L88,000, L72,000 with this book, breakfast extra, Corso Novara 9, tel. 285344, fax 202070) is a fine establishment run with panache by English-speaking Nicola (Danny DeVito). Clean, good beds, brown and gray tones and all the comforts in sterile surroundings, which is exactly what you're after in Naples. Ask to see the hall lighting ambience.

Hotel Ginerva (D-L50,000, DBWC-L60,000, no breakfast, across the street from the Eden and down Via Genova to #116, tel. 283210) is bright and cheery. Little English spoken, but they try hard. New beds, floral wallpaper, and the owner will let you use his washing machine for only L3,000 per load.

Ostello Mergellina (L18,000 beds including sheets and breakfast, D-L40,000, non-members pay extra, small rooms with 2-6 beds, Metro: Mergellina, take two right turns, and walk 15 minutes to Salita della Grotta a Piedigrotta 23, tel. 7612346, closed 9:00-16:00 and at 24:00, cheap meals) is well run, cheap, and pleasant but a headache to get to.

Train Connections

Trains run from Naples to **Rome** (hrly, 2-3 hrs), **Brindisi** (ferries to Greece, 2/day, 7 hrs, overnight possible), **Milan** (4/day, 7-9 hrs, overnight possible, more with a change in Rome), **Nice** (4/day, 13 hrs), **Paris** (3/day, 18 hrs), and **Venice** (4/day, 8-10 hrs).

The Circumvesuviana: **Naples, Herculaneum, Pompeii,** and **Sorrento** are all on the handy commuter train, the Ferrovia Circumvesuviana, 2/hr from the basement of Naples' central station (clearly sign-posted). The Circumvesuviana also has its own terminal, one stop or a 5-minute walk beyond the central station. Take your pick. Trains marked Sorrento get you to Herculaneum (Ercolano) in 15 minutes, Pompeii in 40 minutes, and Sorrento, the end of the line, in 70 minutes (L4,000 one-way, cheaper round-trip, no train passes). When returning to Naples on the Circumvesuviana, get off at the Collegamento FS or Garibaldi stop for the main train

station (just up the escalator). Naples train information:
tel. 081/554 3188.

Sorrento

Wedged on a ledge under the mountains and over the Mediterranean, surrounded by lemon and olive groves, Sorrento is
an attractive resort of 20,000 residents and easily as many
tourists. It's as well located for regional sightseeing as it is a
pleasant place to stay and stroll. And there's not a hint of
Naples. The Sorrentines have gone out of their way to create
a pleasant, completely safe, and relaxed place for tourists to
come and spend money. Everyone seems to speak fluent
English and work for the Chamber of Commerce. This
gateway to the Amalfi coast has a pleasant and unspoiled
old quarter, a lively main shopping street, and a spectacular
cliffside setting. Skip the port and its poor excuse for a
beach unless you're taking a ferry.

Orientation (tel. code: 081)

Sorrento is long and narrow. The main drag, Corso Italia
(50 meters in front of its Circumvesuviana train station), runs
parallel to the sea from the station through the town center
and out to the cape, where it's renamed Via Capo. Everything
mentioned (except the Via Capo hotels) is within a 5-minute
walk of the station.

Tourist Information

"Soggiorno e Turismo:" (from station, go left on Corso Italia,
walk 5 minutes to Piazza Tasso [Sorrento's main square],
right at end of square down Via L. de Maio through Piazza
Sant Antonino to the Foreigners' Club mansion at #35; 8:30-
14:00, 17:00-20:00, tel. 8074033; get free *Sorrentum* magazine with great map, and boat, bus, and events schedules).
You'll pass many fake "tourist offices" on the way (travel
agencies selling bus and boat tours) which, with longer
hours and town maps, can be helpful.

Getting Around

Orange city buses run from the station to the Punta del
Capo, and down to the port (L1,000 tickets within the
center, good for 90 minutes, sold at *tabacchi* shops). Rental

mopeds (L35,000) and Vespas (L50,000 plus L650,000 plus tax if it's stolen, tel. 8781386) are at Corso Italia 210. In summer, forget renting a car unless you enjoy traffic jams in the Italian sun.

Helpful Hints

The Foreigners' Club (behind the TI, city discount cards, public WC) provides reasonably priced snacks and drinks, relaxation and views, and a handy place for visitors to meet locals. It's lively, with music, on summer evenings. If you need immediate tanning, you can rent a chair on the pier by the port, though the best nearby sandy beach is at Punta del Capo (see below). There's a handy coin-op laundromat at Corso Italia 30.

Sights—Sorrento

▲▲**Central Sorrento**—Take time to stroll and explore the surprisingly pleasant old city between Corso Italia and the sea. The evening *passegiata* (along the Corso Italia and via San Cesareo) peaks around 22:00. Check out the old-boys' club playing cards, oblivious to the tourism under their portico at Via San Cesareo and Via Tasso.

▲**Punta del Capo**—For clean water and a free pebbly beach on the tip of a peninsula, walk to Punta del Capo. From Sorrento, walk 40 minutes or take the 10-minute bus ride (orange city bus from Piazza Tasso, 2 departures/hr, L1,000) to the end of the road for a rocky but accessible, traffic-free swimming area and a stunning view of Sorrento and Naples. The very ruined Roman Villa di Pollio marks this discovered but beautiful cape. From the American Bar, turn right and amble down the covered walkway.

Sleeping in Sorrento

(L1,600 = about $1; tel. code: 081, zip code: 80067)
Unlike many resorts, Sorrento offers the whole range of rooms. If you splurge, get a balcony and view. (Ask "*con balcon, con vista sul mare.*") "*Tranquillo*" is taken as a request for a room off the street. Hotels listed here are either near the station and city center or out toward the Punta del Capo, a good 30-minute walk from the station. The TI can book you a L50,000 double in a private home. While many hotels

Sorrento

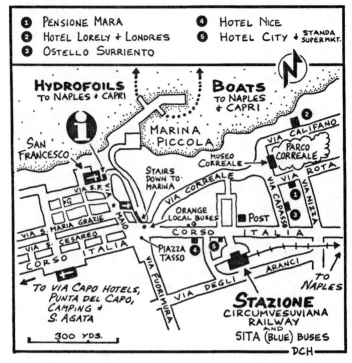

close for the winter, you'll have no trouble finding a room off-season. Note: the spindly and more exotic Amalfi Coast town of Positano (see Amalfi Coast below) is also a good place to spend the night.

Sleeping near the Train Station and in the Town Center

From the station, turn right onto the Corso Italia, then left down Via Capasso for the first three listings. For the others, turn left toward the town center on Corso Italia.

Pension Mara (D-L50,000, DBWC-L60,000, T-L70,000, TBWC-L90,000, cheap quads, optional breakfast-L5,000; friendly Adelle, the English-speaking owner, can be talked out of her "quasi-obligatory" L60,000 per person half-board policy in August, ask for a balcony; from Via Capasso, turn right onto the unmarked Via Rota just past the youth hostel and police station, Via Rota 5, tel. 8783665) provides simple, clean rooms in a dull building with a good location.

Hotel Lorely and Londres (D-L70,000, DBWC-L90,000 with breakfast; in July, August, and September half-pension, L80,000 per person, is required, but the food is delicious; follow Via Capasso to the water and turn right to see the big rose-colored hotel at Via Califano 2, tel. 8073187, CC:VM, easy free parking on the street), a reasonable exception in an expensive neighborhood, is drunk with character. This rambling, spacious, colorful old Sorrentine villa is ideal for those wishing to sit on the bluff and contemplate their own (or anyone else's) navel. Seaside rooms have balconies and great views. Avoid the noisy street-side rooms. Don't avoid the elevator down to the hotel's private beach.

Ostello Surriento (L15,000 beds in 6- to 20-bed dorms, including breakfast, closed tightly from 9:30-17:00 and at midnight, rarely full except in August, no card required, easy to find, 3 minutes from the station at Via Capasso 5, tel./fax 8781783) is relaxed, friendly, bright, and basic, offering firm beds and the hope of warm water. Girls get the big rooms on the top with a view of the gulf. Helpful, English-speaking Piero runs the place and is a wealth of information.

Hotel City (SBWC-L50,000, DBWC-L60,000, TBWC-L90,000, breakfast-L5,000, CC:VM, handy location near Piazza Tasso at Corso Italia 221, tel. 8772210) is small and bright. The manager, Gianni, caters to budget English-speaking travelers and runs a newsstand and travel agency in his lobby.

Hotel Nice (SBWC-L48,000, DBWC-L75,000 with breakfast, third and fourth roommates-L20,000 each; Corso Italia 257, tel. 8781650) is a good, basic value very near the station on the busy main drag. Ask for a room off the street.

Hotel Del Corso (D-L60,000, DBWC-L70,000, breakfast-L10,000; half-pension at L75,000 per person required in July and August; CC:A; in town center, Corso Italia 134, tel. 8781299), a well-worn Old World hotel is clean and comfortable, with spacious rooms and urban noise. I'm not sure if the manager is wry or unfriendly.

Sleeping with a View on Via Capo

These hotels are outside of town near the cape (straight out the Corso Italia, which turns into Via Capo; 30 minutes on foot, L15,000 by taxi, or a L1,000 bus ride away). It's an easy walk to the Punta del Capo from here. If you're in Sorrento to stay put and luxuriate, these are best (although, I'd rather luxuriate on the Amalfi Coast).

Pension La Tonnarella (DBWC-L90,000-L110,000 with view and breakfast; obligatory L80,000 per person half-pension with a fine dinner in the summer; many rooms with view balconies; Via Capo 31, tel. 8781153, fax 8782169, family Gargiulio) is a worthwhile splurge. A classic Sorrentine villa is beautifully maintained inside and out with several terraces, stylish tiles, killer views, and an elevator down to its private beach. Reserve long in advance for summer visits.

Hotel Desiree (DBWC-94,000, shares La Tonnarella's driveway and beach, at Via Capo 31, tel./fax 8781563), run by helpful Ingeborg Garguilio, is a simpler affair with humbler views but all the comforts and no half-board requirements.

Hotel Minerva (SBWC-L95,000, DBWC-L150,000, TBWC-L180,000 with breakfast and no summer half-pension requirement, CC:VMA, at Via Capo 30, tel. 8781011, fax 8781949). The friendly, English-speaking owners have lovingly restored this dream palace. Riding the elevator to the fifth floor, you'll step into a spectacular terrace with outrageous Mediterranean views and a cliff-hanging swimming pool complementing large tiled rooms with balconies. Peasants sneak in a picnic dinner and enjoy just hanging out here.

Pension Elios (D-L64,000, DBWC-L70,000, including breakfast, Via Capo 33, tel. 8781812), run by Luigi and Maria, offers simple but spacious rooms, many with balconies and views, and a fine roof terrace.

Eating in Sorrento

Dining out can be reasonable here. If you fancy a picnic dinner on your balcony, on the hotel terrace, or in the public garden, you'll find many markets and take-out pizzerias in the old town. The supermarket at 223 Corso Italia has it all (open until 21:00).

In the city center: **Sant Antonino's** offers friendly service, red-checkered tablecloths, an outdoor patio, decent prices, and good pasta (just off the P. Sant Antonino on Santa Marie delle Grazie 6). The nearby and smaller **Pizzeria Da Gigino** (first road to the right of Sant Antonino) is also good. **Pizzeria Giardiniello** (Via Accademia 7) is a family show offering good food at good prices. The **Osteria Gatto Nero**, a hole in the wall at via Santa Maria della Pieta 36 (tel. 878-1582, closed Monday), is a mom-and-pop place that respects its budget eaters. The restaurant on the terrace of **Hotel Lorely and Londres** serves the best reasonably priced great-view meals in town.

For a splurge, **La Tonnarella** (see Sleeping for directions, a 20-minute walk from the Piazza Tasso) offers fine views, terraces, and exquisite Sorrentine cooking. **Parrucchiano** (Corso Italia 71) is venerable, expensive, and a decent splurge for fine regional cooking.

For cheap eats, skip the center and the views and walk a couple of blocks past the station on Corso Italia to **Master Hosts** (cheap good pizza and pasta) or **"CCC"** with a more varied menu. Then stroll the center for coffee.

Transportation Connections
From Sorrento to Positano and Capri by boat: Sorrento's busy port launches ferries to Capri, Ischia, Positano, and Naples (schedules available at TI, walk or shuttle bus to port from Piazza Tasso). To **Positano** (L7,000, July and August only). To **Capri** (about hourly, L5,000). Several lines compete, using boats and hydrofoils. Buy only one-way tickets (there's no round-trip discount) for schedule flexibility so you can take any company's boat back. Prices are the same. (15-minute hydrofoil and "jet-boat" crossings, L7,500.) Check times for the last return crossing upon arrival.
From Sorrento to the Amalfi Coast by bus: Blue SITA buses depart from Sorrento's train station about every 2 hours and stop at all Amalfi Coast towns (Positano in 45 minutes for L1,800, Amalfi in 90 minutes), ending up in Salerno at the far end of the coast in just under 3 hours. Buy tickets at the tobacco shop nearest any bus stop before boarding. (There's a *tobac* at the Sorrento station.) You may have to change in Amalfi to get to Salerno. Leaving Sorrento, arrive early to grab a seat on the right for the best views (left seats are seriously

deficient). There are often two or three buses leaving at the
same time.

**From Sorrento to Pompeii, Herculaneum, and Naples
by Circumvesuviana train:** This handy commuter train
runs at least hourly between Naples and Sorrento. From
Sorrento, it's 30 minutes to Pompeii, 45 minutes to Herculaneum, and 70 minutes to Naples (L4,000 one-way,
cheaper round-trip). See the Naples chapter for tips on
arriving smartly there.

The Amalfi Coast

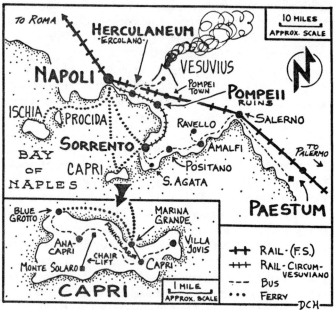

Sights—The Amalfi Coast

▲▲▲**Bus ride along Amalfi Coast**—One of the world's
great bus rides, this trip from Sorrento along the Amalfi Coast
will leave your mouth wide open and your film exposed. You'll
gain respect for the Italian engineers who built the road—
and even more respect for the bus drivers who drive it. The
hyperventilation caused by winding around so many breathtaking cliffs makes the Mediterranean, 500 feet below, really
twinkle.

Cantilevered garages, hotels, and villas cling to the vertical terrain, and beautiful sandy coves tease from far below and out of reach. Gasp from the right side of the bus as you go and the left on the way back (if you return by bus). Those on the wrong side really miss out. Traffic is so heavy that in the summer, local cars are allowed to drive only every other day—even-numbered license plates one day, odd the next. (Buses and tourists foolish enough to drive are exempt from this system.)

The Amalfi Coast towns are pretty to look at but generally touristic, congested, overpriced, and a long hike above tiny beaches. The real thrill here is the scenic drive. Catch a blue SITA bus from the Sorrento train station (see above for details).

▲▲**Positano**—Specializing in scenery and sand, Positano sprawls halfway between Sorrento and Amalfi on the most spectacular stretch of the coast. The village, a three-star sight from a distance, is a pleasant (if expensive) gathering of women's clothing stores and cafés with a superb beach. There's little to do here but enjoy the beach and views and window-shop. Consider a day trip from Sorrento; take the bus out and the afternoon ferry home.

To minimize your descent, use the last Positano bus stop (on the Amalfi town side, ask for "Sponda"). It's a 15-minute stroll/shop/munch from here to the beach. To catch the bus back to Sorrento, remember it may leave from "Sponda" 10 to 15 minutes before the main Positano departure, which is at the other end of town. You can also take the orange bus up to the highway and catch the SITA bus from the small town square (2/hr, tickets from the adjacent café). Boats to Sorrento, Amalfi, and Capri depart from Positano. For accommodations in Positano, see Sleeping, below.

Amalfi—I'd skip this most overrated of the Amalfi Coast villages. The waterfront is dominated by a bus station, a parking lot, and two gas stations. The main street through the village, hard for pedestrians to avoid, is packed with cars and bully mopeds. Neighboring Atrani, a 15-minute walk away, and Minori, a bit further on, are far more pleasant.

▲**Bus ride to Sant Agata and Sorrento's Peninsula**—The trip from Sorrento to Sant Agata is a beautiful cliff-hanger punctuated by lemon groves, olive orchards, and wild flowers.

Catch the sunset here for the single best view over both
sides of the peninsula. From the end of the line, Sant Agata,
walk toward Sant Agata's church. Follow signs to the
monastery, Il Deserto. Go through the gate and climb into
and on top of the monastery for the views surveying both the
Golfo di Napoli and the Golfo di Salerno (ask for *"Colle di
Fontanelle."*) The village of Sant Agata is nothing special, but
you'll find it refreshingly unspoiled. It's a decent place for
dinner or a *"Granita coffee con panna"* at the old wooden bar
about 100 meters from the bus stop (20 min one-way, departures via blue SITA bus about every 30 min from the
Sorrento station, buy two one-way L1,800 tickets in the
station café).

   This is the gateway to the scenic but ignored Sorrento
peninsula that stretches 20 kilometers from Sorrento to the
Campanella point. From Sant Agata, the bus continues to
Termini. From there a 7-kilometer walk takes you to the
point under a ruined Norman Tower where you can almost
reach out and touch Capri. (Bring water, get local directions,
not good for swimming.)

Sleeping on the Amalfi Coast
(L1,600 = about $1, zip code: 84017)

Sleeping in Positano
These hotels, arranged by altitude from nearest the bus to
nearest the beach, are on Via Colombo, which leads from the
"Sponda" SITA bus stop down into the village. **Albergo
California** (DBWC-L120,000 including optional breakfast,
CC:A, Via Colombo 141, tel. 089/875382) has great views,
spacious rooms, and a comfortable terrace. **Residence La
Tavolozza** (DBWC-L90,000, also a royal family apartment,
Via Colombo 10, tel. 089/875040) is a tiny, unassuming hotel
warmly run by Celeste. Flawlessly restored, each room comes
with view, balcony, fine tile, and silence. **Hotel Bougainville**
(DBWC-L90,000 with views, L70,000 without, breakfast
included only with this book; Via Colombo 25, tel.
089/875047, fax 811150), is a fine, spotless place with
eager-to-please owners and comfortable rooms. The pizzerias
on the beach are a bit overpriced but pleasant. Consider a
balcony, terrace, or beach picnic dinner.

If marooned in Amalfi, stay at the **Hotel Amalfi** (DBWC-L80,000-L100,000 with breakfast, Via dei Pastai 3, tel. 089/872440) or hike 15 minutes (or ride the bus) to the tiny town of Atrani, right on the beach, and stay in **A' Scalinatella** (L15,000 per bed, D-L30,000, DBWC-L50,000, tel. 089/871492, 84010 Atrani). This informal hostel with dorm beds, private rooms, family apartments, and a guest washer and drier is ideal for a small town Amalfi hideaway without the glitz and climbing of Positano. Owner Filippo speaks English and is eager to please (near main square, tel. 871492).

Capri

Made famous as the vacation hideaway of Roman emperors Augustus and Tiberius, these days Capri is a world-class tourist trap packed with gawky tourists in search of the rich and famous and finding only their prices. The 4-mile-by-2-mile "Island of Dreams" is a zoo in July and August. Other times of year it provides a relaxing and scenic break from the cultural gauntlet of Italy. While Capri has some Roman ruins and an interesting 14th-century Carthusian monastery, its chief attraction is its famous Blue Grotto, and its best activity is a scenic hike.

At the ferry dock, confirm your plans at the tourist information office (tel. 081/8370424 or 8375308, room-finding service, baggage deposit service nearby).

Sights—Capri

Capri and Anacapri—From the ferry dock at Marina Grande, a funicular lifts you 500 feet to the cute but most touristy town of Capri. From there buses go regularly along a cliff-hanging road to the still cute but more bearable town of Anacapri.

Blue Grotto—To most, a visit to the Blue Grotto is an overrated "must." While the standard tour is by ferry from Marina Grande, you can save money by catching the bus from Anacapri and hiking for an hour. Admission, by rowboat with a guide, is L12,000. (Those who hike, dive in for free.) Touristy and commercial as this all is, the grotto, with its eerily beautiful blue sunlight reflecting through the water, is an impressive sight (daily 9:00 until an hour before sunset except in stormy weather).

Hike down Monte Solaro—From Anacapri, ride the

chairlift to the 1,900-foot summit of Monte Solaro for a commanding view of the Bay of Naples and a pleasant downhill hike through lush vegetation and ever-changing views, past the 14th-century Chapel of Santa Maria Cetrella, and back into Anacapri.

Villa Jovis—Emperor Tiberius's now-ruined Villa Jovis is a scenic 1-hour hike from Capri town. Supposedly, Tiberius ruled Rome from here for a decade (in about A.D. 30)

While you can take a boat between Naples and Capri, the ferry from Sorrento is much quicker and cheaper. And there is a Positano-Capri boat. *Capri-Sorrento* boats run about hourly (L9,000 round-trip). For an untouristy alternative to Capri, consider the nearby island of Ischia (easy boat connections from Naples and Sorrento).

Pompeii, Herculaneum, and Vesuvius

Pompeii (▲▲▲), stopped in its tracks by the eruption of Mount Vesuvius in A.D. 79, offers the best look anywhere at what life in Rome must have been like 2,000 years ago. An entire city of well-preserved ruins is yours to explore. Once a thriving commercial port of 20,000, Pompeii grew from Greek and Etruscan roots to become an important Roman city. Then, shake 'n' bake, Pompeii was buried under 30 feet of hot mud and volcanic ash. For archaeologists this was a windfall, leaving a volcanic textbook to teach them about ancient Roman culture. It was rediscovered in the 1600s, and the first excavations began in 1748 (L10,000, open 9:00 to an hour before sunset, 20:00 in summer, ticket office closes an hour before that).

Orientation

Pompeii is halfway between Naples and Sorrento, about a half-hour from either by direct Circumvesuviana train (runs at least hourly). Get off at the Villa dei Misteri, Pompei Scavi stop. (The modern town is Pompei, the ancient sight is Pompeii.) Check your bag at the train station for L1,500 or at the site for free. From the station, turn right and walk down the road to the circus-like entrance. The TI (look for the "i" across the street above the locked door) may have a Pompeii layout. The *Pompeii* and *Herculaneum* "past and present" book has a helpful text and allows you to re-create

Pompeii

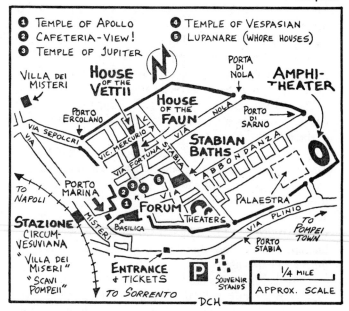

① TEMPLE OF APOLLO   ④ TEMPLE OF VESPASIAN
② CAFETERIA-VIEW!   ⑤ LUPANARE (WHORE HOUSES)
③ TEMPLE OF JUPITER

the ruins with plastic overlays—with the "present" actually
being 1964; L20,000 price but pay no more than L15,000.
To understand what you're seeing, a guidebook is essential.

Touring Pompeii

Allow 3 hours. Entering through the Porta Marina, you'll
walk past the Antiquarium (first building on right, artifacts
and eerie casts of well-preserved victims) to the Forum.

The Forum (Foro), Pompeii's commercial, religious,
and political center, is the most ruined part of Pompeii. It's
nonetheless impressive, with several temples; the "basilica"
(Pompeii's largest building, used for legal and commercial
business); and some interesting casts of volcano victims displayed with piles of pottery behind the fence on the left as
you enter the Forum.

From the Forum, walk toward the volcano—past the
convenient 20th-century cafeteria (decent value, gelati, overpriced cards and books, WCs with rooftop views)—down Via
del Foro, which becomes Via di Mercurio, into Pompeii's
oldest quarter for the most interesting houses. The House of

Vettii (Casa dei Vettii), home of two wealthy merchant brothers who enjoyed erotic wallpaper (notice as you enter), is best. After a wander through the nearby House of the Faun (Casa del Fauno), go back to the Forum and walk left down Via dell' Abbondanza to explore Pompeii's more recent excavations.

The Stabian Baths (Terme Stabiane, public baths, on the left), are the best preserved baths in the city. Behind the baths, the Vico del Lupanare leads to Lupanare, a simple whorehouse with stone beds, stone pillows, and art to get you in the mood.

Continuing down Via dell' Abbondanza, you'll pass a variety of businesses. Ask guards to let you into various houses and buildings, many of which are locked, or tag along with a tour if you can. Inside homes, you'll find frescoes, paintings, and mosaics that give you a feel for (at least the rich man's) workaday Roman life. The flat stones that cross the streets like crosswalks allowed pedestrians keep their sandals dry during rainstorms.

At the far end is the huge, rebuilt Amphitheater (Anfiteatro). It's a long walk, but you'll get a look at the oldest (80 B.C.) and best-preserved Roman amphitheater in Italy. From the top, look into the giant rectangular Palestra, where athletes used to train. (Pompeii's best art is in the Naples museum, described above.)

▲▲**Herculaneum (Ercolano)**—Smaller, less ruined, and less crowded than its more famous big sister, Herculaneum offers in some ways a closer peek into ancient Roman life. Caked and baked by the same eruption in A.D. 79, Herculaneum is a small community of intact buildings with plenty of surviving detail (15 min from Naples and 45 min from Sorrento on the same train that goes to Pompeii, turn right and follow the yellow signs, 5 min downhill from the Ercolano station, L10,000, open 9:00 until one hour before sunset).

▲**Vesuvius**—The 4,000-foot summit of Vesuvius, mainland Europe's only active volcano (sleeping restlessly since 1944) is accessible by car or by the blue Vesuvio bus (from the Herculaneum station, 45-minute ride, irregular, often 5/day, often only taxis). From the bus and car park you'll hike 30 minutes to the top for a sweeping Bay of Naples view, desolate lunar-like surroundings, and hot rocks. On the top, walk the entire

crater lip for the most interesting views. The far end overlooks Pompei. Be still and alone to hear the wind and tum-
bling rocks in the crater. Any steam? Closed when erupting.

Paestum

Paestum is one of the best collections of Greek temples anywhere—and certainly the most accessible to western Europe.
Serenely situated, it's surrounded by fields and wildflowers
and has only a modest commercial strip.

Founded as Poseidonia in sixth century B.C., a key stop
on an important trade route, its name was changed to Paestum
by occupying Romans in third century B.C. The final con-
querors of Paestum, malaria-carrying mosquitoes, kept the
site wonderfully desolate for nearly a thousand years. Rediscovered in the 18th century, Paestum today offers the only
well-preserved Greek ruins north of Sicily (L8,000 tickets
include the museum, daily 9:00 until one hour before sunset, museum closed first and third Mondays, ticket sales end
2 hours before sunset, tel. 0828/811023, TI tel. 811016).

Orientation

Buses from Salerno (see Connections, below) stop at the
"secondary entrance" that leads to the lonely Temple of
Ceres, across from a good bar/café with sandwiches and
cappuccino. Get a feel for the manageable scale of this three-
temple set of ruins by looking through the fence, then visit
the museum, opposite the entrance.

The Museum: Orient yourself at the site plan (upstairs on
the right). If you're not buying a guidebook, establish your
sightseeing plan here. The large carvings overhead adorned
various temples from the nearby city of Hera. Most are scenes
from the life of Hercules. Don't miss the Greek sculptures in
the ground-floor back room. Find the plans for the Temple
of Neptune, the largest and most impressive of Paestum's
temples, and notice the placement of the decorative carvings
and the gargoyle-like heads behind you.

Touring Paestum

Allow 2 hours with the museum. Enter the ruins at the
Ionic Temple of Ceres, the northern end of ancient Paestum
and do a loop through the ruins, exiting where you entered.

The key ruins are the impossible-to-miss Temples of Ceres and Neptune and the Basilica. But the scattered village ruins are also interesting. Faint remains of swimming pools, baths, houses, a small amphitheater, and lone columns will stretch your imagination's ability to re-create this ancient city.

The misnamed Temple of Neptune, a textbook example of the Doric style, constructed in 450 B.C. and dedicated to Hera, is simply overwhelming. Better preserved than the Parthenon in Athens, this huge structure is a tribute to Greek engineering and aesthetics. Walk right in, sit right down, and contemplate the word "renaissance"—the rebirth of this grand Greek style of architecture. Notice how the columns angle out and how the base bows up (scan the short ends of the temple). This was a trick ancient architects used to create the illusion of a perfectly straight building. All important Greek buildings were built using this technique. Now imagine it richly and colorfully decorated with marble and statues.

Adjacent is the almost delicate Basilica (also dedicated to the Goddess Hera, 550 B.C.). Beyond these temples, you'll find traces of the old wall that protected Paestum. If you have time, walk out toward the train station to see the wall's eastern limit.

Should you get stuck in Paestum, the **Albergo della Rosse** (DB-L60,000, tel. 0828/811070), which has a respectable restaurant, is just across from the main entry.

Transportation Connections

Salerno to Paestum: Salerno, the big city just north of Paestum, is your transfer point. From Naples or Sorrento you'll go to Salerno to catch the bus or train to Paestum. Several companies offer a Salerno-Paestum bus service from the same stop (2/hr, 60 min, buy L4,200 ticket on board, schedules are more difficult on Sunday). The Salerno-Paestum train is usually less efficient, but check schedules at the Salerno station. Northbound buses leave Paestum from the far side of the street bordering the ruins. Flag down any bus, ask "Salerno?" and buy the ticket on board. Most buses stop in front of the Salerno train station.

Naples to Salerno by train: (hrly, 1-hr trip).

Sorrento to Salerno by bus: The scenic 3-hour Amalfi Coast drive (blue SITA bus) drops you in Salerno, 75 yards

Salerno Connections

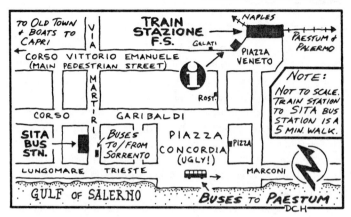

```
TO OLD TOWN    V    TRAIN        ↖ NAPLES
+ BOATS TO     I    STAZIONE
CAPRI          A    F.S.      GELATI      →  PAESTUM +
                                             PALERMO
CORSO VITTORIO EMANUELE          PIAZZA
(MAIN PEDESTRIAN STREET)    M    VENETO
                            A                NOTE:
                            R                NOT TO SCALE.
                            T    ROST.       TRAIN STATION
CORSO          I    GARIBALDI                TO SITA BUS
               R                             STATION IS A
                                             5 MIN. WALK.
SITA               BUSES   PIAZZA
BUS               TO/FROM CONCORDIA  PIZZA
STN.              SORRENTO  (UGLY!)

LUNGOMARE      TRIESTE              MARCONI

GULF OF SALERNO         BUSES TO PAESTUM
                                        DCH
```

from the Paestum bus stop (head toward waterfront) and 150 yards from the train station. Ask the driver to direct you to the station and/or Paestum bus stop. Sorrento to Paestum by train requires a change in Naples. Ride the Circumvesuviana for an hour to Naples and catch the Salerno train at the central station (hrly, 1 hr).

Drivers: While the Amalfi Coast is a thrill to drive, summer traffic is miserable. From Sorrento, Paestum is 3 hours via the coast and a much smoother 2 hours by autostrada. Driving toward Naples, catch the autostrada (direction: Salerno), skirt Salerno staying on the autostrada (direction: Reggio), exit at Eboli, drive straight through the modern town of Paestum, and you'll hit the ruins about when you're worried that you missed a turnoff. Along the way, you'll see signs for *Mozzarella di bufalo*, the soft cheese made from the milk of water buffalo that graze here.

APPENDIX

Telephone Information

Smart travelers use the telephone every day. Hotel reservations by phone on the morning of the day you plan to arrive are a snap. If there's a language problem, ask someone at your hotel to talk to your next hotel for you.

The key to dialing long distance is understanding area codes and having a local phone card. Hotel-room phones are reasonable for local calls, but a terrible rip-off for long-distance calls. Never call home from your hotel room unless your hotel allows toll-free access to your AT&T or MCI operator. (If this doesn't work from your room, try it from the lobby.)

To call from Italy to other countries, dial the international access code (00 in Italy), followed by the country code of the country you're calling, followed by the area code without its zero, and finally the local number. When dialing long distance within Italy, start with the area code (including its zero), then the local number. Post offices have fair, metered long-distance booths. SIP (national phone company) offices are central and filled with (unvandalized) phones.

Italy's phone cards aren't credit cards, just handy cards you insert in the phone instead of coins. The L5,000, L10,000, or L15,000 phone cards (buy at post offices, tobacco shops, and machines near phone booths; many phone booths indicate where the nearest phone card sales outlet is located; rip off the corner to "activate" the card) are much easier to use than coins for long-distance calls. Buy one on your first day to force you to find smart reasons to use the local phones.

Dial slowly and deliberately, as if the phone doesn't understand numbers very well. (Some Italian phones don't.) Repeat as needed.

Telephone Directory

Italy's international access code 00
Italy's country code 39
MCI operator 172-1022
AT&T operator 172-1011
SPRINT operator 172-1877
Emergency (*English-speaking police help*) 113
Emergency (*military police*) 112

Telephone Directory *(continued)*
Road Service 116
Directory Assistance *(a toll-free Italian robot gives
    the number twice, very clearly)* 12
English language telephone help 170
To call Italy from the U.S.A.: 011-39-area
    code without the zero-local number
To call U.S.A. from Italy: 00-1-area
    code-local number

Train Connections (L1,600 = about $1)

from . . . to	duration of trip	frequency	cost 2nd class
Milan-La Spezia	3-4 hours	6/day	L20,000-L25,000
La Spezia-Pisa	1 hour	hourly	L6,000
Pisa-Florence	60-90 minutes	hourly	L7,000-L9,000
Florence-Siena	80-120 minutes	hourly	L7,200
Siena-Orvieto	2-3 hours, 1 change	7/day	L10,000
Siena-Assisi	3½ hours, 2 changes	4/day	L16,000
Assisi-Rome	2-3 hours, 1 change	8/day	L14,000-L20,000
Siena-Rome	3 hours, 1 change	6/day	L20,000-L25,000
Orvieto-Rome	75-90 minutes	10/day	L11,000
Orte-Rome	40-80 minutes	20/day	L7,000
Rome-Naples	2-3 hours	hourly	L16,000
Salerno-Naples	40 minutes	2/hour	L4,500
Rome-Venice	5-7 hours	2/day	L50,000
Venice-Bolzano	3½-4 hours, 1 change	8/day	L20,000-L28,000
Bolzano-Milan	3½ hours, 1 change	8/day	L20,000

Italy's Public Transportation

KEY: —— RAIL   - - - BUS   •••• SHIP
NOT TO SCALE   ◉ OVERNIGHT STOPS (ON 22 DAYS ROUTE)

Italian Hostels

These are near recommended sights but not covered in the text. For a complete listing, pick up the free annual **Italian Youth Hostels** booklet at any hostel in Italy.) Like hotels, hostels are rated with one to four stars (indicated by asterisks below.

Agerola (near town of Amalfi): Beata Solitudo *, Piazza G. Avitabile, tel. 081/8025048.

Como: Villa Olmo***, Via Bellinzona 2, tel. 031/573800 .

Cortona: San Marco ***, Via Maffei 57, tel. 0575/601392.

Domaso (north end of Lake Como): Via Case Sparse 12**, tel. 0344/96094 .

Florence: Europa-Villa Camerata ****, tel. 055/601451.

Lucca (near Pisa, Cinque Terre): Il Serchio***, Via del Brennero 673, tel. 0583/341811.

Marina di Massa e Carrara (near Cinque Terre): Ostello Apuano***, Via delle Pinete 89, tel. 0585/780034.

Milan: Piero Rotta ***, Via Martino Bassi 2, tel. 02/39267095.

Ravenna: Dante ***, Via Aurelio Nicolodi 12, tel. 0544/ 420405.

Verona: Villa Francescatti***, Salita Fontana del Ferro 15, tel. 045/590360 .

Climate Chart

Here is a list of average temperatures and days of no rain.
The first line shows average daily lows; the second line, average daily highs;
the third line, days of no rain.

Rome, Italy

J	F	M	A	M	J	J	A	S	O	N	D
39°	39°	42°	46°	55°	60°	64°	64°	61°	53°	46°	41°
54°	56°	62°	68°	74°	82°	88°	88°	83°	73°	63°	56°
23	17	26	24	25	28	29	28	24	22	22	22

Basic Italian Survival Phrases

English	Italian	Pronunciation
Hello. / Goodbye.	Ciao.	chow
Do you speak English?	Parla inglese?	PAR-lah een-GLAY-zay
Yes. / No.	Sì. / No.	see / noh
I don't understand	Non capisco.	nohn kah-PEE-skoh
I'm sorry.	Mi dispiace.	mee dee-speeAH-chay
Please.	Per favore.	pehr fah-VOH-ray
Thank you.	Grazie.	GRAH-tseeay
Where is...?	Dov'è...?	doh-VEH
...a hotel	...un hotel	oon oh-TEHL
...a youth hostel	...un ostelio della gioventù	oon oh-STEHL-loh DAY-lah joh-vehn-TOO
...a restaurant	...un ristorante	oon ree-stoh-RAHN-tay
...a grocery store	...un negozio di alimentari	oon nay-GOH-tsoh dee ah-lee-mayn-TAH-ree
...the train station	...la stazione	lah stah-tseeOH-nay
...tourist information	...informazioni per turisti	een-for-mah-tseeOH-nee pehr too-REE-stee
...the toilet	...il gabinetto	eel gah-bee-NAYT-toh
men	uomini, signori	WAW-mee-nee, seen-YOH-ree
women	donne, signore	DON-nay, seen-YOH-ray
How much?	Quanto costa?	KWAHN-toh KOS-tah
Cheaper.	Più economico.	peeOO ay-koh-NOH-mee-koh
Included?	È incluso?	eh een-KLOO-zoh
I would like...	Vorrei....	vor-REHee
Just a little. / More.	Un pochino. / Di più.	oon poh-KEE-noh / dee peeOO
A ticket.	Un biglietto.	oon beel-YAYT-toh
A room.	Una camera.	OO-nah KAH-may-rah
The bill.	Il conto.	eel KOHN-toh
one	uno	OO-noh
two	due	DOO-ay
three	tre	tray
four	quattro	KWAHT-troh
five	cinque	CHEENG-kway
six	sei	SEHee
seven	sette	SEHT-tay
eight	otto	OT-toh
nine	nove	NOV-ay
ten	dieci	deeEH-chee
hundred	cento	CHEHN-toh
thousand	mille	MEEL-lay

For another 112 pages of user-friendly Italian, check out *Rick Steves' Italian Phrase Book.*

INDEX

Other Books from John Muir Publications

2 to 22 Days in Asia, 192 pp. $10.95

2 to 22 Days in Australia, 192 pp. $10.95

2 to 22 Days in California, 1995 ed., 192 pp. $11.95

2 to 22 Days in Eastern Canada, 1995 ed., 240 pp $11.95

2 to 22 Days in Florida, 1995 ed., 192 pp. $11.95

2 to 22 Days Around the Great Lakes, 1995 ed., 192 pp. $11.95

2 to 22 Days in Hawaii, 1995 ed., 192 pp. $11.95

2 to 22 Days in New England, 1995 ed., 192 pp. $11.95

2 to 22 Days in New Zealand, 192 pp. $10.95

2 to 22 Days in the Pacific Northwest, 1995 ed., 192 pp. $11.95

2 to 22 Days in the Rockies, 1995 ed., 192 pp. $11.95

2 to 22 Days in Texas, 1995 ed., 192 pp. $11.95

2 to 22 Days in Thailand, 192 pp. $10.95

22 Days Around the World, 264 pp. $13.95

Other Terrific Travel Titles

The 100 Best Small Art Towns in America, 224 pp. $12.95

Elderhostels: The Students' Choice, 2nd ed., 304 pp. $15.95

Environmental Vacations: Volunteer Projects to Save the Planet, 2nd ed., 248 pp. $16.95

A Foreign Visitor's Guide to America, 224 pp. $12.95

Great Cities of Eastern Europe, 256 pp. $16.95

Indian America: A Traveler's Companion, 3rd ed., 432 pp. $18.95

Interior Furnishings Southwest, 256 pp. $19.95

Opera! The Guide to Western Europe's Great Houses, 296 pp. $18.95

Paintbrushes and Pistols: How the Taos Artists Sold the West, 288 pp. $17.95

The People's Guide to Mexico, 9th ed., 608 pp. $18.95

Ranch Vacations: The Complete Guide to Guest and Resort, Fly-Fishing, and Cross-Country Skiing Ranches, 3rd ed., 512 pp. $19.95

The Shopper's Guide to Art and Crafts in the Hawaiian Islands, 272 pp. $13.95

The Shopper's Guide to Mexico, 224 pp. $9.95

Understanding Europeans, 272 pp. $14.95

A Viewer's Guide to Art: A Glossary of Gods, People, and Creatures, 144 pp. $10.95

Watch It Made in the U.S.A.: A Visitor's Guide to the Companies that Make Your Favorite Products, 272 pp. $16.95

Parenting Titles

Being a Father: Family, Work, and Self, 176 pp. $12.95

Preconception: A Woman's Guide to Preparing for Pregnancy and Parenthood, 232 pp. $14.95

Schooling at Home: Parents, Kids, and Learning, 264 pp., $14.95

Teens: A Fresh Look, 240 pp. $14.95

Automotive Titles

The Greaseless Guide to Car Care Confidence, 224 pp. $14.95

How to Keep Your Datsun/Nissan Alive, 544 pp. $21.95

How to Keep Your Subaru Alive, 480 pp. $21.95

How to Keep Your Toyota Pickup Alive, 392 pp. $21.95

How to Keep Your VW Alive, 25th Anniversary ed., 464 pp. spiral bound $25

TITLES FOR YOUNG READERS AGES 8 AND UP

American Origins Series
Each is 48 pages and $12.95 hardcover.
Tracing Our English Roots
Tracing Our French Roots
Tracing Our German Roots
Tracing Our Irish Roots
Tracing Our Italian Roots
Tracing Our Japanese Roots
Tracing Our Jewish Roots
Tracing Our Polish Roots

Bizarre & Beautiful Series
Each is 48 pages, $9.95 paperback, and $14.95 hardcover.
Bizarre & Beautiful Ears
Bizarre & Beautiful Eyes
Bizarre & Beautiful Feelers
Bizarre & Beautiful Noses
Bizarre & Beautiful Tongues

Environmental Titles
Habitats: Where the Wild Things Live, 48 pp. $9.95
The Indian Way: Learning to Communicate with Mother Earth, 114 pp. $9.95
Rads, Ergs, and Cheeseburgers: The Kids' Guide to Energy and the Environment, 108 pp. $13.95
The Kids' Environment Book: What's Awry and Why, 192 pp. $13.95

Extremely Weird Series
Each is 48 pages, $9.95 paperback, and $14.95 hardcover.
Extremely Weird Bats
Extremely Weird Birds
Extremely Weird Endangered Species
Extremely Weird Fishes
Extremely Weird Frogs
Extremely Weird Insects
Extremely Weird Mammals
Extremely Weird Micro Monsters
Extremely Weird Primates
Extremely Weird Reptiles
Extremely Weird Sea Creatures
Extremely Weird Snakes
Extremely Weird Spiders

Kidding Around Travel Series
All are 64 pages and $9.95 paperback, except for *Kidding Around Spain* and *Kidding Around the National Parks of the Southwest*, which are 108 pages and $12.95 paperback.
Kidding Around Atlanta
Kidding Around Boston, 2nd ed.
Kidding Around Chicago, 2nd ed.
Kidding Around the Hawaiian Islands
Kidding Around London
Kidding Around Los Angeles
Kidding Around the National Parks of the Southwest
Kidding Around New York City, 2nd ed.
Kidding Around Paris
Kidding Around Philadelphia
Kidding Around San Diego
Kidding Around San Francisco
Kidding Around Santa Fe
Kidding Around Seattle
Kidding Around Spain
Kidding Around Washington, D.C., 2nd ed.

Kids Explore Series
Written by kids for kids, all are $9.95 paperback.
Kids Explore America's African American Heritage, 128 pp.
Kids Explore the Gifts of Children with Special Needs, 128 pp.
Kids Explore America's Hispanic Heritage, 112 pp.
Kids Explore America's Japanese American Heritage, 144 pp.

Masters of Motion Series
Each is 48 pages and $9.95 paperback.
How to Drive an Indy Race Car
How to Fly a 747
How to Fly the Space Shuttle

Rainbow Warrior Artists Series
Each is 48 pages and $14.95 hardcover.
Native Artists of Africa
Native Artists of Europe
Native Artists of North America

Rough and Ready Series
Each is 48 pages and $12.95 hardcover.
Rough and Ready Cowboys
Rough and Ready Homesteaders
Rough and Ready Loggers
Rough and Ready Outlaws and Lawmen
Rough and Ready Prospectors
Rough and Ready Railroaders

X-ray Vision Series
Each is 48 pages and $9.95 paperback.
Looking Inside the Brain
Looking Inside Cartoon Animation
Looking Inside Caves and Caverns
Looking Inside Sports Aerodynamics
Looking Inside Sunken Treasures
Looking Inside Telescopes and the Night Sky

Ordering Information
Please check your local bookstore for our books, or call **1-800-888-7504** to order direct. All orders are shipped via UPS; see chart below to calculate your shipping charge for U.S. destinations. **No post office boxes please; we must have a street address to ensure delivery**. If the book you request is not available, we will hold your check until we can ship it. Foreign orders will be shipped surface rate unless otherwise requested; please enclose $3 for the first item and $1 for each additional item.

For U.S. Orders

Totaling	Add
Up to $15.00	$4.25
$15.01 to $45.00	$5.25
$45.01 to $75.00	$6.25
$75.01 or more	$7.25

Methods of Payment
Check, money order, American Express, MasterCard, or Visa. We cannot be responsible for cash sent through the mail. For credit card orders, include your card number, expiration date, and your signature, or call **1-800-888-7504**. American Express card orders can only be shipped to billing address of cardholder. Sorry, no C.O.D.'s. Residents of sunny New Mexico, add 6.25% tax to total.

Address all orders and inquiries to:
John Muir Publications
P.O. Box 613
Santa Fe, NM 87504
(505) 982-4078
(800) 888-7504